IMAGES
of America

MONTGOMERY

On the Cover: This glass-negative image was taken in 1877 with a 38-star American flag waving in the gentle breeze.

IMAGES
of America

MONTGOMERY

Jo Fredell Higgins

ARCADIA
PUBLISHING

ISBN 978-0-7385-8301-3

Published by Arcadia Publishing
Charleston, South Carolina

Printed in the United States of America

Library of Congress Control Number: 2011920137

For all general information, please contact Arcadia Publishing:
Telephone 843-853-2070
Fax 843-853-0044
E-mail sales@arcadiapublishing.com
For customer service and orders:
Toll-Free 1-888-313-2665

Visit us on the Internet at www.arcadiapublishing.com

This book is dedicated with loving wishes to my Aunt Phyllis Fredell Hackwith.

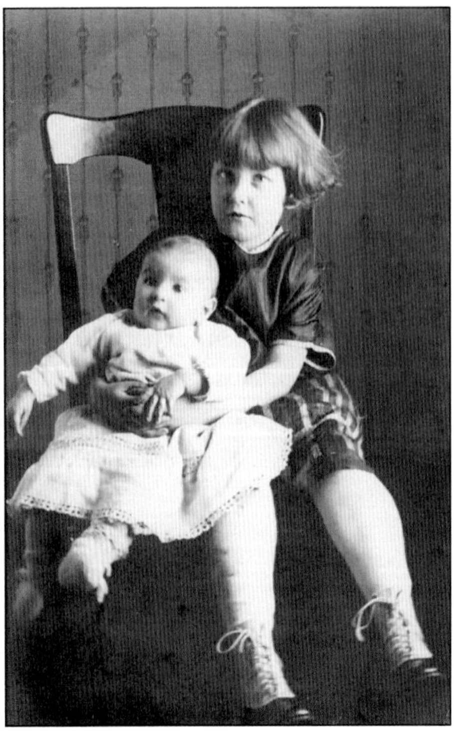

This 1914 photograph shows Aunt Phyllis Fredell as a baby with her sister Aunt Thelma Fredell.

Contents

ACKNOWLEDGMENTS

Nestled along the quiet banks of the Fox River, the Village of Montgomery wakens to each new day. The village was incorporated in 1894, and by 1970 there were 3,258 residents within a radius of 2.8 square miles. Forty years later, the population is estimated to be 18,438 living in 9.35 square miles.

This project would not have been possible without the interest of many citizens who call Montgomery their home. Many other history aficionados provided photographs and memories. The populace of Montgomery was engaging, interesting, informative, and delightful. Arcadia publisher John Pearson, acquisitions editor Jeff Ruetsche, and production coordinator David Mandel offered encouragement and support throughout the book's production. I give my personal thanks to village president Marilyn Michelini, village manager Anne Marie Gaura, state representative Kay Hatcher, village executive assistant Debbie Scheskie Buchanan, village deputy clerk Helen Prester, village volunteer Mark Pawlowicz, Sarah Puleo from Caterpillar Inc., Wynne Swedberg, Carter Crane and Jason Crane from *The Voice* newspaper, Diane Christian, Kathy Priegel, Phyllis Lia, and Ruthmary Wood from the Aurora Public Library, Helen Baker, Brad Baker, Richard "Shorty" Dickson, Marian Dickson, Carolyn Leifheit, Peggy Tegel and Sarah Skilton from the Oswego Public Library, Paul Straits and Vesco Reprographic, James Pfeiffer, Charlene Coulombe-Fiore from the Montgomery Economic Development Commission, Pam Nagel from the Greater Montgomery Area Chamber of Commerce, Harry Hiotis, Gene Michaels, Joan Michaels, Cindy King Adams, Mike Chapin, Veronica Radowicz and Marsha Nilles from the West Aurora School District No. 129, Peter G. Wallers, Beth Petri, alderman Paul J. Hinterlong from the City of Naperville, representative Jesse B. Vazquez on the Kane County Board, Gary Pregel, Mera Johnson, Roger Matile, Mary Baretta, Denise Hansford and Irene Engeln from St. Peter's Church, Vivian Buchtler, Jean Gibson, Jean Hart, John Schaefer, Schaefer's Greenhouse, Jeff Noblitt, Adam Punter and Stephanie Wennemacher from Waubonsee Community College, Elsie Ruth Armbruster Dieterich Wagner, Mary Rohrer, Viola Skogen, Todd Skogen, the Reverend Scott Guhl from St. Olaf Lutheran Church, Howard Hughes, Barbara Mosley Peck, Pat Mosley Torrance, Alice Mosley Seidelman, Jeannie Mosley Wollenweber, Jane Jacobson from the Kendall County Historical Society, police officer Daniel Puskaric, Debbie Olden Gibson, Jenne Olden, Wilma Beyer Hauer, Alice Pocus Sutcliff, Virginia Potter, Ron Potter, director of media relations Al Benson at Aurora University, Al Martner, Claire Martner Erickson, Cecil Piggott Jr., fire chief Tom Meyers Jr., former chief of police Dennis Schmidt, Rene Morales, Ron LaDew, Nancy Touvell Fay, Kim Winkler, police chief Daniel Meyers, Rayanne Carlson, Goldie Carlson, Ione Martin, Brian Kipley, Steve M. Kapas, Linda Eder, Jim Cumpata, Ken Wolf, Dave Chrestenson, Marj Colley, John Wilson, Ken Nagel and Jennifer Karabetsos at Fox River Foods, Jim Spring, Nancy Spring Epley, Juanita Dickson Murst, Ann Wasman, Ginger Lake, Dorothy Gove Bunkofske, Brook McDonald, Kim Dusza, and Jim Drnek from the *Donauschwaben Blaskapelle*.

FOREWORD

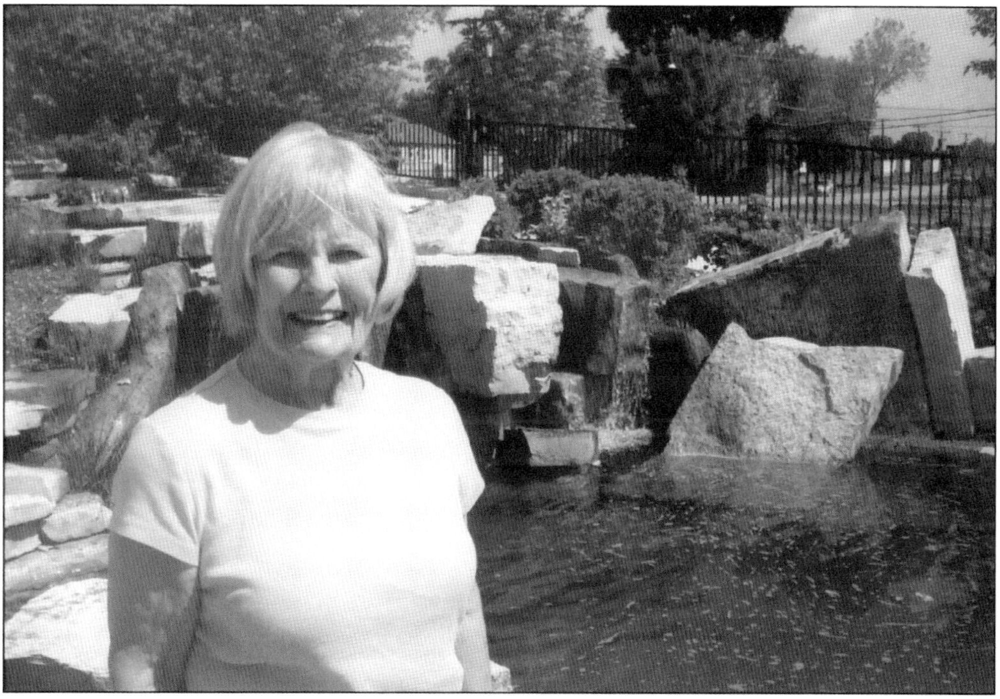

I would like to take this opportunity to welcome you to the Village of Montgomery as seen through the eyes and camera of award-winning photojournalist Jo Fredell Higgins. Diligent research and attention to detail has created an outstanding portrait of the Village.

The Village of Montgomery was first surveyed not long after Daniel Gray's arrival in 1835. Land was cheap, and a Mr. Elijah Pierce bought the rights to a claim of 380 acres on the east side of the Fox River for $7 from the federal government. On October 30, 1852, the town, without a name, was registered and recorded in Plat Book 4, page 93. Between 1852 and 1854, a new railroad was constructed connecting Montgomery and the surrounding areas. Listed in the 1888 directory of the Village were butchers, market gardeners, milkmen, a blacksmith, carpenters, and a general merchant and postmaster.

The Village now has over 18,000 residents who enjoy the scenic views of the Fox River for all seasons. During the anniversary year, our motto "Bridging the Past to the Future" truly expresses our desire to honor the past while building for a bright future. This book details every aspect of society from its early beginnings to the present-day celebrations of Montgomery's 175th anniversary. The photographs, documents, and postcards will enhance the lively narrative to create a truly memorable book of Montgomery history.

—Marilyn Michelini
Village President

INTRODUCTION

Memory, that library of the soul from which I will draw knowledge and experience for the rest of my life.

—Tove Ditlevsen

Long ago, Kendall County was located in the southeast corner of barren rock. A part of Chicago was under water. Morris and Streator were part of a vast swamp where evergreens grew. The prairies, covered with grass and spangled with flowers, were undisturbed. There were droves of passing deer or Indian travelers following their trail in single file. The rivers and creeks, stocked with fish, flowed by quietly. The solitude of the groves was unbroken except by the wolves howling or the occasional sound of an Indian's musket. That was the medieval time in the state's physical history.

Illinois became a state on December 3, 1818. Shadrach Bond was the first governor. In 1820, Indian agent Alexander Wolcott from Chicago wished to be united to Ellen M. Kinzie in matrimony. He was obliged to go down the Fox and Illinois valleys to Fulton County, and Wolcott needed to find a justice of the peace to perform the ceremony. The *American Atlas*, published in 1822 at Philadelphia, stated, "Illinois has 19 counties and 55,000 inhabitants. The settlements at present are confined to the southern portion of the state in the neighborhood of the great rivers. The country is under good cultivation."

Waubonsie was the Pottawatomie chief who had headquarters at Aurora and a smaller camping ground at the mouth of Waubonsie creek in Oswego. As the younger brother of Black Partridge, Waubonsie was born in Indiana in 1785 and died in 1848. He is described as a "giant in size and a devil in nature." Waubonsie stood at six feet four inches and weighed 200 pounds. His tribe was a wandering and unsettled people. Most of the village was composed of movable wigwams, and they emigrated south for each winter. Waubonsie was as strong and barbarous as a grizzly bear, and his people dreaded him. He was feared and avoided by the white colonists. Waubonsie claimed to own 800 ponies, some of superb stock. In Illinois, an Indian encampment was a novel sight, and it was described as a scene with "lazy men, homely working squaws, ponies, dogs, and children." During those times, trading with the Indians involved swapping bread and tobacco for fish.

Many immigrants came from England, Germany, Canada, Scotland, Ireland, and Switzerland to Illinois, like Samuel Dickson in 1835 and John Lilly in 1842. Ephraim DeGroff came from Holland in 1846. The Reverend John. F. Okerstein came from Sweden in 1865. William H. Hillman arrived from Ireland in 1880, and in 1836, Gilbert Denslo Henning came from Scotland to work as a grain dealer. From Somersetshire, England, the Lye family immigrated to Kendall County in 1836. Aaron Lye was a farmer, harness maker, and saddler by trade. The Tebay family arrived from England in 1840. From Sweden came the Dahlins.

The Village of Montgomery had an auspicious beginning. Let us journey forward and explore Montgomery's intricate past as the Village celebrated its 175th anniversary.

One

Set Stones of Strength
Daniel S. Gray

History hath triumphed over time which besides it nothing but eternity hath triumphed over.

—Sir Walter Raleigh

Daniel Samuel Gray was born in 1795 in Montgomery County, New York, and visited the West in the autumn of 1835. His brother Nicholas located there the previous spring, and he lived on a farm within the limits of Kendall County. New York County was named after Richard Montgomery, who was a general in the Revolutionary War and died in the Battle of Quebec. Gray made immediate preparations to settle in Kane County, and in the following fall he built the first frame house in the village. He named the area after the county he left. After he arrived with his family in Kane County, he set about to build a store, two foundries, a reaper-and-header manufacturing shop, and a stone grist mill. His success as a businessman created employment for more than 30 hands. Graytown came to be called Montgomery by July 1849. In the census of 1850, Gray's wealth was listed as $30,000. That figure included farmland, his reaper-and-header factory, foundries, blacksmith shop, worker's residences, his former home that became an inn, and his new home near the mill. During the harsh winter of 1854, the area had 42 snowstorms through March. On October 22, 1854, Gray died of dysentery when he was 60 years old. Daniel left behind his wife, Margaret, and five children.

The Village of Montgomery was first surveyed shortly after Gray's arrival. It was then platted at a location somewhat below its present site. The first school building was put up in 1838. Jacob Keck sold the post office, store land, and building for $6,000 in 1842. On July 27, David Dunham recorded that transaction at 3:00 p.m. Ralph Gray's marriage was the earliest marriage recorded within the corporate limits in 1843. In the fall of 1841, the death of Dewitt, one of Gray's sons, was the earliest recorded within the same perimeter.

In 1857, there were many occupations listed in the *Gazetteer* directory, including a carpenter, millwright, merchant, general dealer, machinist, clergyman, teacher, shoemaker, depot agent, sash maker, and farmer. Montgomery was about two and a half miles south of Aurora. The city was described as "beautifully situated on the west side of Fox River. There is a bridge across the river to the east side, where the groves of trees render the location inviting for residents. There is a good school house in the village."

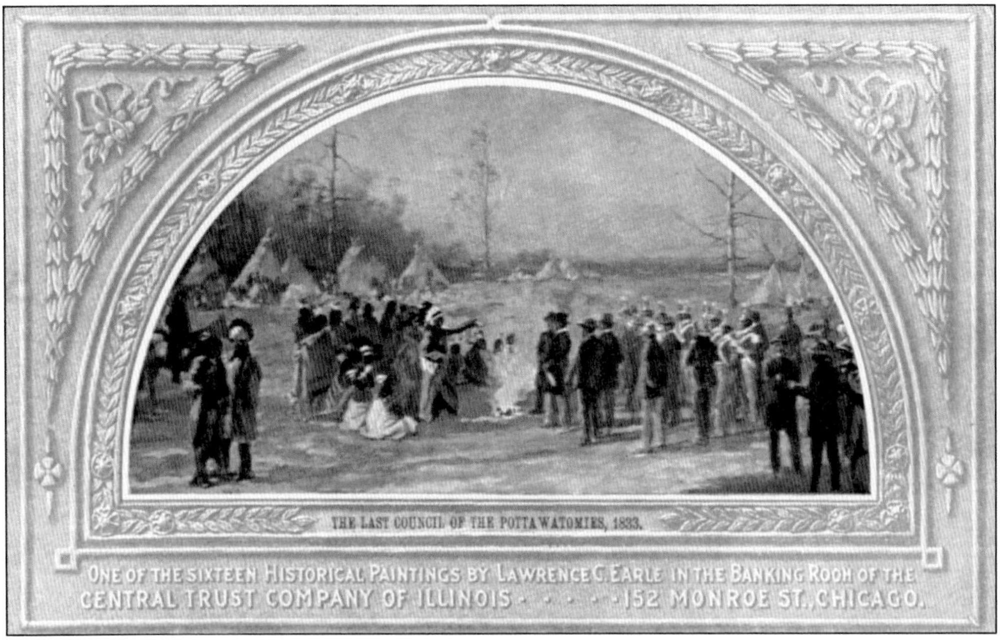

This postcard shows the last council of the Pottawatomies in 1833. The Potawatomi was a powerful tribe that used the Montgomery area as a home and hunting ground. In 1673, the Algonquian languages were the only ones that echoed through the woods and rolled over the prairie. The 18th century brought the English language, as the trapper hunters arrived from the Ohio territory. The land was largely black soil with some clay, sand, and gravel. After 1835, the fame of the soil fertility brought hundreds of sturdy pioneers from New England. (Author's collection.)

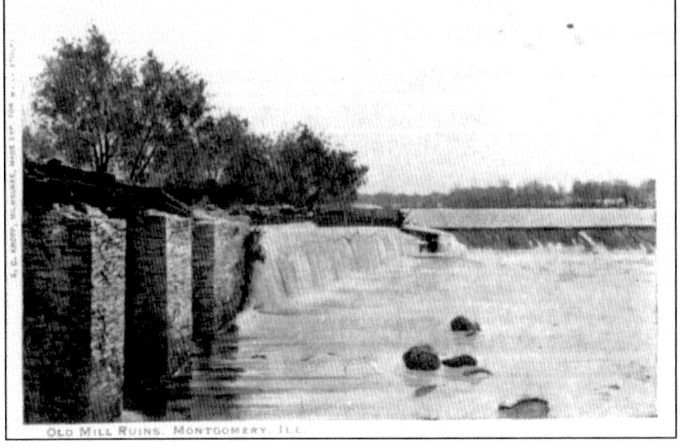

The Fox River was once called Pistakey by the Indians. The name was forgotten because the tribes were driven westward by treaties with the colonizers. Among the first settlers were Jacob and Nancy Cook Keck. Their family numbered 40 people in all. The range of the Fox River in Kane County was described as "thickly settled, and birch-bark cradles could be seen hanging from the tall trees." (Courtesy of Montgomery Archives.)

The Village of Montgomery, Aurora Township, is shown in this 1909 map. The water goes underneath the mill. The Illinois and Peoria Indians lived and hunted in the northern reaches of the river valley. Along the Fox River were abundant groves of oak, ash, and elm. The vastness, the grandeur of the natural prairie included the "music of the big frogs and prairie chickens." (Courtesy of Virginia Potter.)

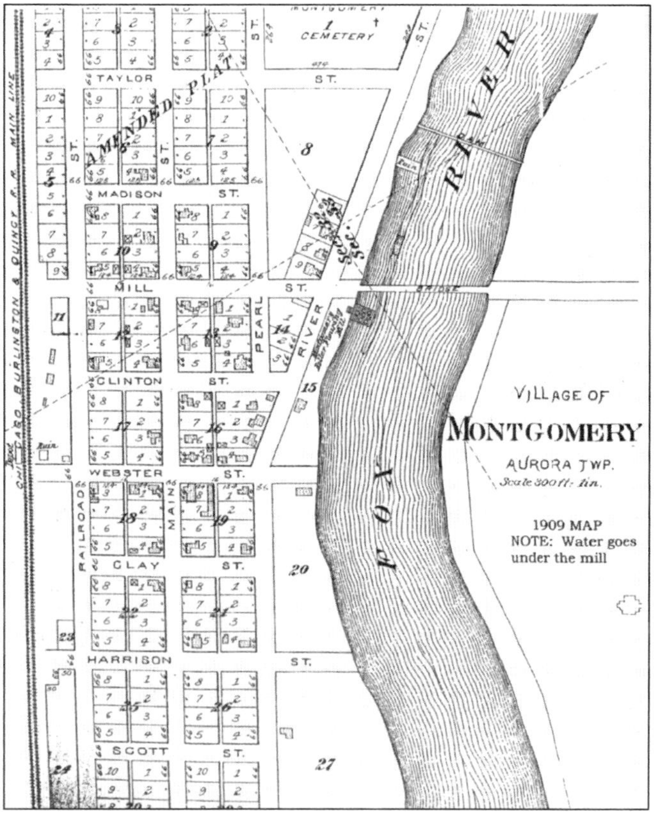

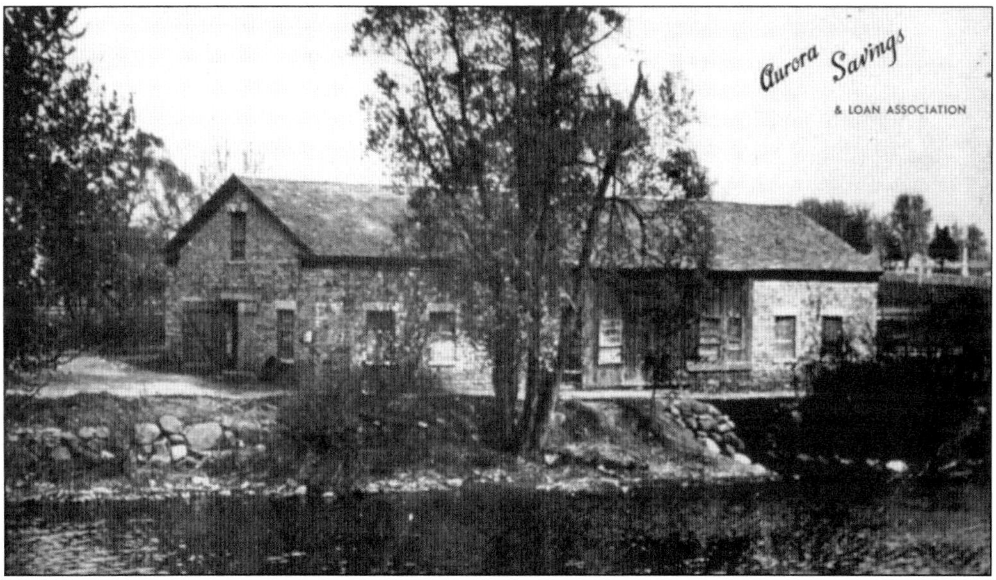

The Keck families sold their homes in the Mohawk Valley of New York. They came to the West in wagons pulled by horses and oxen. Along the way, the group divided. In the autumn of 1840, each family purchased a few acres of timber, which is now known as Boulder Hill. This postcard shows the old Montgomery mill, which was 100 feet long and was operated by waterpower. (Courtesy of Mary Rohrer and Aurora Historical Society.)

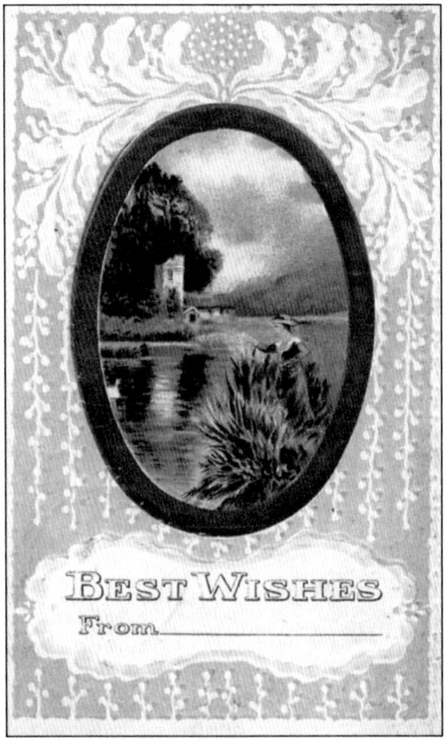

In the 1878 *Past and Present of Kane County Illinois*, a Mr. Wm. T. Elliott took up a claim in June 1834 and reported that he had seen "forty people—men, women, children—packed away in promiscuous order for the night upon the floor." At that time, no government surveys had been made anywhere in the vicinity. All were squatters and all were obliged to travel to Ottawa for transaction of public business. This 1901 postcard was mailed from Montgomery. (Author's collection.)

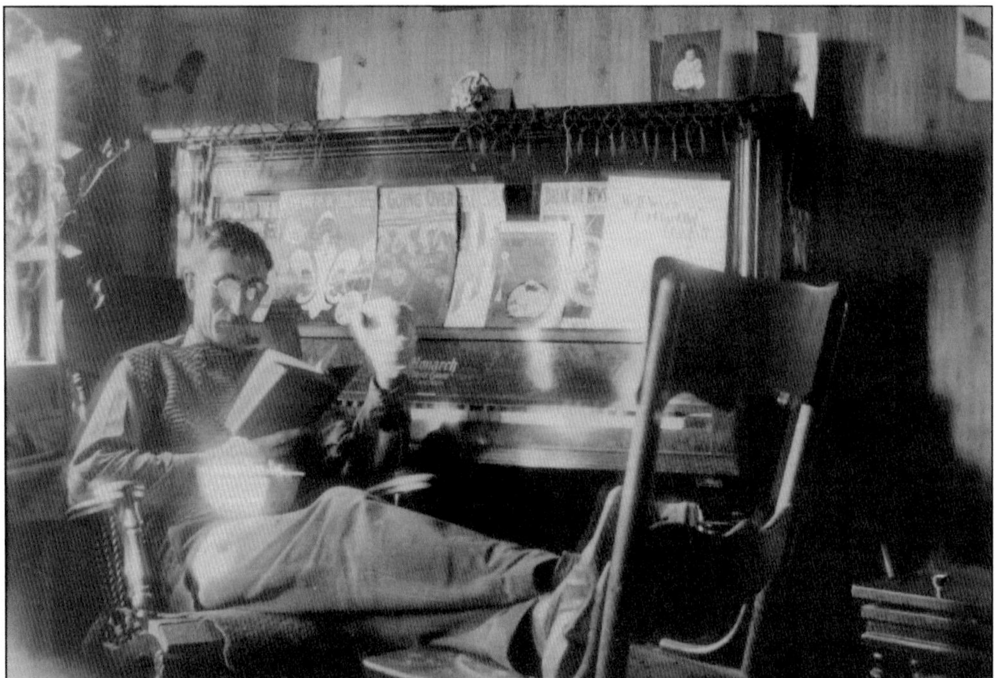

George LaDew sits reading in 1935 at his 320 North River Street home. He lost the fingers on his left hand due to a corn picker accident. Four generations lived in this house. (Courtesy of Ron LaDew.)

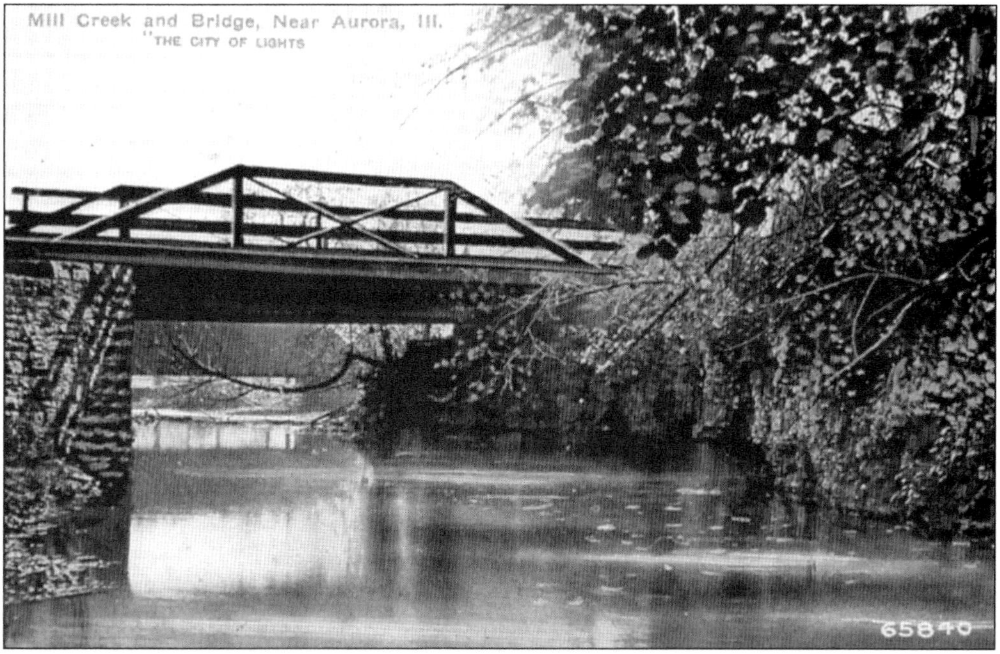

The Royal Neighbors was organized in 1898. In the beginning, the members met at one another's homes or beside the flowing Fox River. Later, they rented the upper floor of Beher's grocery store and post office, which was on the corner of Webster and Railroad Streets. They held card parties and box socials. They also provided assistance in time of emergencies. Membership dues of 10¢ were collected at each meeting. This postcard shows the bridge at Mill Creek. (Courtesy of Montgomery Archives.)

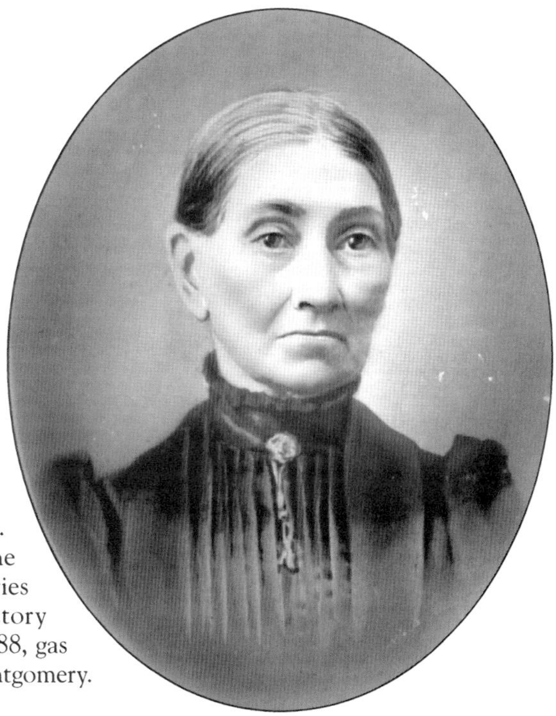

Taken in the late 1880s, this portrait shows a relative from the Livsey family. The Livsey family often bought groceries at Beher's Store. At that time, bread was 5¢ a loaf, milk was 28¢ a gallon, butter was 25¢ a pound, and gas was 4¢ a gallon. The average home cost $3,395, and the annual income was $1,004. Early industries included a window sash-and-blind factory and a cotton-batting manufacturer. In 1888, gas pipes were extended from Aurora to Montgomery. (Courtesy of Montgomery Archives.)

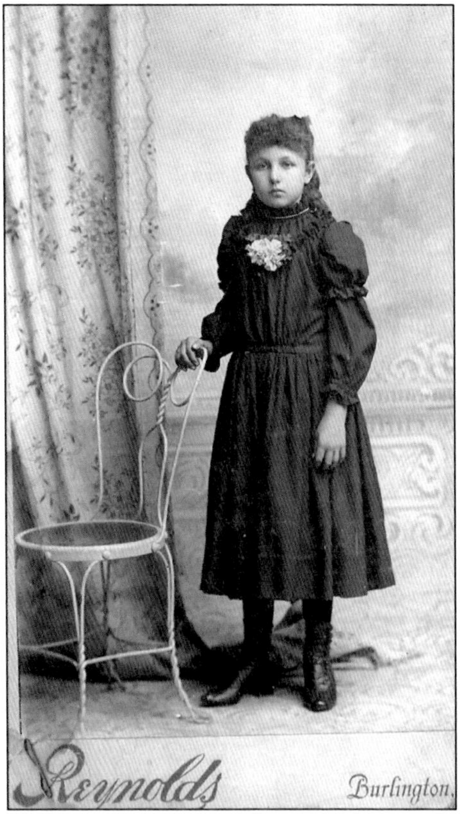

This 1905 portrait shows a young Josie Ellen Moore. During 1905, only 8 percent of homes had a telephone, and only 14 percent had a bathtub. The average life expectancy was only 47 years, and the average wage was 22¢ an hour. Twenty percent of adults in the United States could not read or write. The American flag had 45 stars. (Courtesy of Montgomery Archives.)

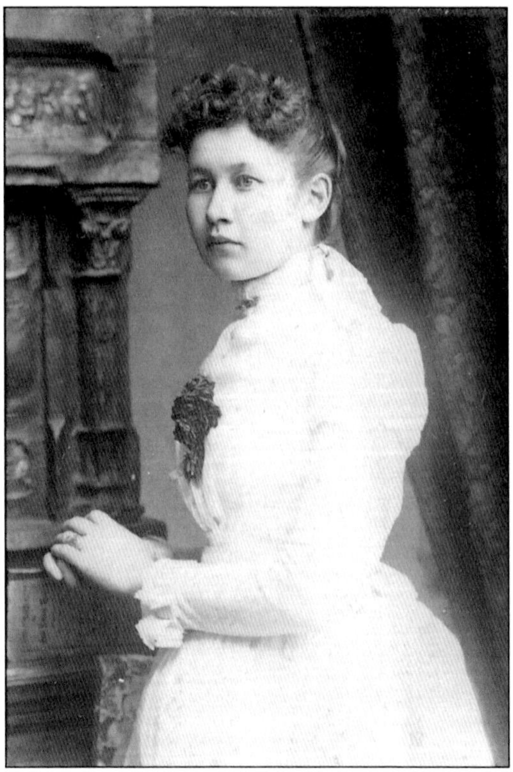

This is a beautiful 1918 portrait of Josie Moore McClain. The late 1910s and early 1920s were a turbulent period for Americans. In 1918, the influenza outbreak killed millions. The banker James T. Woodward coined the phrase, "America is the envy of the world." During this time, Thomas Edison invented the alkaline battery. A postage stamp cost 3¢. The general attitude in America was that anything was possible. (Courtesy of Montgomery Archives.)

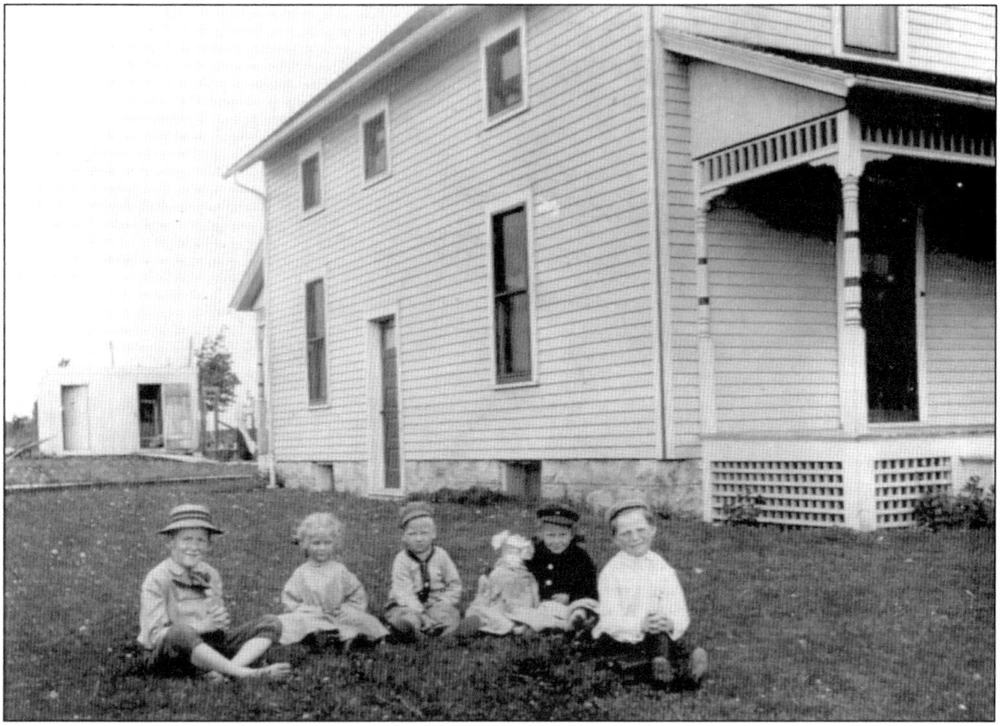

Charlie Gaylord was born in 1904. In this 1910 photograph, Gaylord is sitting with his neighborhood playmates at 322 South River Street. (Courtesy of Montgomery Archives.)

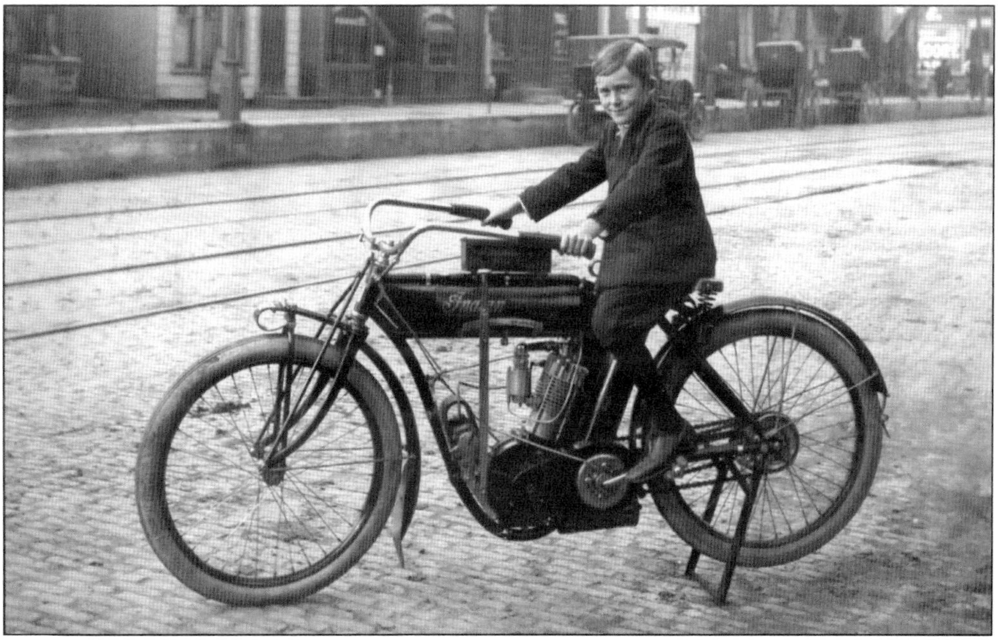

This 1912 photograph shows Charlie Gaylord enjoying a ride on his motorbike. Gaylord had won the bike at an event in Riverview Park, but his mother sold it to buy a piano. It was said that Charlie hated the piano lessons and wanted his motorbike back. He told colleagues that he never learned how to play the piano. (Courtesy of Montgomery Archives.)

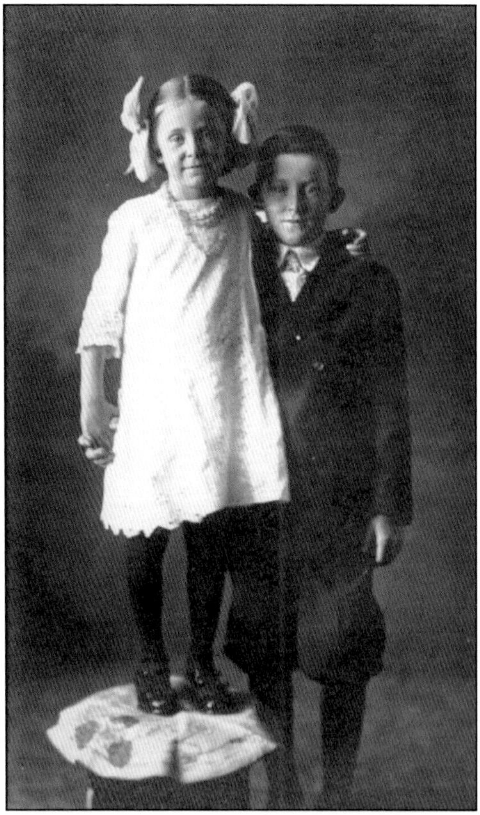

This 1912 photograph shows Lelia Gaylord and her brother Chuck. In 1912, Louis Armstrong dropped out of Fisk School at age 11 and joined a quartet of boys who sang on the streets for money. During this time, New Mexico and Arizona became the 47th and 48th states admitted to the Union. (Courtesy of Montgomery Archives.)

This 1837 photograph shows Alexander Patterson and his wife, Nancy Stocksledger. On a centennial farm application filed in 1972, it was noted that Indians "would chin themselves to peak [*sic*] in the windows in the 1840s." It was also noted that the original purchase of 135 acres was consummated on February 1, 1840. (Courtesy of Shorty Dickson.)

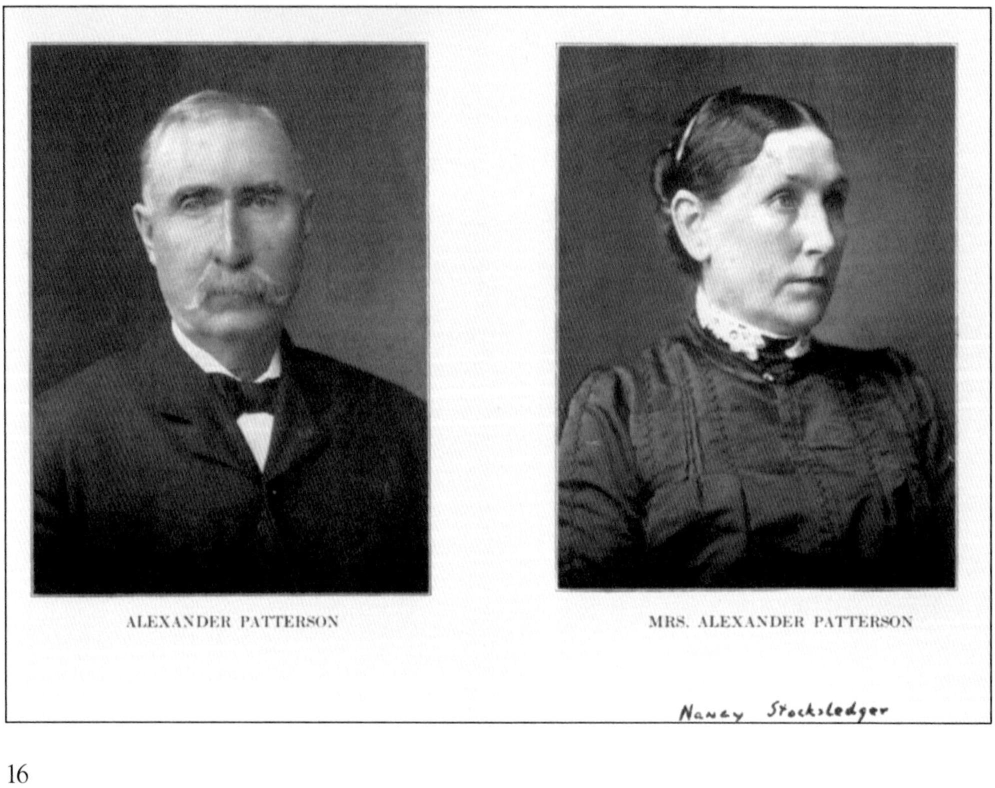

On March 27, 1860, Janet V. Patterson married Simon Dickson Jr. Janet was born in 1839. During that year, the first state law permitting women to own property was passed in Jackson, Mississippi. (Courtesy of Shorty Dickson.)

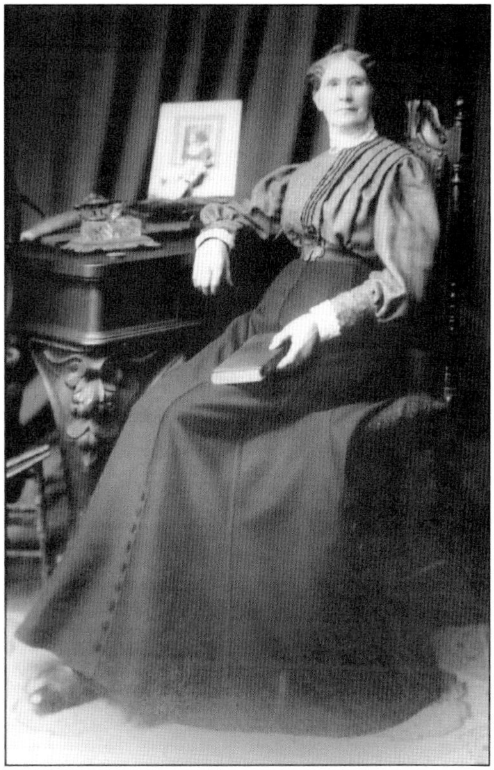

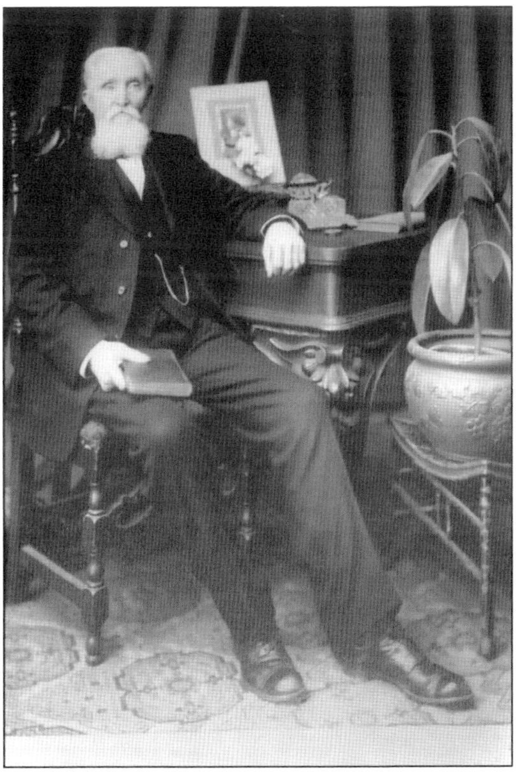

This photograph shows Simon Dickson Jr. striking a thoughtful pose. Dickson Jr. was born in 1836. Improvements to the original farm property included a frame house with high windows. The original house was built around 1880, and it was remodeled into a two-story house in 1947. After staking a claim, the settlers had to live on the land for 14 months, improving it with fences and plowed fields. It was possible to buy it from the federal government for $1.25 an acre up to 160 acres. (Courtesy of Shorty Dickson.)

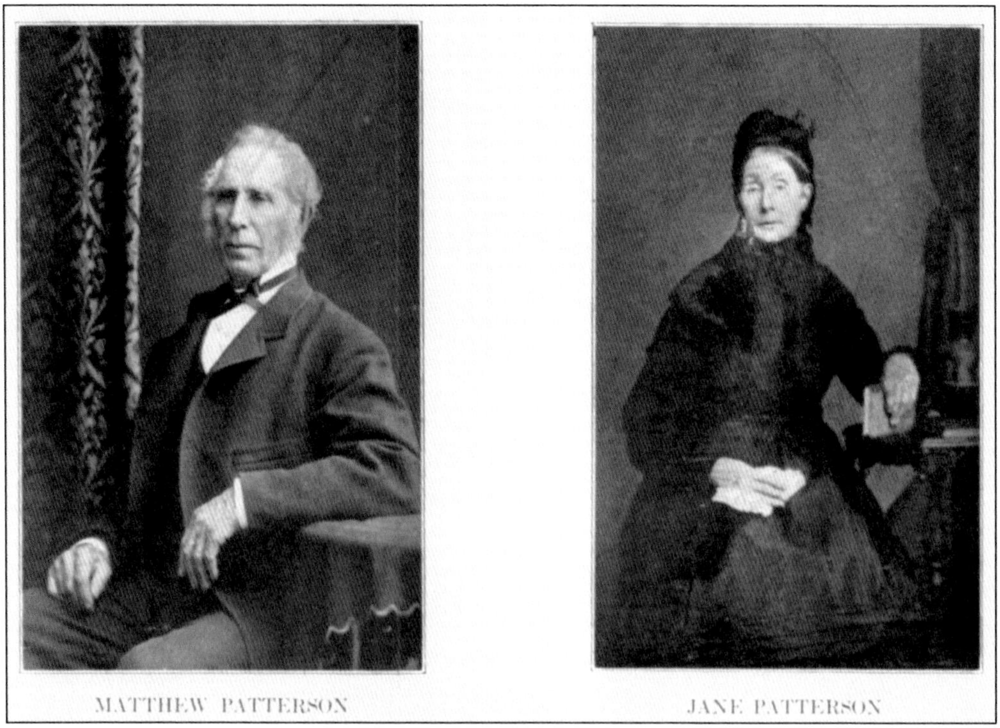

This 1837 photograph shows Matthew Patterson and his wife, Jane Patterson. Born in 1812, Matthew immigrated to Kendall County from Scotland in 1835. Together, they raised seven children. Matthew was the original owner of the 135 acres located in the township of Bristol. Matthew's sister was Janet V. Patterson. (Courtesy of Shorty Dickson.)

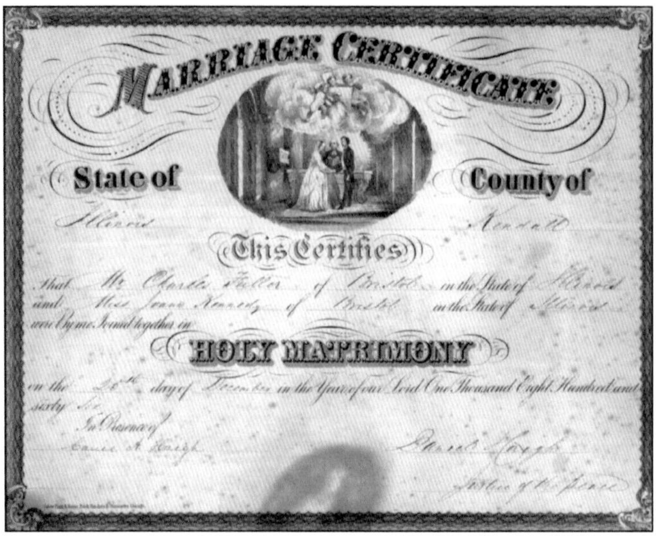

This marriage certificate was dated on December 25, 1866, and shows the union between Charles Fuller and Joann Kennedy. Charles was the brother of Grace Dickson Fuller and Shorty Dickson's grandfather. He and his wife were both from Bristol, which is Kendall County's smallest township. On February 19, 1841, the Illinois State Legislature organized Kendall County, naming it in honor of Amos Kendall, a successful journalist, politician, and businessman. (Courtesy of Shorty Dickson.)

Two

Thus They Would Learn and Gladly Teach

Then followed that beautiful season, summer . . . filled was the air with a dreamy and magical light and the landscape lay as if new created in all the freshness of childhood.

—Henry Wadsworth Longfellow

Montgomery was an agrarian society that consisted of families, homes, schools, and churches. Education was very important to frontier families. As T. Cogan penned, "The education of the human mind commences in the cradle." In 1838, a young lady named Mrs. Ellis taught in a small frame house. During that winter, it was recorded that Mrs. Carpenter sent her two sons to that school, and teachers were paid by subscription. The building was later converted into a dwelling, and another school was built in 1858. By 1878, the house was owned by Harrison Young. After the one-room schoolhouse, a redbrick building was built on Main Street in 1891. It was named the Montgomery School, and the property was a gift of Vine Watkins. There were four rooms, and the school taught grades one through eight. Silas B. Hallock became the first principal.

In 1915, an additional frame was built for the school when Grace M. Nicholson became principal, after Ella Mead's retirement. Nicholson was a graduate of West Aurora High School and had begun teaching at Montgomery School in 1902. She retired in June 1949. She had used her personal funds to start the first school library in 1911. Nicholson also instituted the first kindergarten. In 1929, Mrs. John Erickson and Nicholson began the School Mother's Club, which became the first PTA group. It had 20 original members, and Mildred Swanson became its first president in 1930. In 1932, Beatrice Stone was named the second PTA president. A gymnasium/auditorium was added in 1938.

In 1955, the Montgomery School became part of the West Aurora School District No. 129, and graduating students were required to attend high school at West Aurora. On March 11, 1962, the school was renamed as Grace M. Nicholson School. The new principal was Wilman Favero, who retired in 1981. Today, Nicholson has a diverse group of 365 students under the leadership of Principal David Russell.

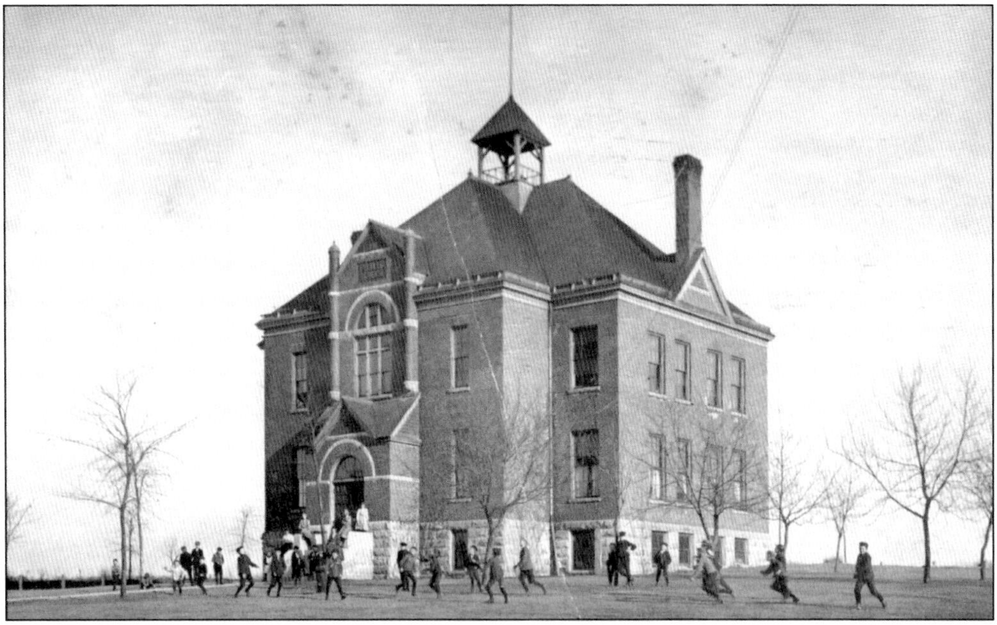

The American people have always felt strongly about education. Once pioneers settled in a new territory, a school was soon built. The Northwest Ordinance reinforced this inclination on July 13, 1787. In 1850, the Illinois General Assembly approved using of property taxes to finance public schools. This photograph shows the old Montgomery School that was built in 1891, and during that time the population was 263 residents. (Courtesy of Paul Straits.)

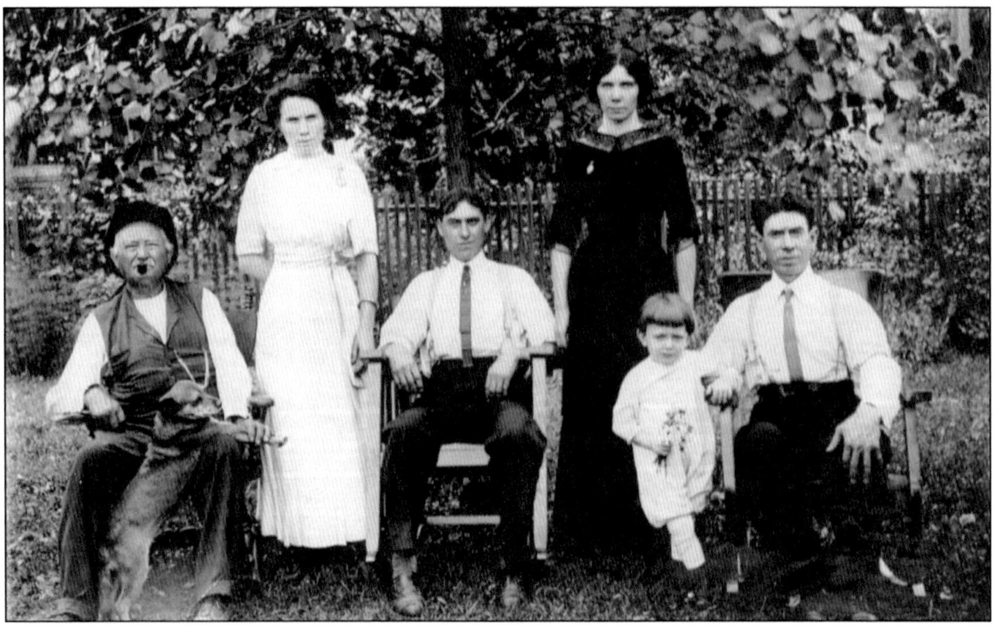

Grandfather Frederick Beyer fought in the Civil War. When he returned home to Montgomery, he built buggies and wagons. He joined the silent choir on March 4, 1916. As a member of Aurora Post No. 20, Frederick was accorded military honors. In this 1898 photograph, pictured from left to right are Frederick Beyer, Mae Beyer, Ben Beyer, Lena Beyer and her husband Joe, Joey Beyer, and the family dog Davey. (Courtesy of Wilma Beyer Hauer.)

This letter from Gov. Adlai Stevenson congratulates Grace M. Nicholson as she retired. A community reception took place to honor her. The original Montgomery School was replaced. In the early 1960s, a new school was built with an 11-classroom wing, and the price tag was $272,192.42 without furniture. In 1962, the school was renamed the Grace M. Nicholson School. (Courtesy of West Aurora District No. 129 and Veronica Radowicz.)

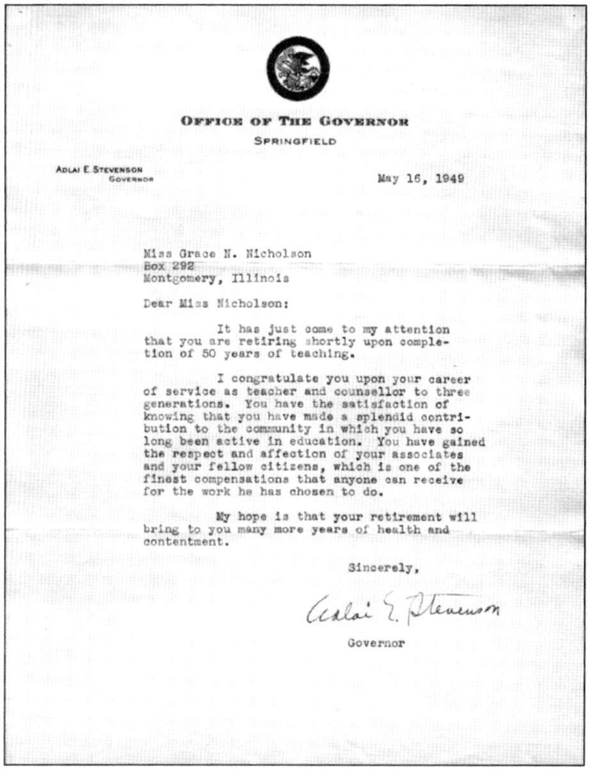

OFFICE OF THE GOVERNOR
SPRINGFIELD

ADLAI E. STEVENSON
GOVERNOR

May 16, 1949

Miss Grace M. Nicholson
Box 292
Montgomery, Illinois

Dear Miss Nicholson:

It has just come to my attention that you are retiring shortly upon completion of 50 years of teaching.

I congratulate you upon your career of service as teacher and counsellor to three generations. You have the satisfaction of knowing that you have made a splendid contribution to the community in which you have so long been active in education. You have gained the respect and affection of your associates and your fellow citizens, which is one of the finest compensations that anyone can receive for the work he has chosen to do.

My hope is that your retirement will bring to you many more years of health and contentment.

Sincerely,

Adlai E. Stevenson

Governor

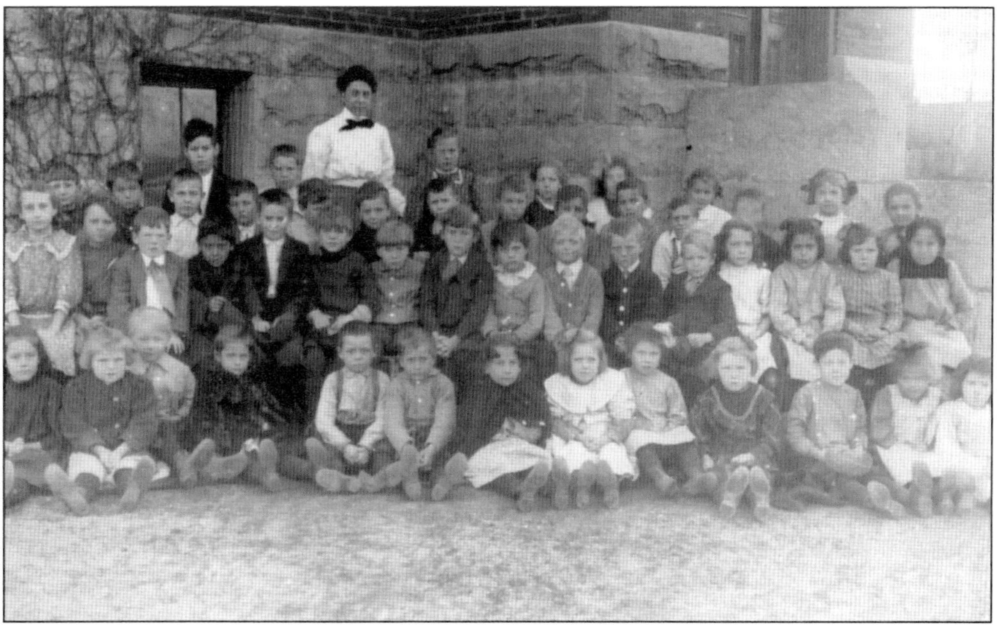

This photograph shows a class of Montgomery School in 1915. It was a time of crochet, capelets, and chemises in Montgomery. Village residents could attend the Grand Opera House in Aurora for 25¢ a ticket. *Beacon News* advertisements were 1¢ per word. Words in vogue were coterie, rueful, ebullition, and demurred. According to the census, the town's population was 371 residents during that year. (Courtesy of Montgomery Archives.)

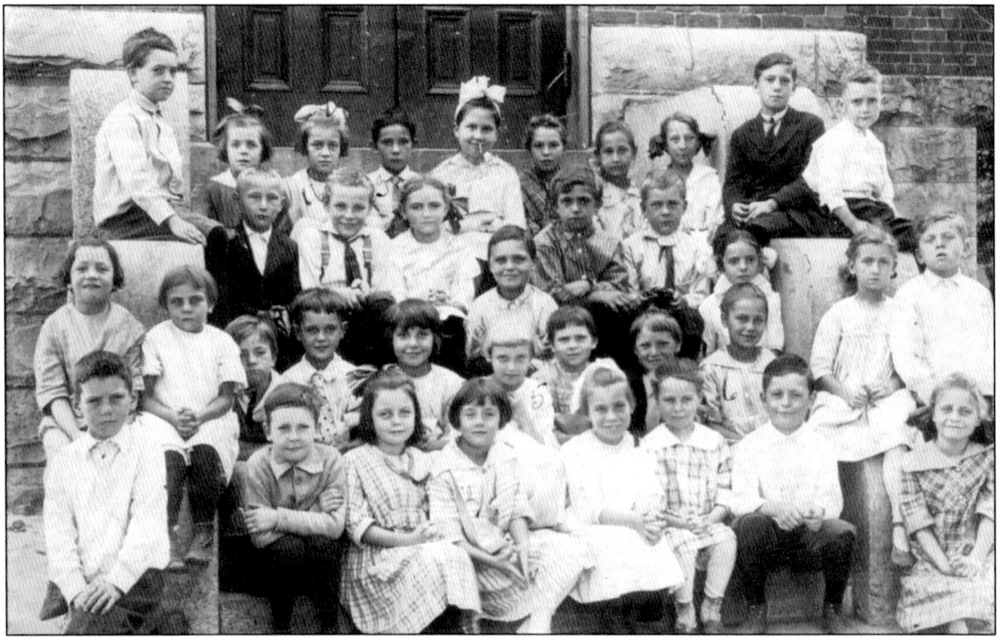

Shown is a third-grade class from Montgomery School in 1916. The United States acquired the Virgin Islands in 1916. Jeannette Rankin, who was from Montana, was the first woman elected to the US House of Representatives. As a lifelong pacifist, Jeannette was called the "Lady of the House." She remains the only woman elected from Montana to this date. (Courtesy of Montgomery Archives.)

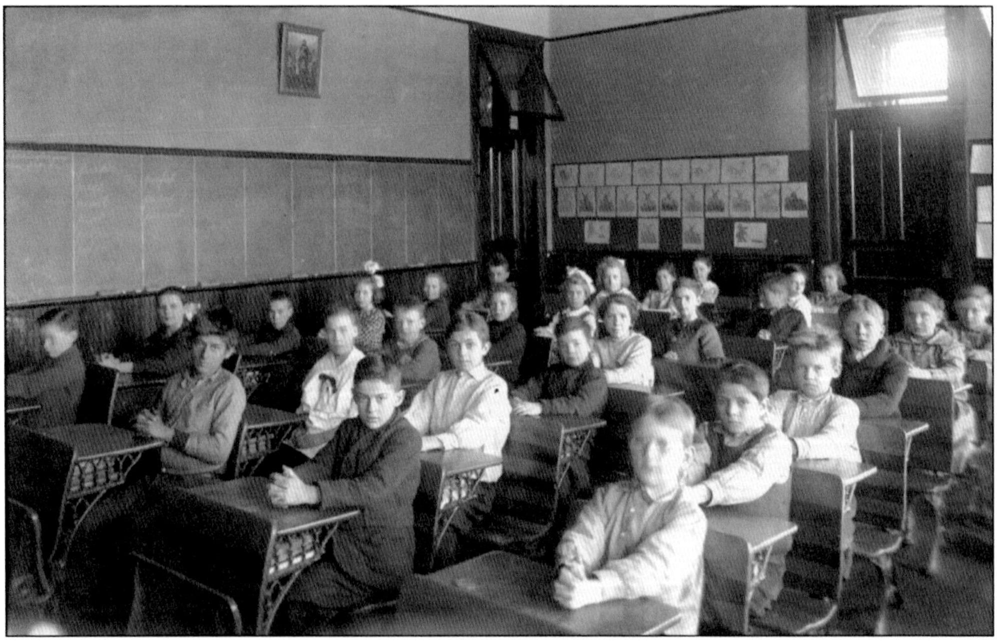

This 1922 photograph shows a class from Montgomery School. Did the children enjoy playing with paper dolls? In the early 1900s, paper dolls were very popular and were sold at 5¢ a doll and 10¢ a boxed set. Bessie Bright, Pansy Blossom, and Little Henry were the most popular boxed paper-doll sets. (Courtesy of Montgomery Archives.)

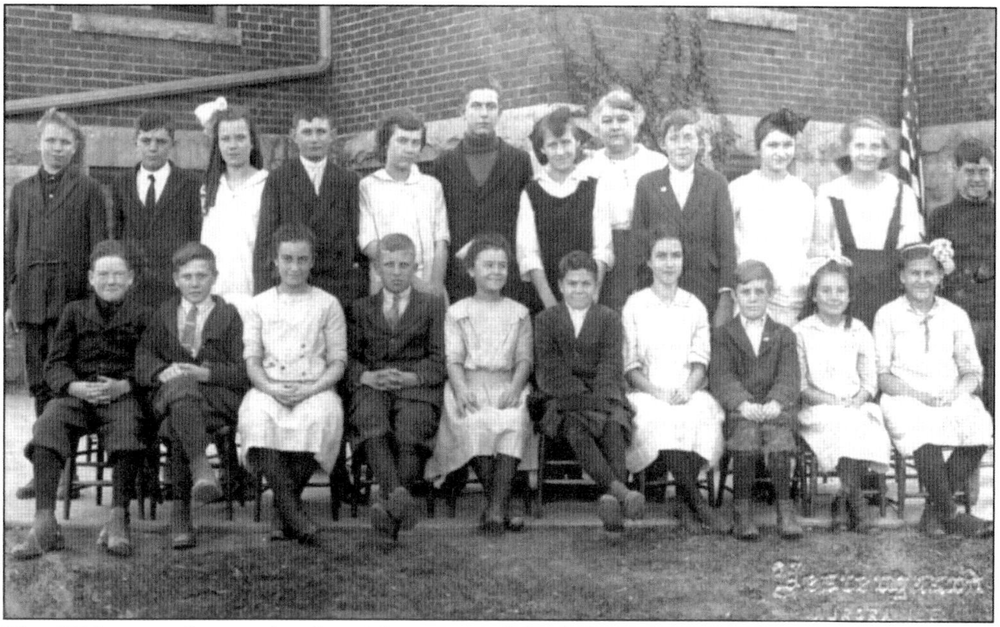

This 1930 picture shows a class from Montgomery School. According to 1930 census, the population was listed as 546. During this period, music became very popular and reflected the cultural and social conditions of the time. The sweet sounds of Guy Lombardo and the dance bands from the Jazz Age gave way to the swing era of the late 1930s. (Courtesy of Montgomery Archives.)

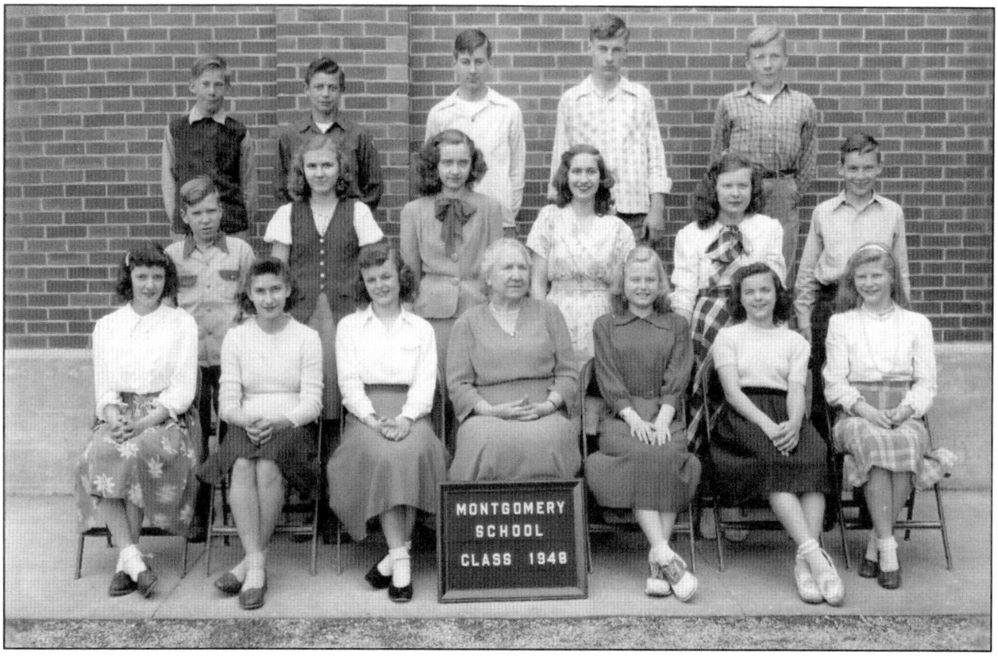

This 1948 photograph shows a class from Montgomery School. Ella Appel was the 11th president of the school's PTA. Its theme for that year was "We Meet Our Challenge." In 1949, Pres. Harry S. Truman unveiled his Fair Deal program. Nereid, a moon of planet Neptune, was discovered. According to the national census, Montgomery's population stood at 773. (Courtesy of Montgomery Archives.)

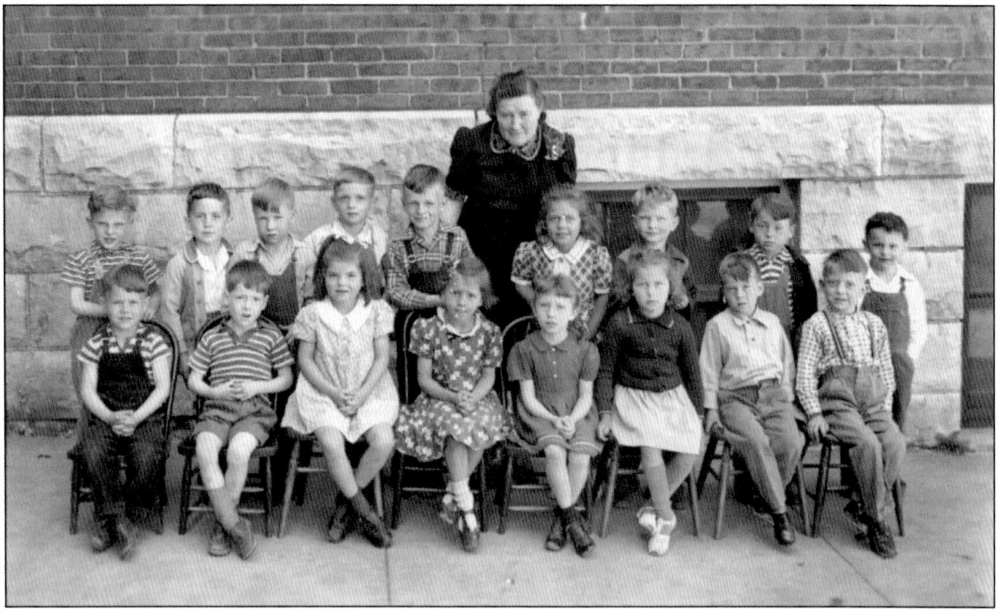

This 1949–1950 photograph shows children with their teacher at the Montgomery School. Grace M. Nicholson recalled her memories at the school and said, "I have always said my heart belongs to Montgomery." Throughout her 47 years of teaching, Nicholson missed only one day of school when she fell and broke her wrist. Although she was taken to the hospital in Aurora, she was back in time for the closing bell that day. (Courtesy of Montgomery Archives.)

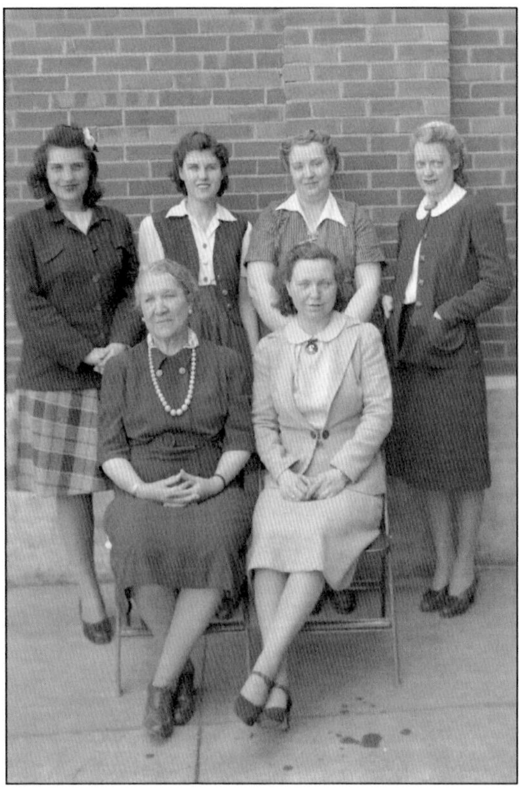

Friends of Grace Nicholson called her Nicky. In 1902, she began her teaching career in Montgomery. The school consisted of three rooms, three teachers, and 100 students. For the last 15 years, Nicholson was the principal of Montgomery School and was considered to be "very distinguished and helpful." This photograph shows Nicholson with her faculty in the early 1940s. Pictured from left to right are (first row) Nicholson and Grace Merrill; (second row) Betty Harding, Dorothy London, Helen Eck, and Myrta Coddington. (Courtesy of Veronica Radowicz.)

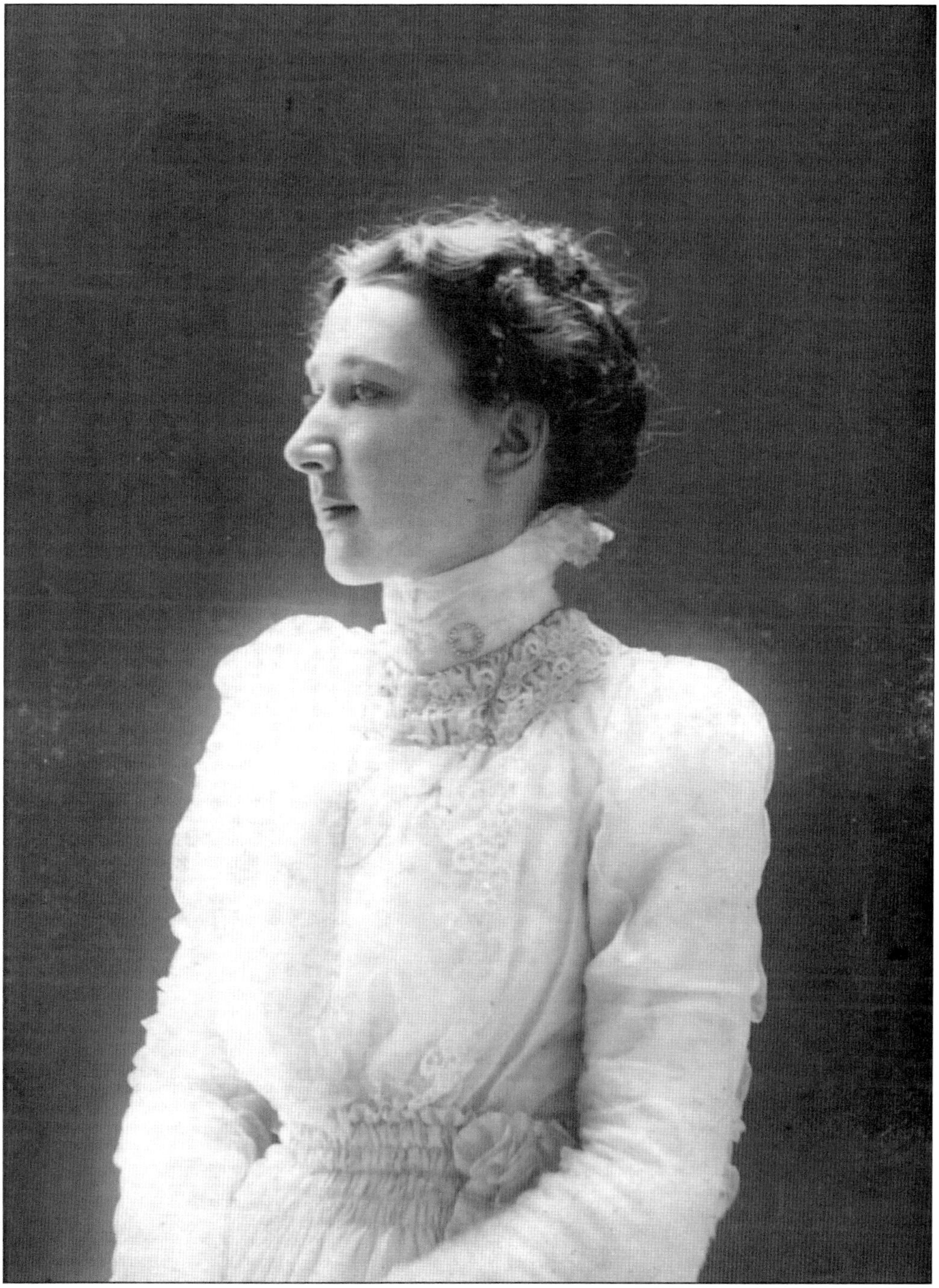

Grace Nicholson was born in Rock Island, Illinois, in 1879. Her parents were Edward and Maria Nicholson, and they bore eight children, four girls and four boys. When Grace was twelve years old, the family moved to Aurora on 418 North View Street. She attended public school in Aurora and graduated from West Aurora High School. She then attended college at the Northern Illinois State Normal School in DeKalb, which had opened in an unfinished building on September 1, 1899. Grace passed a peaceful death on November 29, 1966. (Courtesy of Veronica Radowicz.)

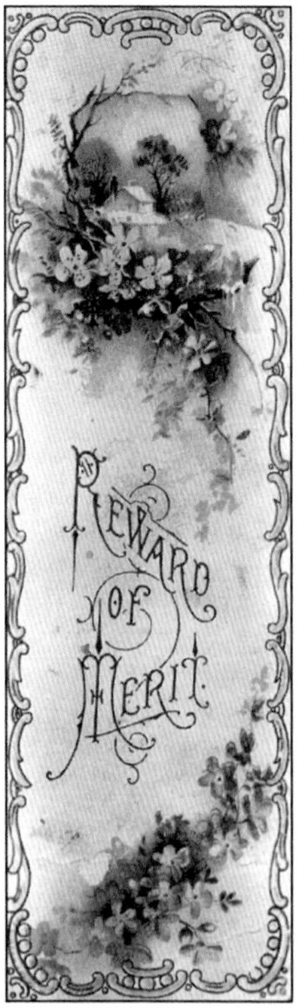

For special occasions, good behavior, or as a reward for outstanding student achievements, this bookmark would be given to the students at Montgomery School. These cards were often put into scrapbooks to show school performance, for punctuality, attendance, or proper conduct. According to the 1970 census, Montgomery had a population of 3,278. (Author's collection.)

This photograph shows the staff and principal of Nicholson School in 1989–1990. (Courtesy of Veronica Radowicz.)

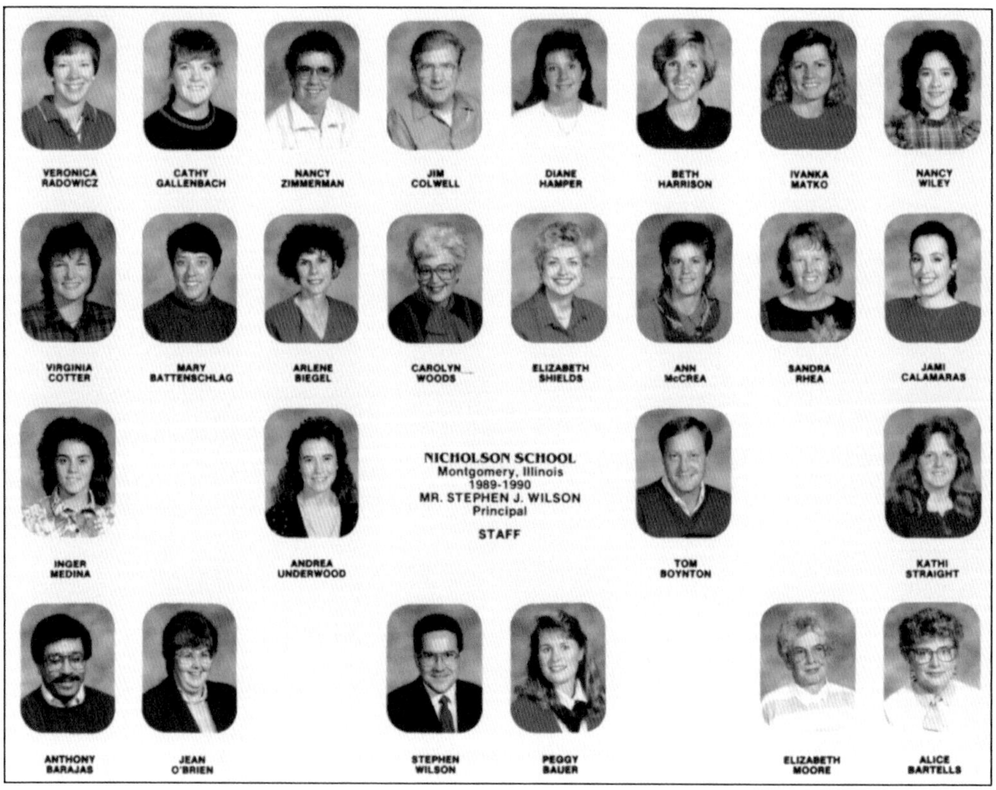

Ed Moore was featured in an article from the *Beacon-News* on February 6, 2000. He was a volunteer for the Adult Literacy Project at Waubonsee Community College. Moore, who was 81 years old, was a retired electronics mechanic and had been a tutor for 18 years. He began tutoring at St. Mary's Church in Aurora and once said, "My star pupils bring great satisfaction." Moore and his wife, Toni, lived in Montgomery. (Author's collection; *Beacon News* photograph.)

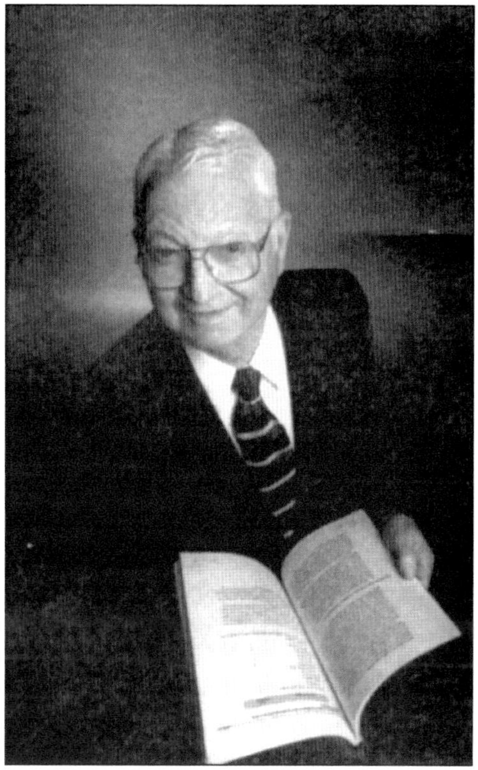

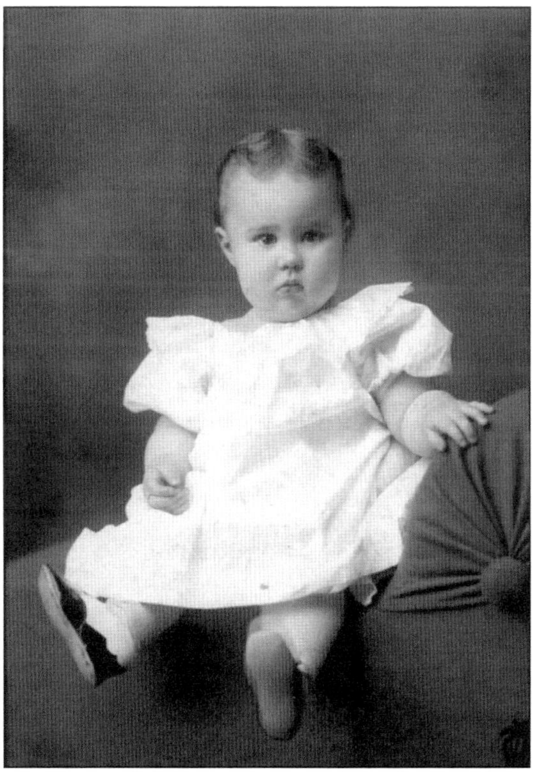

Simon W. Dickson, age one, sits pensively for the camera. He was born in Bristol on August 12, 1903, and was the son of Robert and Grace Fuller Dickson. He lived and farmed in Bristol his entire life until death approached on August 21, 1991. Simon was a community leader who served on the Oak Grove Cemetery Board, the Yorkville School District Board, the Farm Bureau, Kendall County Historical Society, and Bristol Township Board. (Courtesy of Juanita Dickson Murst.)

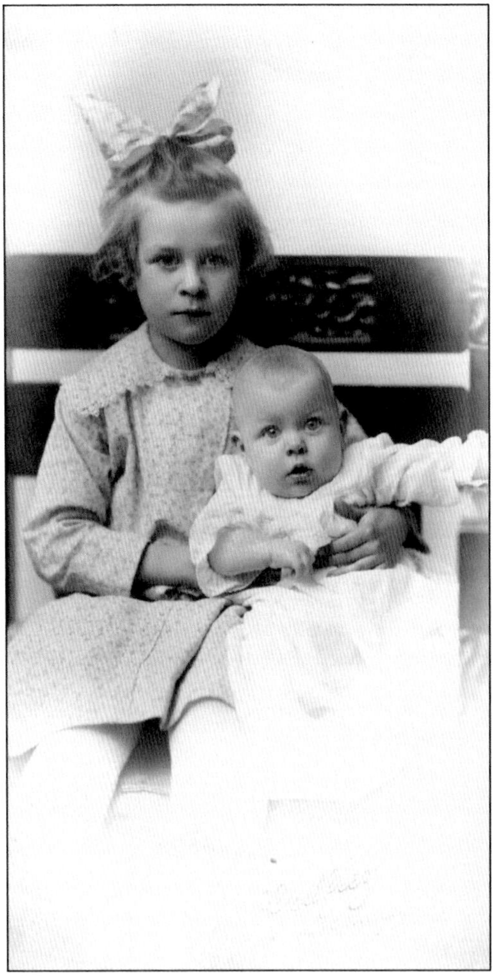

In this lovely 1918 photograph, Thelma Wedemaier holds her baby sister Margaret. Margaret was born on June 21, 1917. She wed John Kiro on February 18, 1945, and they had four children, Marsha, Sharon, Janice, and William. There are now six grandchildren and six great-grandchildren. Margaret is a spry 93-year-old and did not stop driving until she was 91 years old. (Courtesy of Juanita Dickson Murst.)

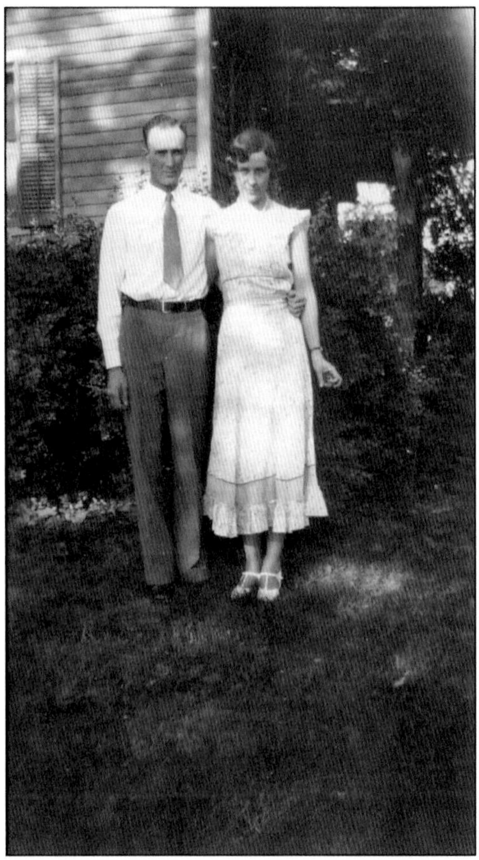

Simon and Thelma Wedemaier Dickson married on June 24, 1933, in the front room of the family farm on By-Pass Route 30. Thelma did not wear a wedding dress. They spent their first night at the Baker Hotel in St. Charles. They celebrated their 50th anniversary with an open house at the Beecher Community Building in Yorkville. Their three children are Richard, Juanita, and Lorene. (Courtesy of Juanita Dickson Murst.)

On December 23, 1956, Juanita Dickson married John Murst at the Bristol Methodist Church. The Reverend Hughes B. Morris Jr. officiated the ceremony. Attendants were Lorene Dickson and Cliff George. They have three children, Robert, Thomas, and Julie. They also have three grandchildren and three great-grandchildren. (Courtesy of Juanita Dickson Murst.)

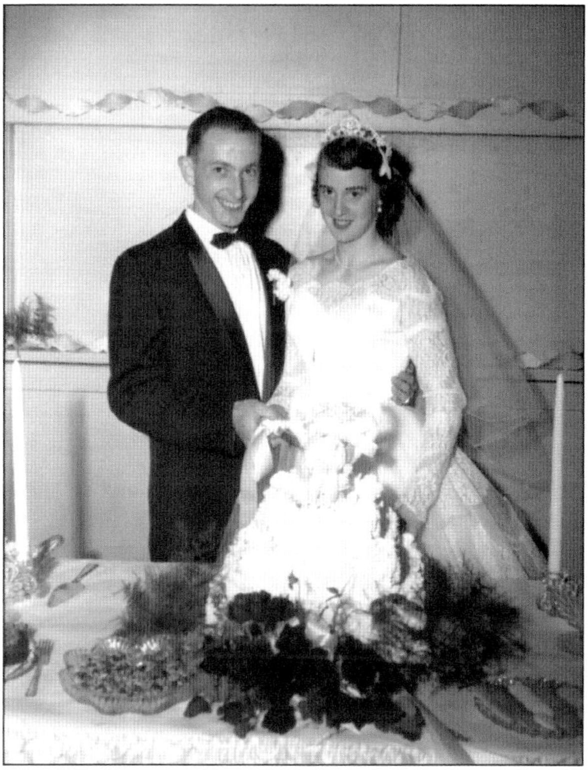

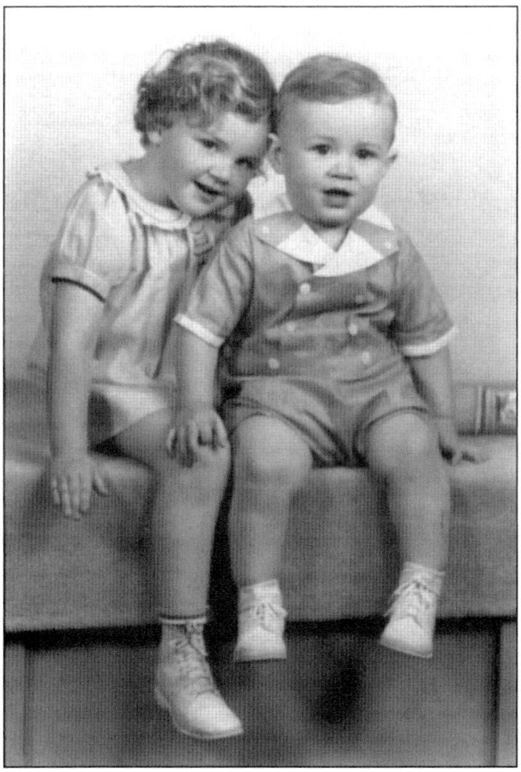

This photograph shows a young Lorene and Richard "Shorty" Dickson. In those days, neighbors helped one another on the farms. If there were illness or accident, neighbors would work the farm fields until their neighbor was back on his feet, said Lorene. (Courtesy of Juanita Dickson Murst.)

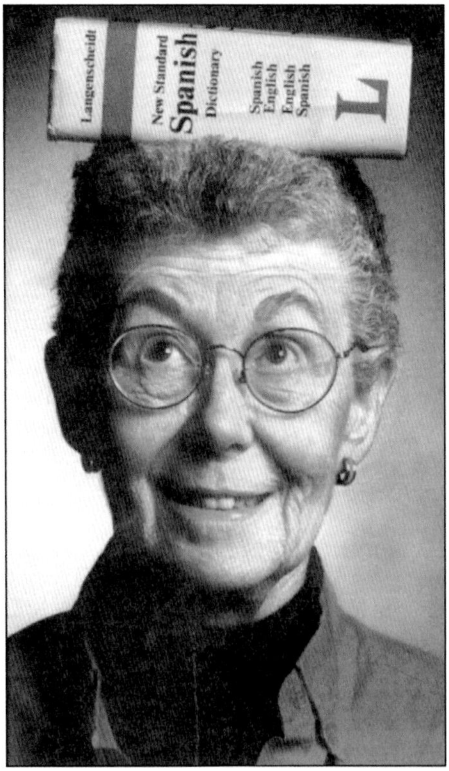

Helen Baker was featured in an article from the *Beacon-News* on February 6, 2000. Helen was head of the nursing department at Waubonsee Community College and an adult literacy volunteer for three years. She holds a doctorate in education from Northern Illinois University. (Author's collection; *Beacon News* photograph.)

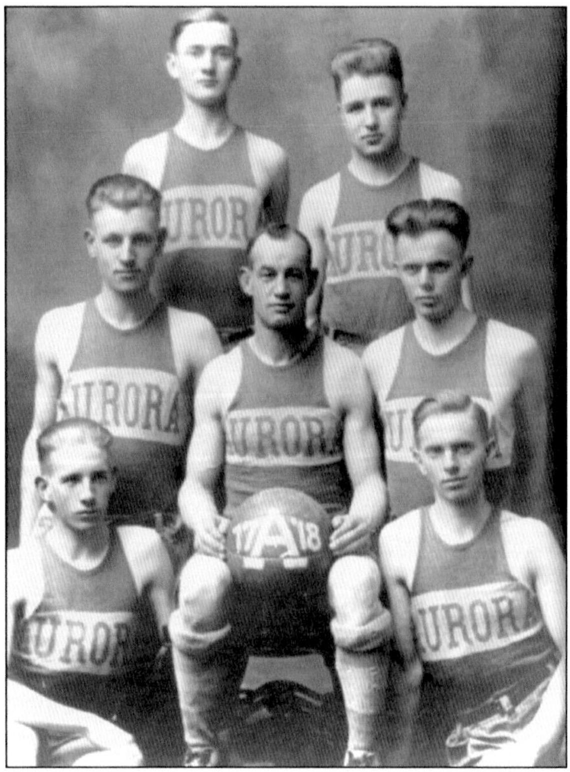

This 1907 photograph shows the serious faces of the men's basketball team at Aurora University. Records are unavailable before 1912, and many were lost in the area flood of 1996. Today, the basketball coach is James Lancaster. He holds a 296-132 record for the last 16 seasons. The Spartans won the 2009–2010 Northern Athletics Conference Men's basketball championship and the 2010 NCAA Division Three championship. (Courtesy of Aurora University Archives.)

This is the earliest known 1947 photograph of cheerleaders at Aurora College. Since 1912, the university has served residents of Montgomery and is located at 347 South Gladstone in Aurora. The college was rechristened Aurora University in 1985. (Courtesy of Aurora University Archives.)

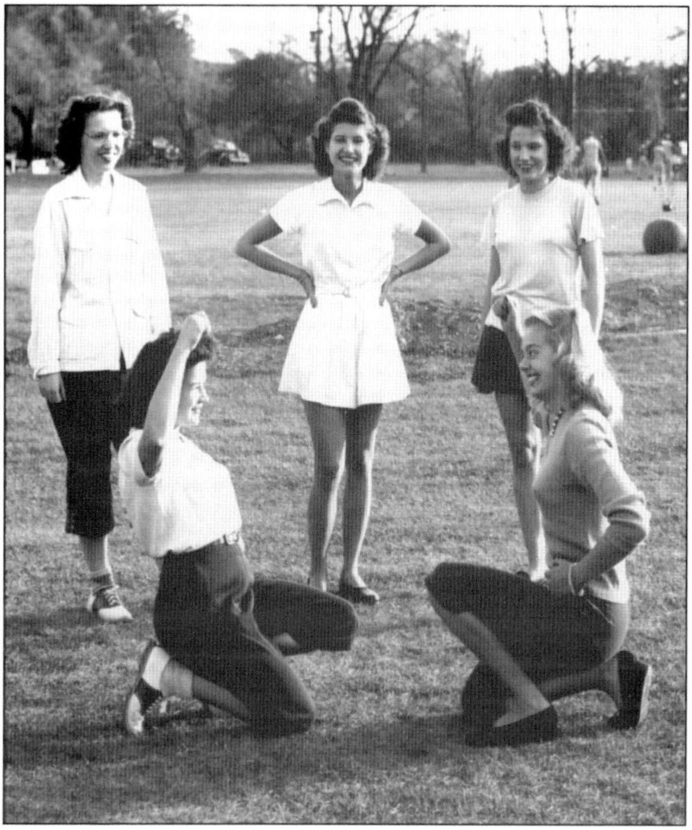

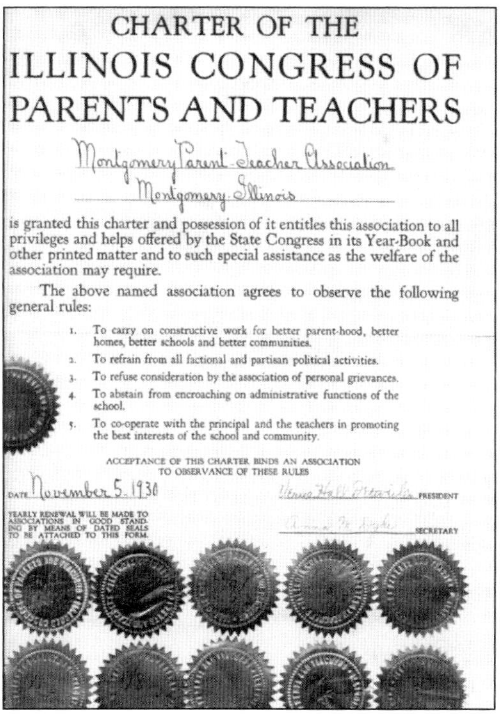

CHARTER OF THE

ILLINOIS CONGRESS OF PARENTS AND TEACHERS

Montgomery Parent-Teacher Association

Montgomery Illinois

is granted this charter and possession of it entitles this association to all privileges and helps offered by the State Congress in its Year-Book and other printed matter and to such special assistance as the welfare of the association may require.

The above named association agrees to observe the following general rules:

1. To carry on constructive work for better parent-hood, better homes, better schools and better communities.
2. To refrain from all factional and partisan political activities.
3. To refuse consideration by the association of personal grievances.
4. To abstain from encroaching on administrative functions of the school.
5. To co-operate with the principal and the teachers in promoting the best interests of the school and community.

ACCEPTANCE OF THIS CHARTER BINDS AN ASSOCIATION TO OBSERVANCE OF THESE RULES

DATE November 5, 1930 PRESIDENT

YEARLY RENEWAL WILL BE MADE TO ASSOCIATIONS IN GOOD STANDING BY MEANS OF DATED SEALS TO BE ATTACHED TO THIS FORM.

SECRETARY

This Illinois charter was given to the Montgomery Parent Teacher Association on November 5, 1930. (Courtesy of Veronica Radowicz.)

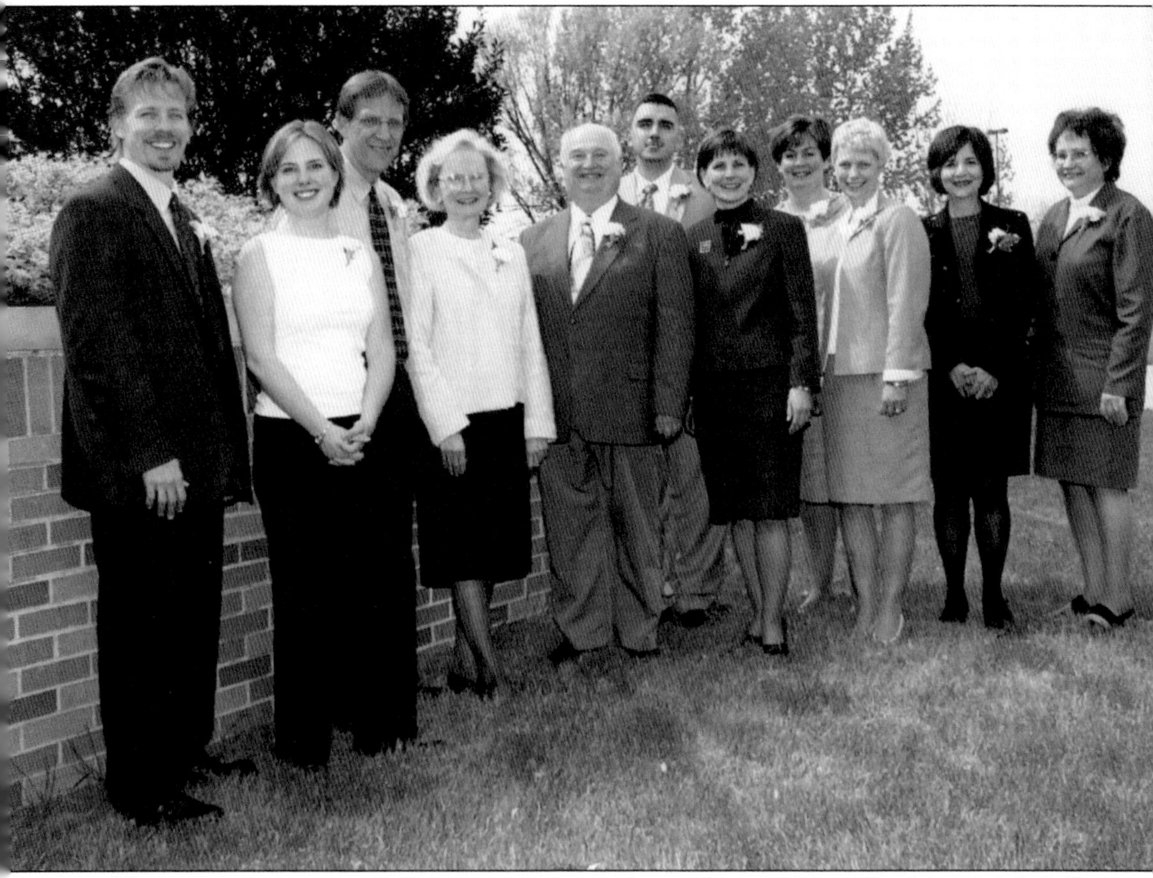

Waubonsee Community College began to serve the residents of Kane, Kendall, Will, LaSalle, and DeKalb Counties on August 22, 1966. The Vision Writing Team collaborated for several months to format the college's vision statement. On May 5, 2004, this photograph was taken of the committee members led by Dr. Wayne Stone. Pictured from left to right are Mike Vester, Joy Baish, Larry Modaff, the author, Dr. Wayne Stone, Danny Jaquez, college president Dr. Christine J. Sobek, Ellen Lindeen, Jill Wold, Dr. Maria Bakalis, and Rita Brubacher. (Author's collection.)

Three

Excel in This Grace of Giving

But just as you excel in everything, in faith, in speech, in knowledge, in complete earnestness and in your love for us, see also that you excel in this grace of giving.

—II Corinthians 8:7

The Village of Montgomery sits in both Kane and Kendall Counties, 38 miles west of the Chicago Loop. The earliest settler was Jacob Carpenter, who arrived from Ohio in November 1832. In 1833, he built a log house on the east side of the Fox River, the first house built in the township of Aurora. His wife, Nancy Pierce Carpenter, gave birth to their son Elijah P. Carpenter on May 25, 1834, and the baby boy was the first white child born in Aurora Township. In 1834, the Chicago-Galena road crossed the Fox River and traversed the land that would become Montgomery. The location was a day's stagecoach journey from Chicago, and so a traveler's inn was built there. Elijah Pierce's tavern and Daniel Gray's tavern soon faced each other across the river. The blacksmith William T. Elliott arrived in 1834, and he served travelers, settlers, and the remaining Potawatomi population. Stagecoaches delivered Montgomery's mail biweekly from Naperville, which was 10 miles away. The arrival of the McCormick Works at Chicago doomed Montgomery's reaper plant. Likewise, the railroad nexus at Aurora made it difficult for Montgomery to compete economically. Population diminished and industry stagnated. However, in 1880, relief began when the Chicago, Burlington & Quincy Railroad constructed a station for livestock that was en route to Chicago's stockyards. By 1960, the Chicago yards were the largest worldwide. Also, the railroad shipped Montgomery's produce and spring water to the Chicago markets.

In 1904, the city directory listed many different occupations, such as crockery making, coppersmith, cutlery, dressmaker, embroider, fresco painter, confectionery, gasfitter, milliner, scroll sawing, and silk sales.

In 1906, Lyon Metallic was the first modern factory to move to Montgomery from Chicago. Montgomery and Aurora have remained inextricably linked. Along with North Aurora, the three cities formed the Fox Valley Park District, which allowed their students to share a school district. Many residents attend church in Montgomery, but they also attend churches in the surrounding communities of Oswego, Aurora, Yorkville, and North Aurora.

For many years, Montgomery retained its small-town ambience even though its population was rapidly growing. In 2000, Montgomery had a population of 5,471, and 84 percent of the residents were white, 13 percent were Hispanic, and 3 percent were African American. Before the completion of the census in 2010, the population was listed as 17,062. As in the past, Montgomery's identity is closely tied to the Fox River.

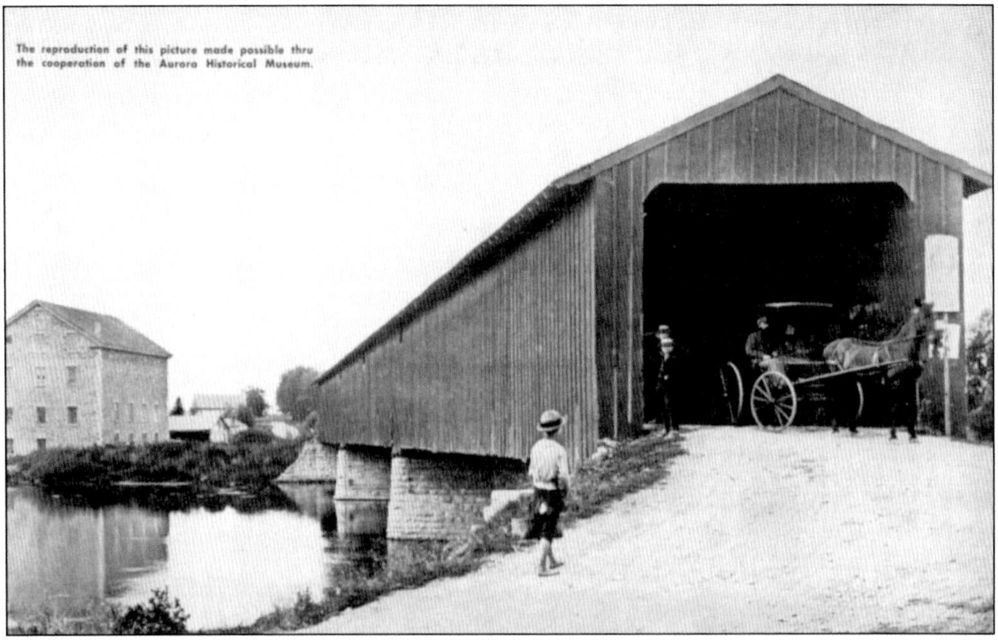

The covered bridge had been dismantled and rebuilt in Montgomery in 1868 because Aurora's city fathers thought the original would not last. Covered bridges kept rain and snow off the timbers, and the covers added more years to the life of the bridge. It also prevented horses from shying at the running water below. The covered bridge had a sign that read, "There is a $5 fine for driving faster than a walk on this bridge." The bridge was removed in 1915. (Courtesy of Alice Pocus Sutcliff.)

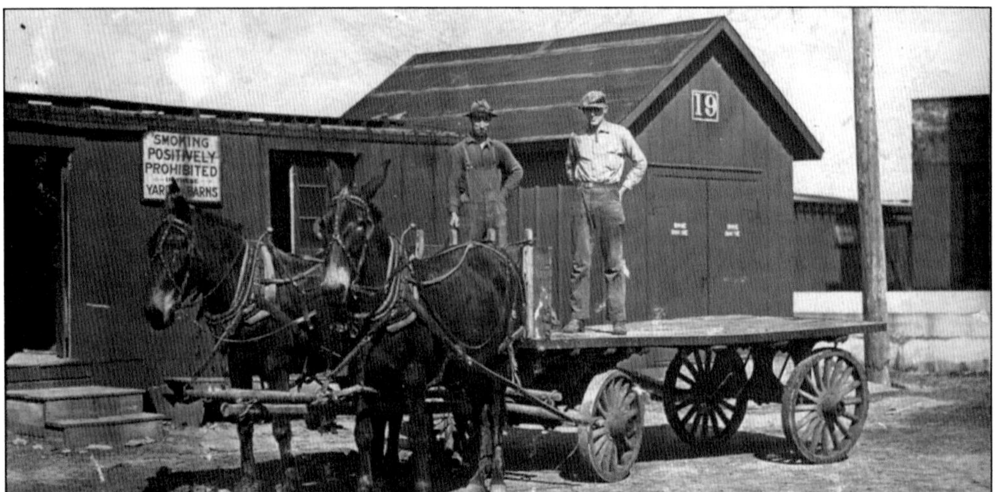

The general farm data for Kendall County from the 1910 census showed a 10,777 population with 1,258 farms. According to the report, 923 farmers were native born, 334 farmers were nonnative born, and there was one black farmer. Farmland composed of 94.4 percent of the land area. The average farm had 155.6 acres. Farm property value was set at $29,630,229. There were 15,052 heads of cattle valued at $456,907. A dinner of "delicious tee-bone steak with French fried potatoes, salad, hot biscuits and syrup, tea, or coffee" only cost 45¢. (Courtesy of Montgomery Archives/Sheep Yards.)

This 1888 photograph shows the Ladies Aid Society of St. Olaf Lutheran Church. They performed many good works for those in need in the community. In 1966, plans were approved for construction of a new church on the same property as the parsonage. Ground breaking was held on October 11, 1968. The new church was built at a cost of $306,000. (Courtesy of Viola Skogen.)

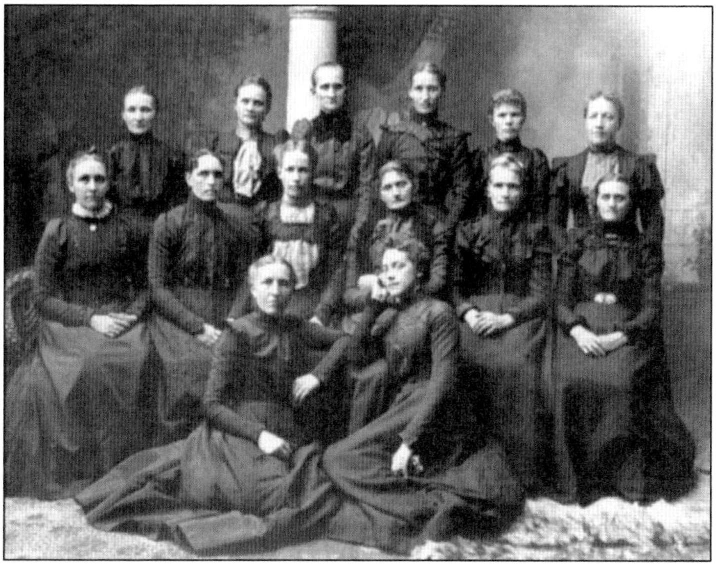

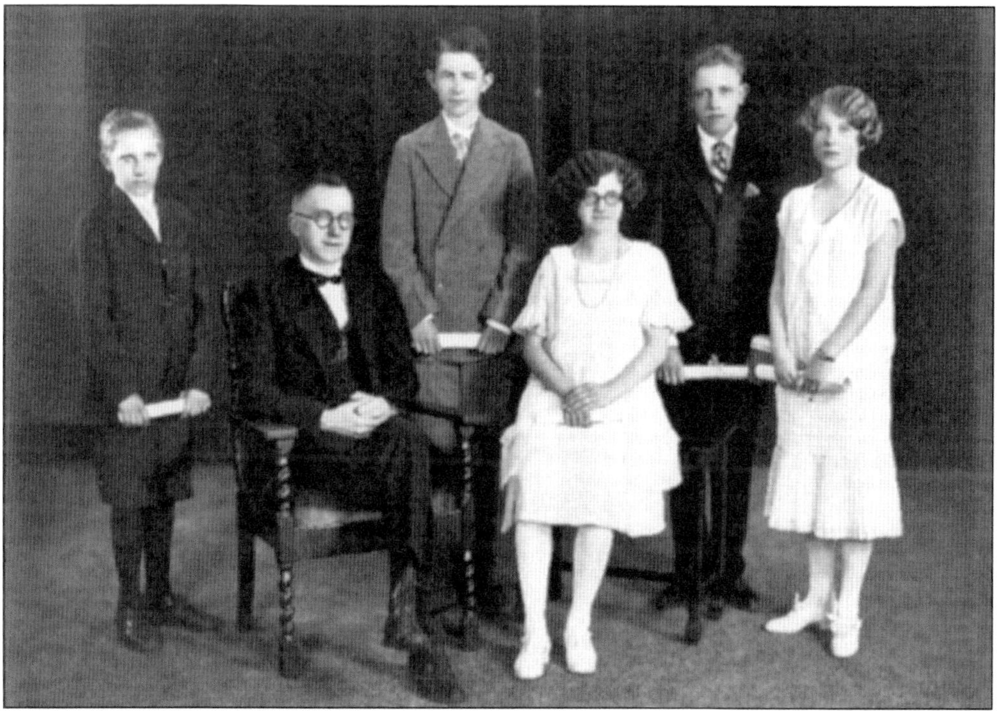

Oscar J. Johnson, the pastor at St. Olaf Lutheran Church, was born in 1921 and passed away in 1963. This 1925 photograph shows him conferring the rite of confirmation on these five students. During this time, the radio was a popular media in Montgomery. In the summer of 1895, Marconi signaled 1.5 kilometers and took British patent No. 7,777. The first audio transmission occurred in 1919. By 1931, the *Aurora Beacon-News* had an advertisement for a Philco Transitone Automobile radio for $65 that was "sold on easy terms." The station KYW produced the *Garden Hour* that aired at 2:30 p.m. and was sponsored by Erlenborn's on South River Street in Aurora. (Courtesy of Viola Skogen.)

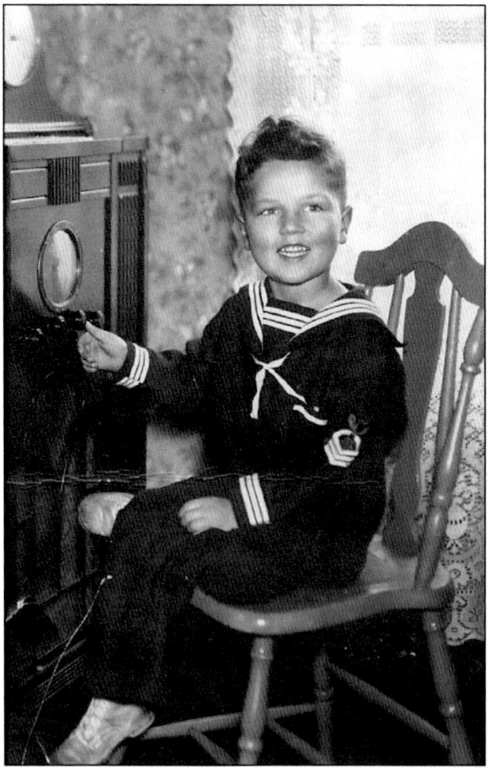

This adorable 1936 photograph is of Larry D. McClain at age six. In 1936, the popular radio programs included Bing Crosby, who hosted the *Kraft Music Hall* and *The Ziegfeld Follies of the Air*. In 1897, there was an ordinance that granted certain rights to the Chicago Phone Company in Montgomery. (Montgomery Archives.)

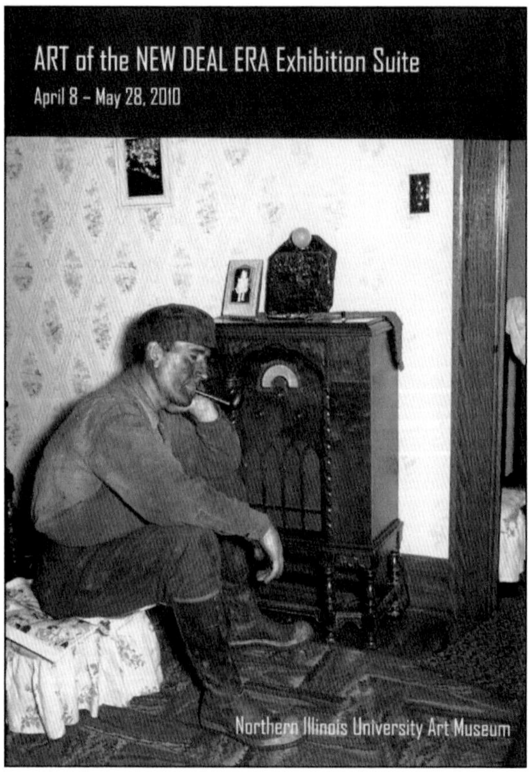

Montgomery is situated very close to many attractions and events, including the Sugar Grove Corn Boil, Swedish Days in Geneva, the Sandwich Fair, or the Blues on the Fox in Aurora. At Northern Illinois University in DeKalb, the university's art museum sponsored the Art of the New Deal Era exhibit April 8 to May 28, 2010. This program cover shows a man listening to the radio. (Author's collection.)

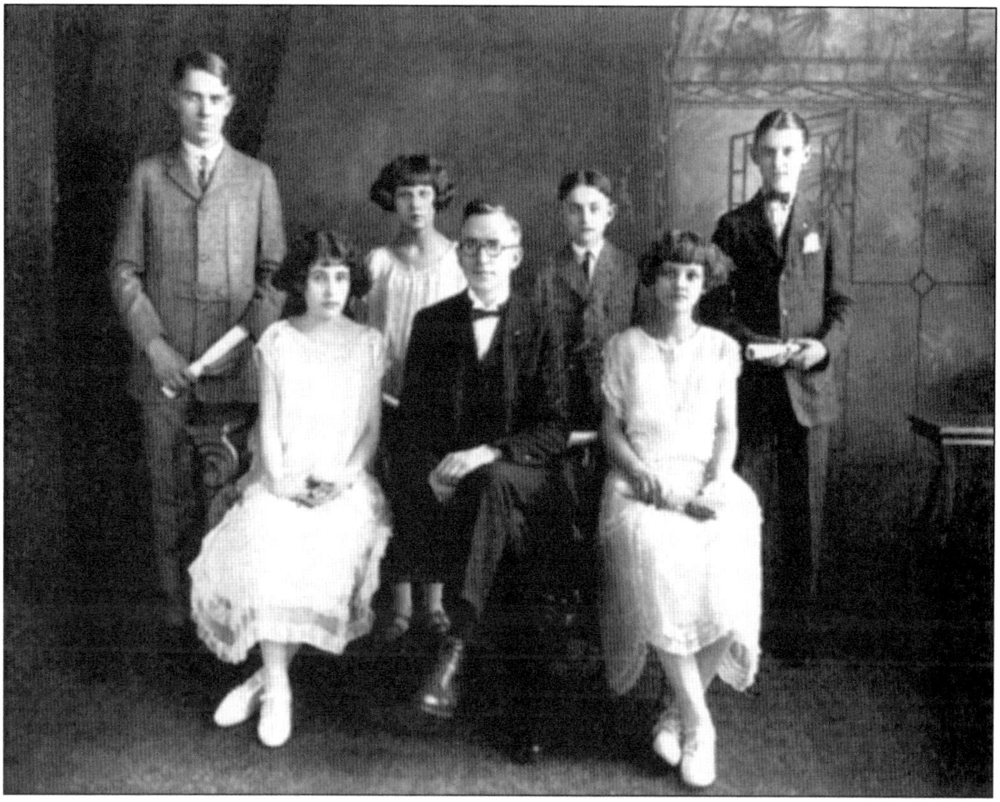

This 1924 photograph shows a confirmation class at St. Olaf Lutheran Church. The students wore lovely white dresses and suits. (Courtesy of Viola Skogen.)

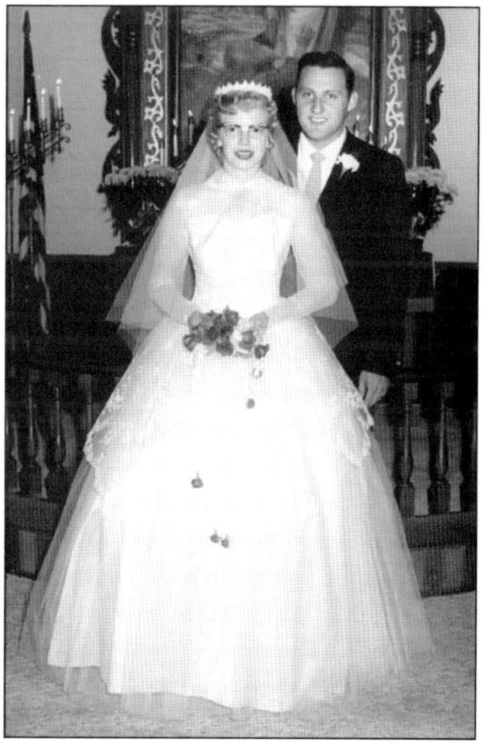

Thomas Skogen and Viola Hoff were married on October 4, 1958. They celebrated their 50th wedding anniversary on October 4, 2008. They have two children, Todd Skogen (married to Linda) and Tracy Skogen Larsen (married to Jim Larsen). Their grandchild is Michael Skogen. Tom is retired from the Burlington Northern Santa Fe Railroad, and Viola is the historian for St. Olaf Lutheran Chuch. They have lived in Montgomery since 1962. (Courtesy of Viola Skogen.)

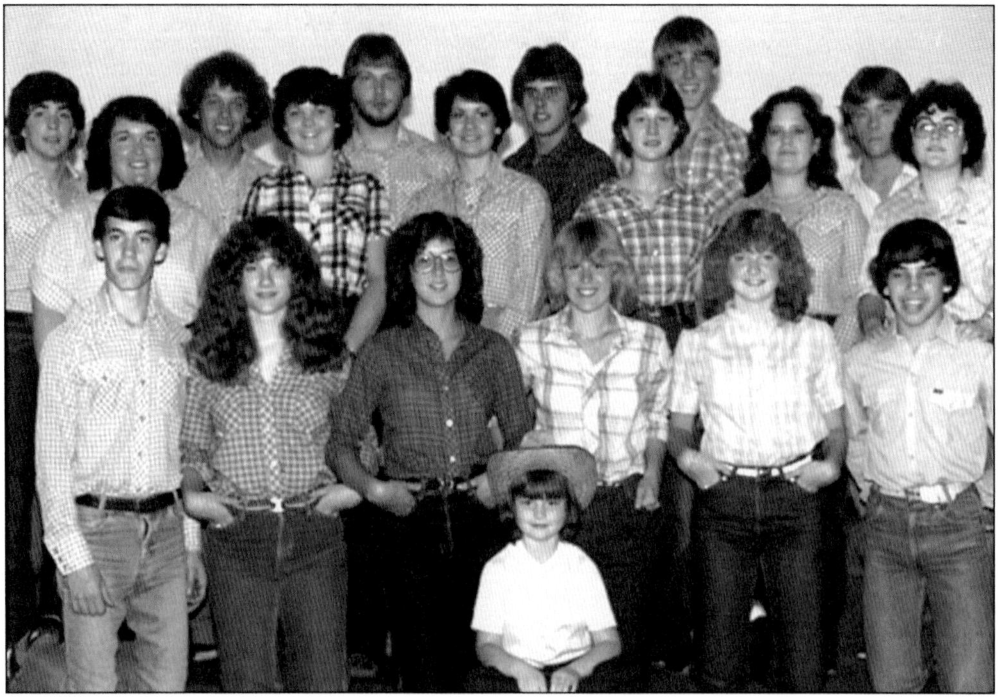

The year was 1981. This photograph shows the singing-group Reflections at the St. Olaf Lutheran Church. In 1979, they had traveled to a state fair in Wyoming to present the choral "Backpackers Suite." During this time, the church pastor was Rev. William H. Hutter (1964–1979), and the director was Doris Pittman. The group performed for three years in the area and traveled as far south as Texas. (Courtesy of Viola Skogen.)

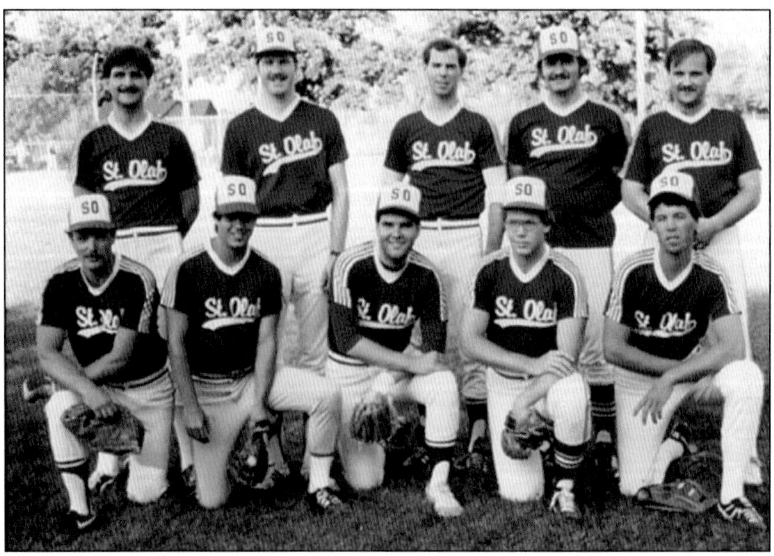

Members of the softball team of St. Olaf Lutheran Church pose in 1984. During this time, the church pastor was Rev. Robert Kasperson, and pastor Brian J. Pearson succeeded Kasperson in 1994. The team's coach was Greg Morris. (Courtesy of Viola Skogen.)

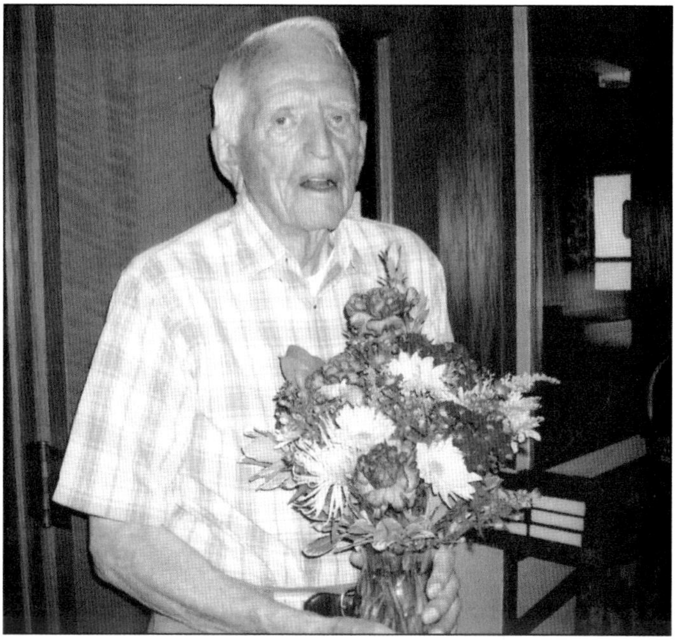

Howard Hughes attends the St. Olaf Lutheran Church, where he has served three terms as a trustee. Howard is 92 years old and was born on July 13, 1918. He enlisted in the Air Force and served 3.5 years in North Africa and Italy. He and Ida Chally married on June 18, 1946, and they have two children, Laurie Church (married to Collin Church) and David Hughes (married to Donna). Their two grandchildren are Bradley and Megan Hughes. Howard has ordered and delivered altar flowers since 1996. (Author's collection.)

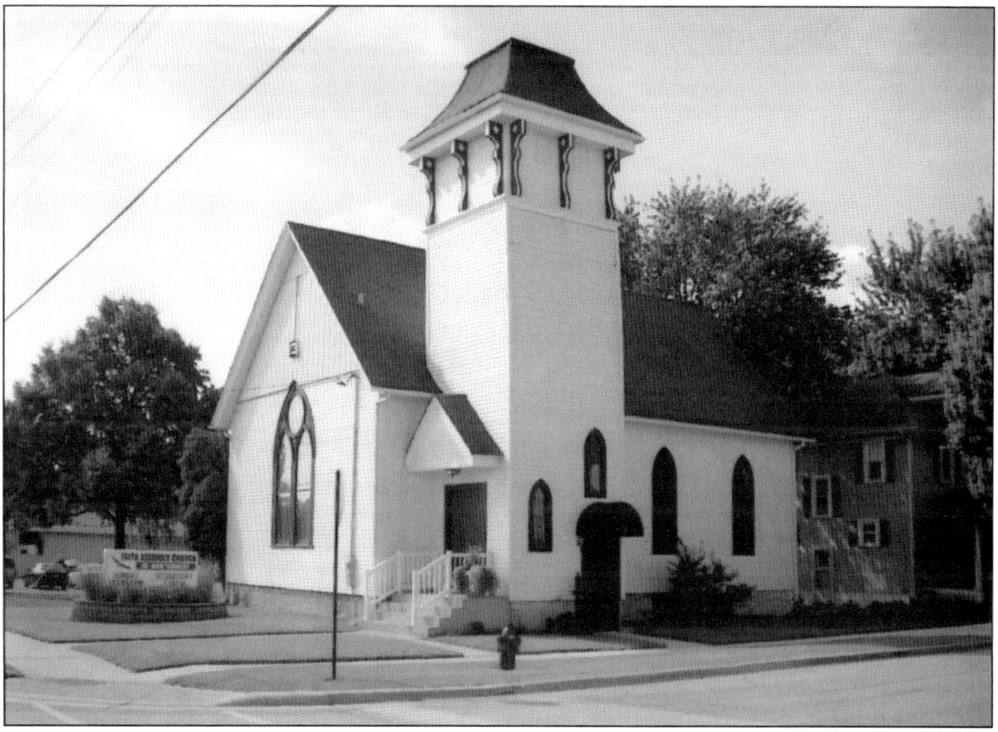

Montgomery Methodist Church was the first congregation in the village. The congregation has ties to the Wesley Methodist Church of Aurora. In 1883, it was known as the First Methodist Episcopal Church of Montgomery. In 1985, the church celebrated 100 years of Christian worship and fellowship. In 1997, because of declining membership, they merged with the Bristol United Methodist Church. The building on Webster and Main Streets is currently occupied by Faith Assembly Church. (Author's collection.)

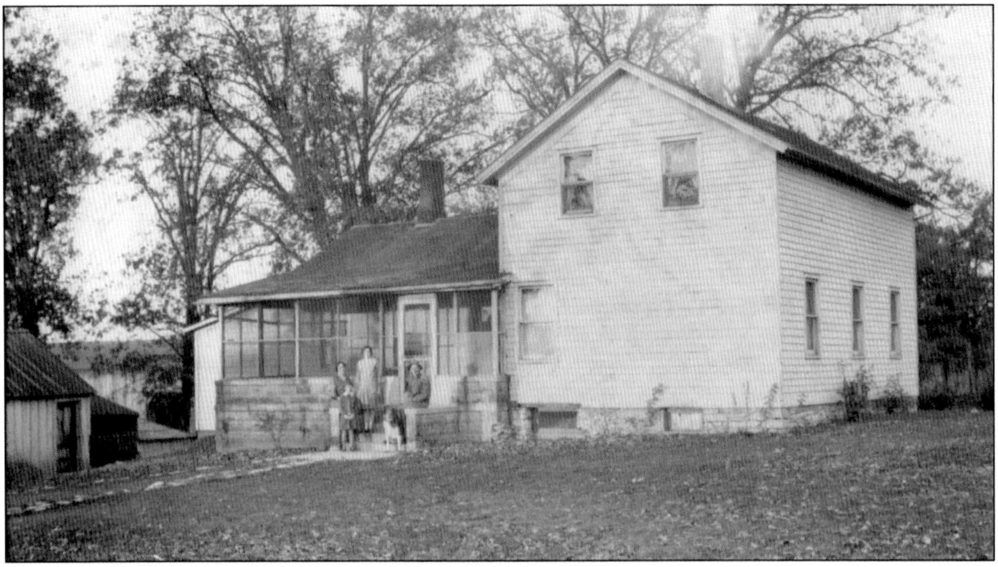

This 1920 photograph shows the family home of Elsie Ruth Armbruster in NaAuSay Township, Minkler Road, in Kendall County. Pictured from left to right are Mary Helene; her sister Hazel; her mother, Elise Ruth; Herman, her father; and Sport, the family dog. During this time, the mail carrier would arrive on Monday nights around sunset. The mail carrier would then travel as far as Colonel Seward's home, which was on the way to Springfield and on the northern terminus of the mail route. (Courtesy of Ruth Armbruster Dieterich Wagner.)

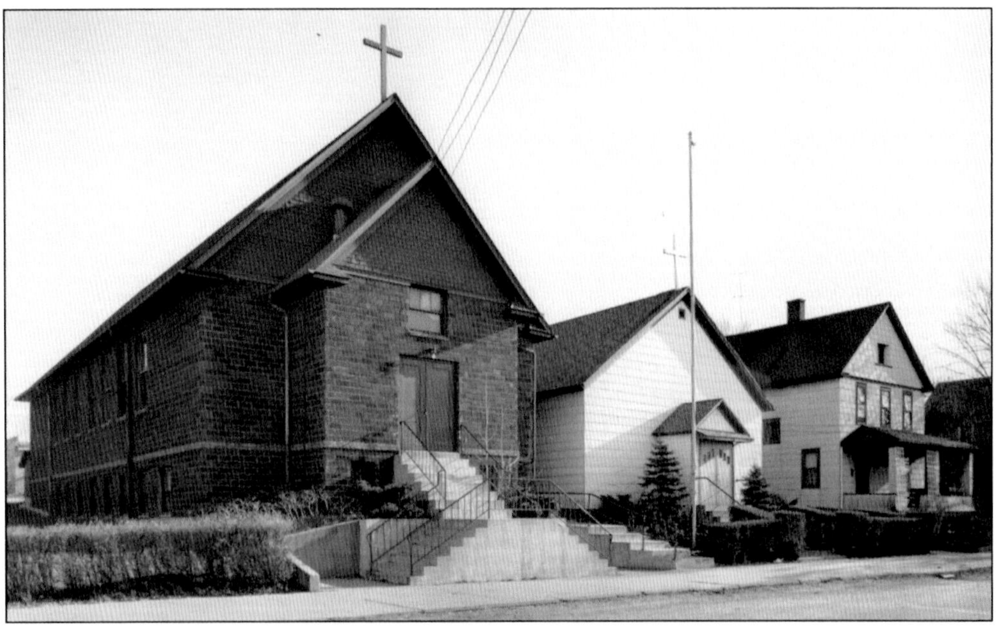

St. Peter's Church began in 1925 as a mission of the Holy Angels Parish in Aurora. Immigrants from Italy, Lithuania, Ukraine, and Germany lived in this area. Father Rojemann later requested that the mission become a parish. Bishop Hoban granted this request in April 1929. Sister Evelyn and Sister Mary Alacoque began to teach 17 children in kindergarten. In 1932, a first grade was added. (Courtesy of St. Peter's Church.)

STATE OF ILLINOIS }
Kane COUNTY } SS

Aurora, Ill., December 3 1958

To All Whom It May Concern

WHEREAS WE the undersigned, P. A. THRALL & SONS, INC. General contractor have been employed by St. Peter's Church of Aurora to furnish labor and materials to complete the St. Peter's School Building

for the building located at Sard Avenue, Aurora

NOW, THEREFORE, KNOW YE, That We the undersigned, for and in consideration of Twelve Thousand Seven Hundred Sixty One & 24/100 ($12,761.24) Dollars and other good and valuable considerations, the receipt whereof is hereby acknowledged, do We hereby waive and release any and all lien, or claim, or right of lien on said above described building and premises under "An Act to Revise the Law in Relation to Mechanics' Liens, approved May 18, 1903, and in force July 1, 1903," on account of labor or materials, or both, furnished by the undersigned to or on account of the said St. Peter's Church of Aurora for said building or premises.

Given under my hand and this 3 rd. day of December 1958

P. A. THRALL & SONS, INC.

Per Philip A. Thrall

In the early 1930s, many financial obstacles necessitated that St. Peter's Church reduce its tuition from 25¢ a month to 10¢ a month. The church buildings badly needed repairs, and the new pastor Joseph A. Rzeszotko prayed, "I came here out of obedience, Lord, now please help me." Father Rzeszotko became a monsignor and remained the church's pastor for 48 years. (Courtesy of St. Peter's Church.)

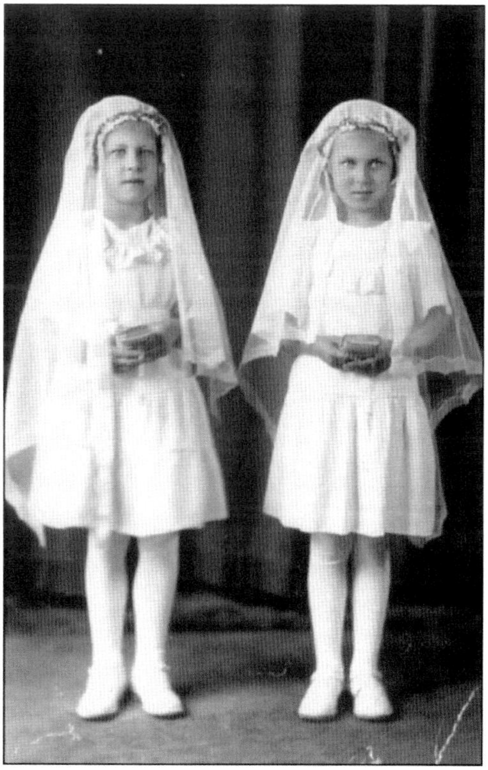

Cousins Nina and Margaret Weber pose for their 1936 first communion at St. Peter's Church. (Courtesy of Barbara Peck.)

This envelope was mailed from the Vatican on October 9, 1964. What a treasure! Pope Paul VI, Giovanni Montini, was the leader of the Roman Catholic Church, bishop of Rome, and sovereign of Vatican City from 1963 to 1978. He toured the Holy Land in 1964—the first pope to leave Italy in 150 years. (Courtesy of St. Peter's Church.)

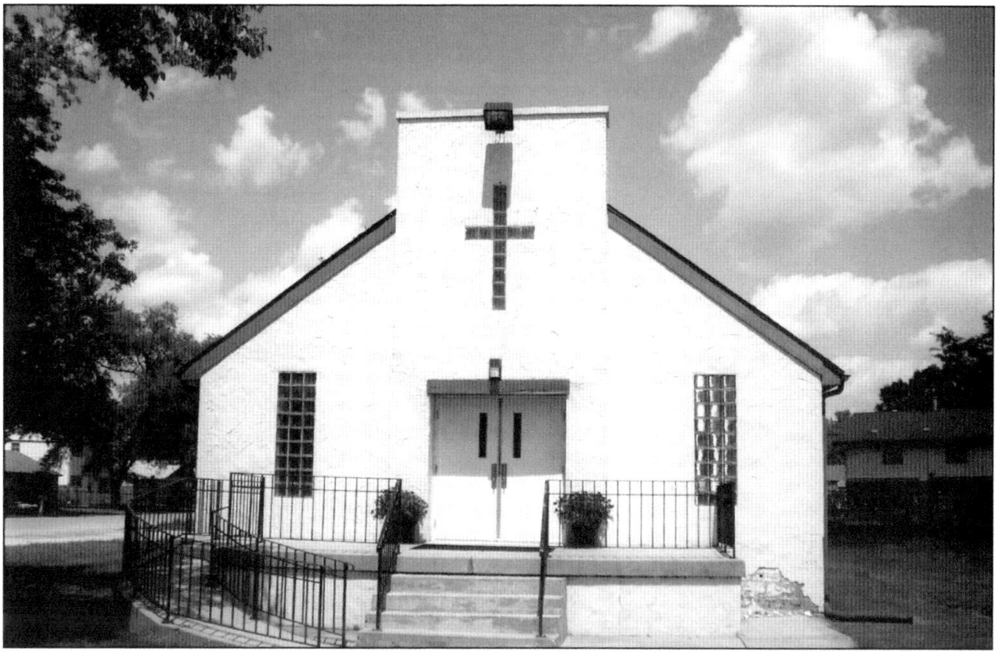

Abundant Life Church is located at 402 Sherman Avenue in Aurora. On September 30, 2010, pastors Jeff and Christine Miller celebrated 20 years as a nondenominational church. Their three children are Elizabeth, Timothy, and Kaitlin. (Author's collection.)

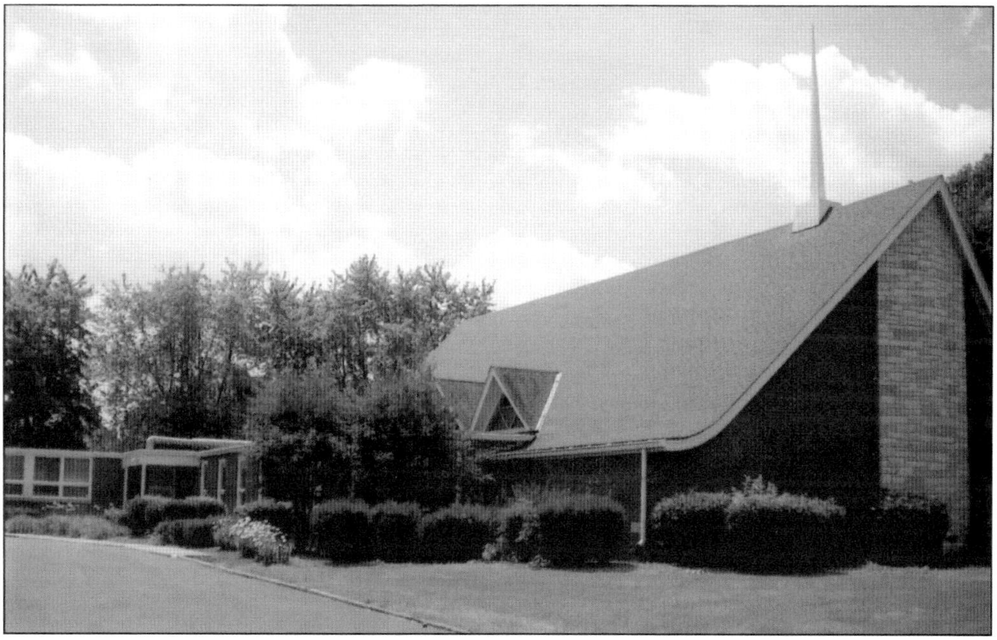

First Congregational Church was organized in 1838 and met in several locations. The first building was constructed on West Park Place in Aurora, but later the congregation moved to East Park Place. In 1857, the congregation moved to East Galena, where it remained for over 100 years. Later on, the church building moved to Montgomery. In the 1990s, it became the Pathway Community Church. In 2000, there was a merger with the Naperville Community Christian Church. The first services were held on March 17, 2002, with 600 in attendance. (Author's collection.)

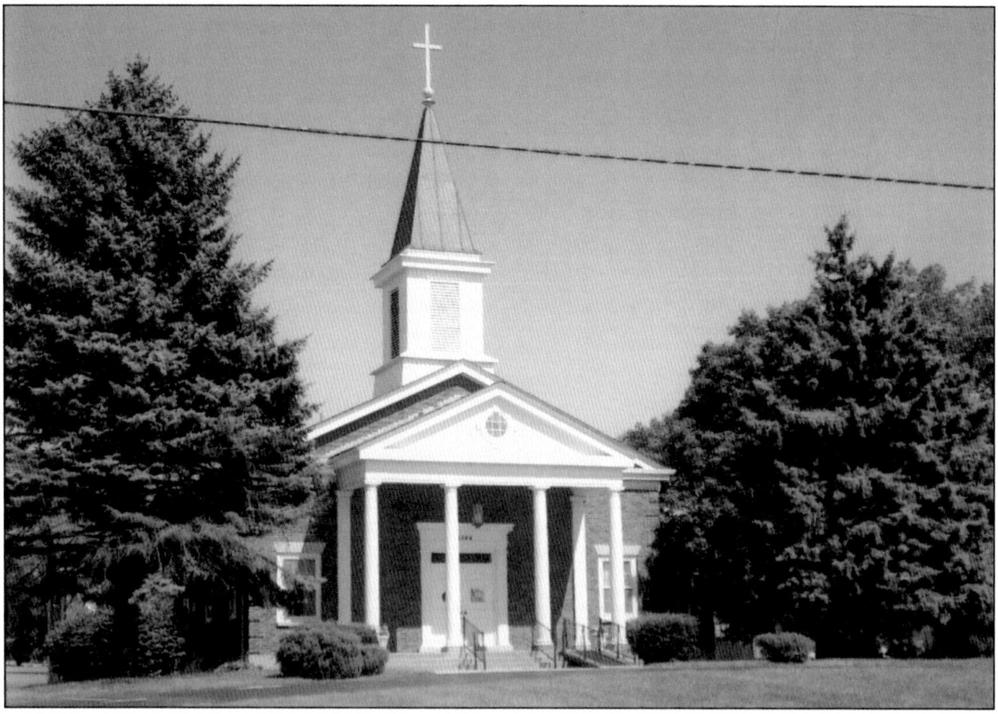

Park Place Baptist Church was known to be a major stop on three routes of the Underground Railroad through Illinois. Several church members conducted slaves through the states as they were on their way to Canada. The church planned to move from Aurora to a new building on Montgomery Road in 1967. The old church was located at 22 West Park Place, and it was torn down. Its altar, cross candles, and pipe organ were saved. Then, on July 6, 1969, the first service was held at the new location. Today, the pastor is Barry Norris. (Author's collection.)

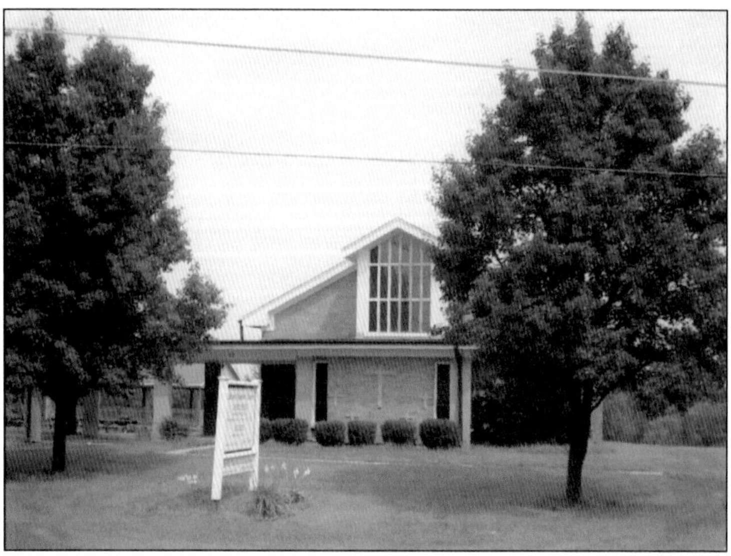

Calvary Baptist Church has served the people of Montgomery since 1953. The church is located at 140 Montgomery Road. Reverend Jim Woods has been the church's pastor since 2001. The state flower of Illinois, the purple violet, can be found on the church grounds every spring. (Author's collection.)

Shown are Aljene Hauer and her mother, Wilma Beyer Hauer, in 1949. Aljene was born on November 6, 1943. They lived on River Street. The rent was $25 a month, and Wilma's monthly income was $82. Wilma was born on November 28, 1919. A coal stove provided heat. On July 5, 1866, Wilma's brother Frederick Beyer and Catherine Anna Webber were married in Aurora by the attorney Squire Murphy. In 1879, William Beyer, the father of Wilma and Frederick, was born in Montgomery and served in the Spanish-American War with Theodore Roosevelt's infamous Rough Riders. He joined the silent choir on March 27, 1960. (Courtesy of Wilma Beyer Hauer.)

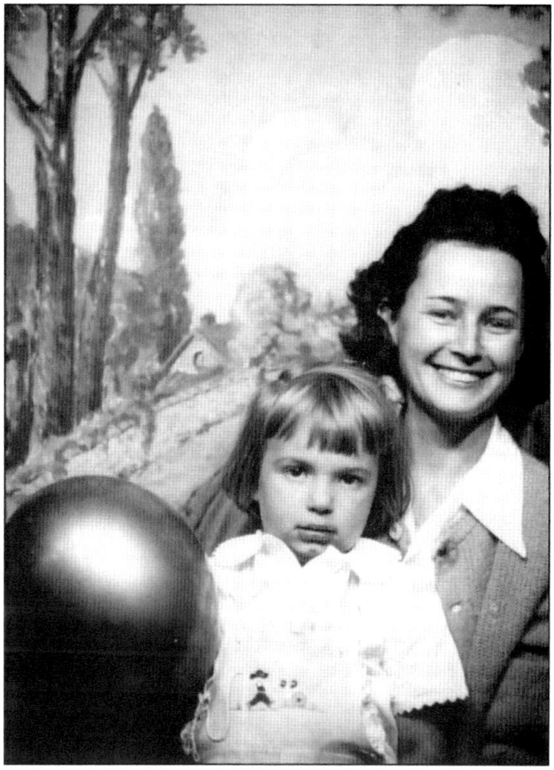

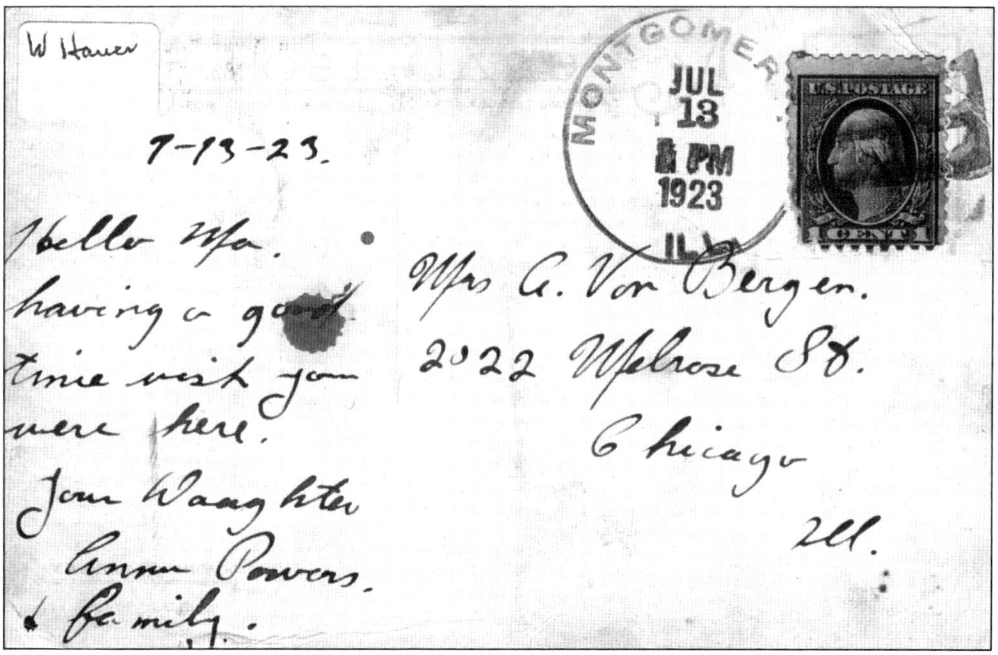

W Hauer

7-13-23.

Hello Ma. having a good time wish you were here. Your Daughter Anna Powers & family.

Mrs A. Von Bergen.
2022 Melrose St.
Chicago
Ill.

This penny postcard was mailed from Montgomery on July 13, 1923, to Mrs. A. Von Bergen, who lived on 2022 Melrose Street in Chicago. Helen told her friend Agnes about the butchering of a hog that day: "We cooked everything but the oink." Under the hay moon of that July, the family watched the silver stars cascade across the darkening sky. (Courtesy of Wilma Beyer Hauer.)

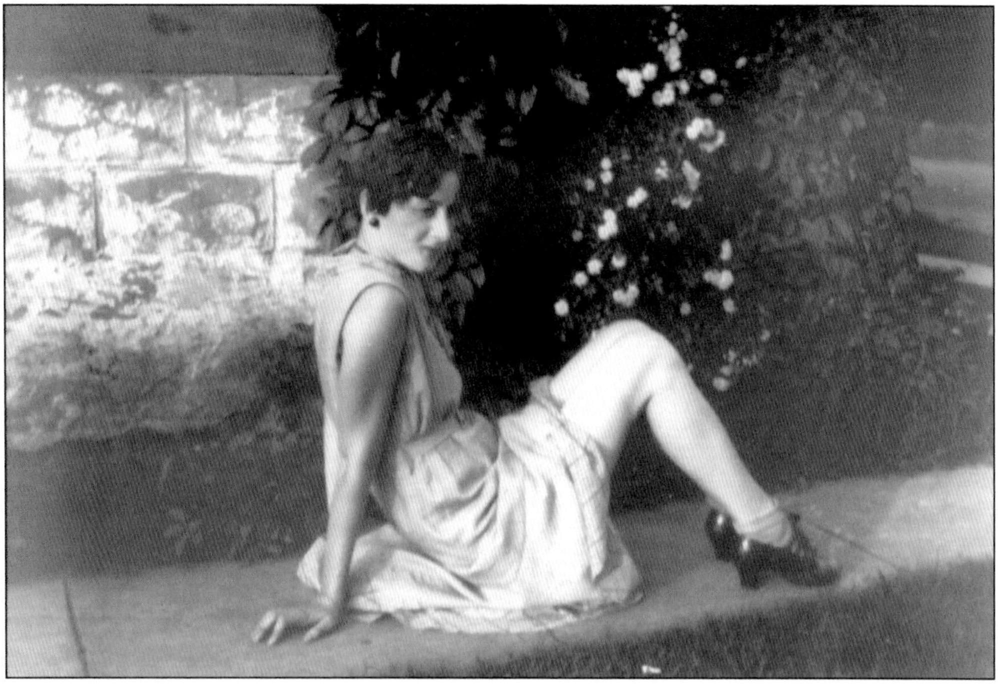

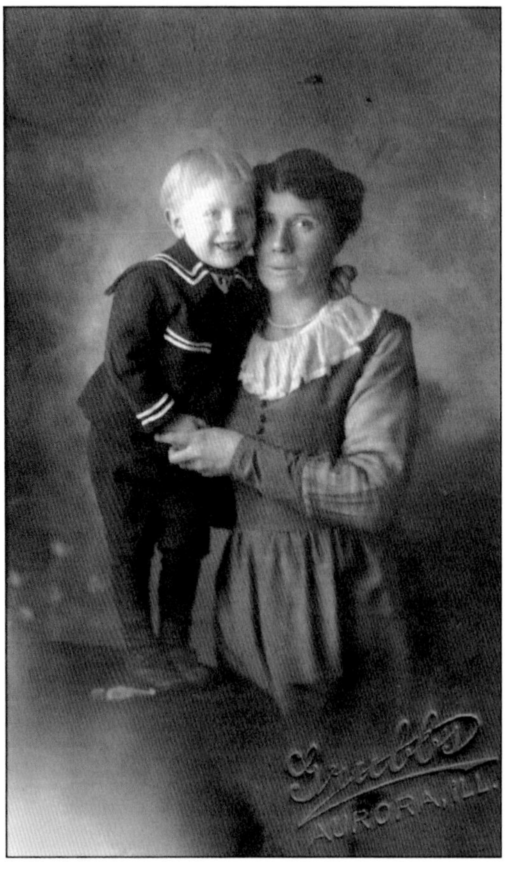

This 1937 photograph shows Myrtle Beyer. What a saucy pose! She was born in 1914. She first married Arthur Ode in 1934, but he died in 1953. She then married Robert Royer, who passed away in 1972. Arthur and Myrtle had adopted one daughter Ramona. Myrtle worked at Stoner's Manufacturing in Aurora for 20 years. The manufacturing company made jukeboxes and conducted war work in the 1940s. Myrtle died in July 2005 at age 91. (Courtesy of Wilma Beyer Hauer.)

Mae Beyer and her son Robert pose happily in 1918. Ten years later, tragedy struck the family when Robert fell on the ice and a streetcar ran over him. He was decapitated and placed in a rubber sack so that the family did not have to view his body. They buried him at Mount Olive Cemetery in Aurora. He was 12 years old. (Courtesy of Wilma Beyer Hauer.)

Pictured in 1902 is George Dahlin Sr., who became a member of the Aurora Zouaves drill team. Four generations of the Dahlin family lived in 1850 house of Daniel Gray. (Courtesy of Montgomery Archives.)

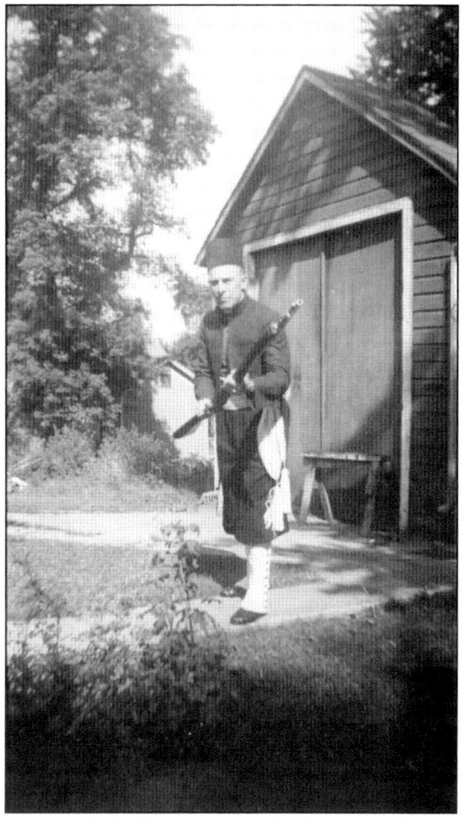

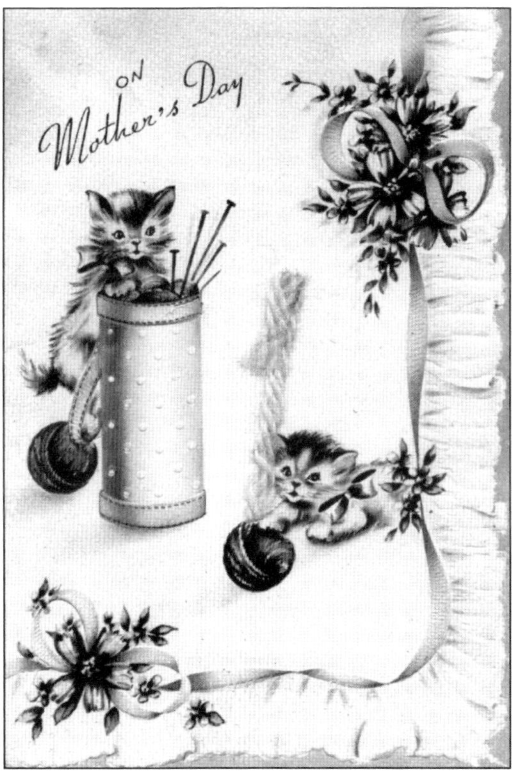

This is a greeting card for Mother's Day that was sent in 1945. In 1908, the holiday was created by Anna Jarvis and became a day to honor mothers. Pres. Woodrow Wilson made it a national holiday in 1914. (Author's collection.)

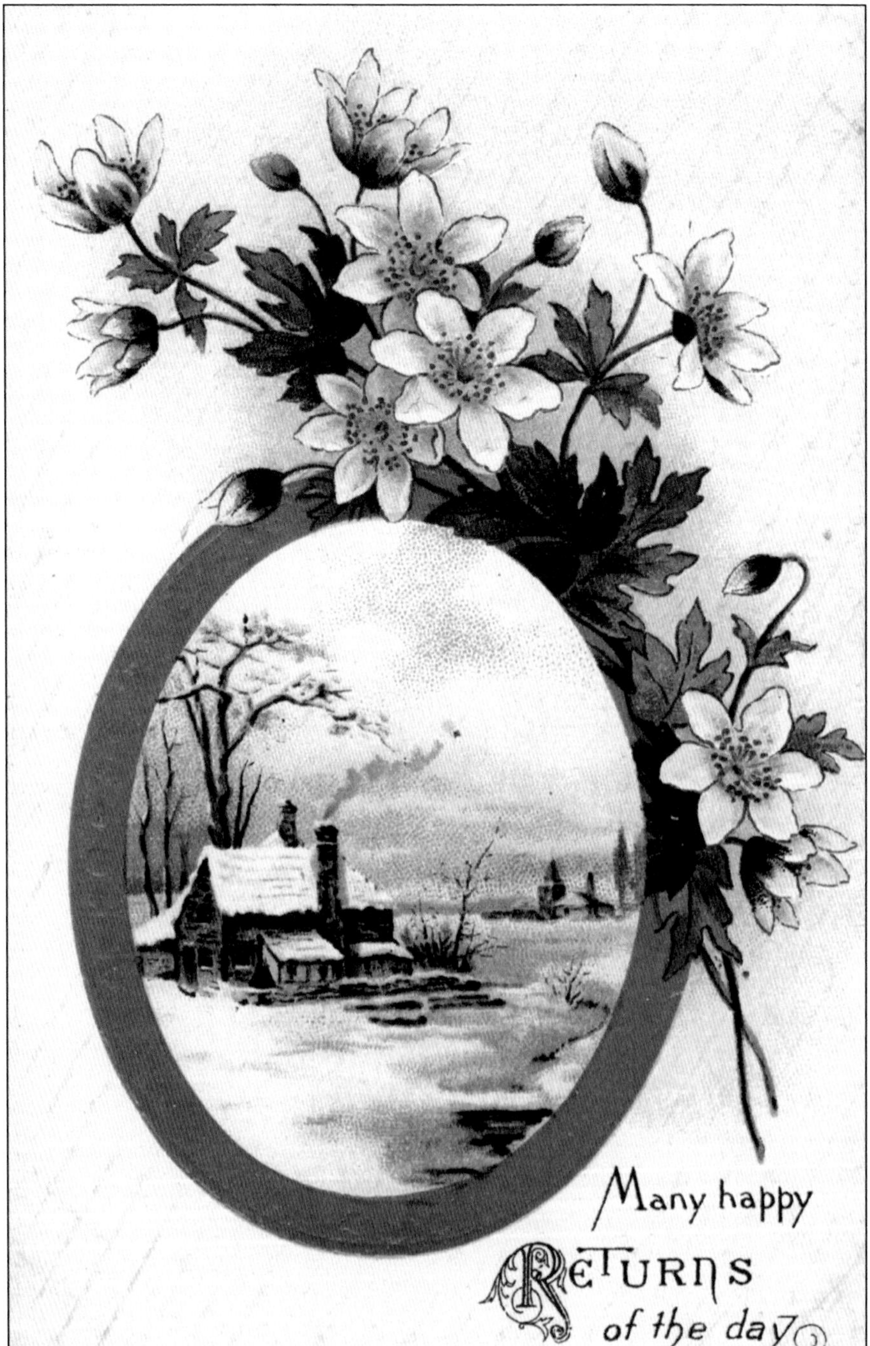

This postcard was mailed from Jackson, Missouri, on August 7, 1913. It was a birthday greeting for William Beyer. In the United States, the first postcard was a privately printed card that was copyrighted in 1861 by J.P. Carlton. The copyright was later transferred to H.L. Lipman. The Lipman postcards were on sale until 1873, when the penny postcards made by the US Government replaced them. In 1889, a Heligoland postcard was considered the first multicolored card ever printed. (Courtesy of Wilma Beyer Hauer.)

Four

Scent of Old Wood and Rosettes

Summer afternoon, summer afternoon. To me those have always been the two most beautiful words in the English language.

—Henry James

By 1858, there were 240 residents and 35 homes in the village. Business included the Montgomery Flouring Mill, Gronberg & Lindgren Mower and Reaper Factory, and a Sash Factory that was on the millrace north of the bridge. A railroad depot was built along the new railroad tracks. On February 17, 1858, a vote was taken for incorporation. There were 30 votes in favor and four votes against. Azariah Rodney Palmer was president of the organizational meeting. A. Tracy Palmer served as clerk. The village limits were located at the Fox River on the east and the railroad tracks on the west.

An ordinance was passed in 1912 to form a fire department. A lumber wagon was purchased for use as a truck. It was fitted with oak ladders and three leather pails on each side. The equipment was stored in a stall of a garage on the corner of Clay and Railroad Streets. Later, a Ford truck was added to the fire department's inventory, with a road speed of 10 miles per hour. The first ambulance was a converted secondhand panel truck.

In 1944, the village bought a $500 siren. Chief Charlie Gaylord devised an alarm system in a basement workshop at his home, assembling components from a discarded pinball machine. When an alarm box received a call, a marble ran down a chute and made contact, electrically sending code impulses that made the siren blow. For more than a year, the chief and his nine firemen worked at wiring call boxes in the village. Five years later, the village hired an answering service. In 1952, the village and the surrounding five-mile area became part of the Montgomery and Countryside Fire Protection District. Money was borrowed to purchase a new truck. Montgomery was the first in the area to have a volunteer fire department that had a sophisticated alarm system, radio, its own base station, and a fog nozzle.

Montgomery installed the original water system in 1928. The original Well No. 1 pumped at 100 gallons per minute into the distribution system and then into a 50,000-gallon elevated tank that was located at Clay and Railroad Streets. The original system was financed through revenue bonds of $15,000. In 1929, there were 50 customers on the system. A second well was constructed in 1949. Deep wells No. 3 and No. 4 were constructed in 1958.

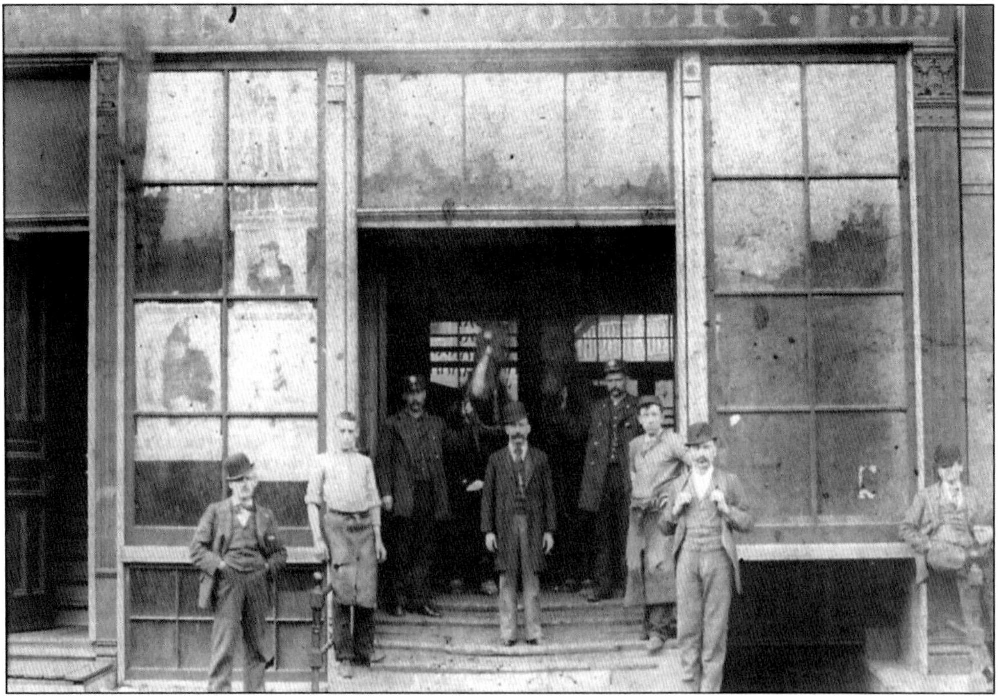

This 1900 photograph shows horses and uniformed firemen posing on the steps. In the 1930s, the fire chief was Ed Rector, who was the earliest recorded chief in the village's fire department. In 1944, the village bought a siren. Chief Gaylord used his electrical engineering skills to draw and assemble the alarm system. (Courtesy of the Kendall County Historical Society.)

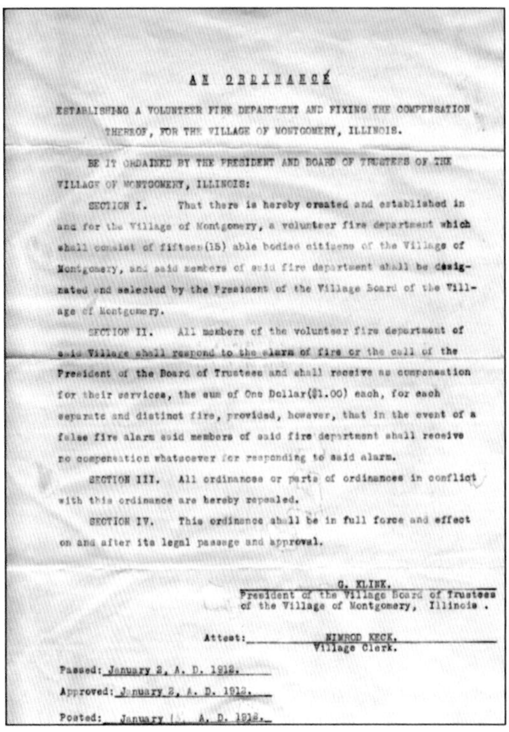

AN ORDINANCE

ESTABLISHING A VOLUNTEER FIRE DEPARTMENT AND FIXING THE COMPENSATION THEREOF, FOR THE VILLAGE OF MONTGOMERY, ILLINOIS.

BE IT ORDAINED BY THE PRESIDENT AND BOARD OF TRUSTEES OF THE VILLAGE OF MONTGOMERY, ILLINOIS:

SECTION I. That there is hereby created and established in and for the Village of Montgomery, a volunteer fire department which shall consist of fifteen(15) able bodied citizens of the Village of Montgomery, and said members of said fire department shall be designated and selected by the President of the Village Board of the Village of Montgomery.

SECTION II. All members of the volunteer fire department of said Village shall respond to the alarm of fire or the call of the President of the Board of Trustees and shall receive as compensation for their services, the sum of One Dollar($1.00) each, for each separate and distinct fire, provided, however, that in the event of a false fire alarm said members of said fire department shall receive no compensation whatsoever for responding to said alarm.

SECTION III. All ordinances or parts of ordinances in conflict with this ordinance are hereby repealed.

SECTION IV. This ordinance shall be in full force and effect on and after its legal passage and approval.

G. KLINK.
President of the Village Board of Trustees of the Village of Montgomery, Illinois.

Attest: NIMROD KECK.
Village Clerk.

Passed: January 2, A. D. 1912.

Approved: January 2, A. D. 1912.

Posted: January [illegible], A. D. 1912.

This ordinance established a volunteer fire department and was passed on January 2, 1912. All volunteer members received a compensation of $1.00 for each fire. In the event of a false fire alarm, the document said that members would receive no compensation whatsoever. The ordinance was signed by G. Klink, president of the Village Board of Trustees, and Nimrod Keck, the village clerk. In 1912, the village's legal services amounted to $65, and the balance was paid in 1913. (Courtesy of Chief Thomas P. Meyers Jr.)

This contract is from the Babcock Fire Extinguisher Company that was located at 373 Wabash Avenue in Chicago. It was dated on August 4, 1909, as a receipt for a chemical engine that was complete with a pair of five-pound extinguishers and a hook-and-ladder truck, amounting to $982.00. Also, it shows a tax invoice for $482.00, which was to be used for fire protection payable from the general fund. Axel Nelson, the village president, signed the document. (Courtesy of Chief Thomas P. Meyers Jr.)

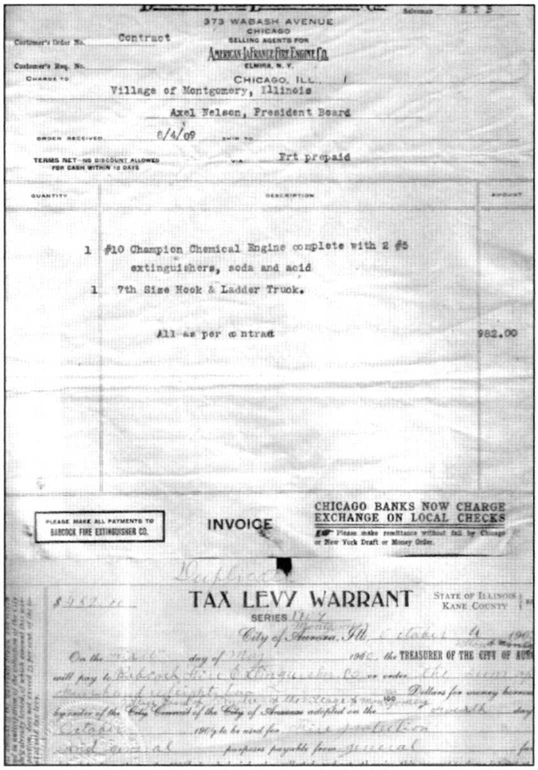

373 WABASH AVENUE
CHICAGO
SELLING AGENTS FOR
AMERICAN-LAFRANCE FIRE ENGINE CO.
ELMIRA, N. Y.

Customer's Order No. Contract
Customer's Req. No.
CHARGE TO
CHICAGO, ILL.
Village of Montgomery, Illinois
Axel Nelson, President Board
ORDER RECEIVED 8/4/09 SHIP TO
TERMS NET—NO DISCOUNT ALLOWED FOR CASH WITHIN 10 DAYS
VIA Frt prepaid

QUANTITY	DESCRIPTION	AMOUNT
1	#10 Champion Chemical Engine complete with 2 #5 extinguishers, soda and acid	
1	7th Size Hook & Ladder Truck.	
	All as per contract	982.00

PLEASE MAKE ALL PAYMENTS TO BABCOCK FIRE EXTINGUISHER CO.

INVOICE

CHICAGO BANKS NOW CHARGE EXCHANGE ON LOCAL CHECKS
Please make remittance without fail by Chicago or New York Draft or Money Order.

Duplicate

TAX LEVY WARRANT
STATE OF ILLINOIS
KANE COUNTY
City of Aurora, Ill.
On the ___ day of May 1910 the TREASURER OF THE CITY OF AURORA will pay to Babcock Fire Extinguisher Co. or order
Dollars for money borrowed by order of the City Council of the City of Aurora adopted on the ___ day of October 1909 to be used for Fire protection purposes payable from general fund

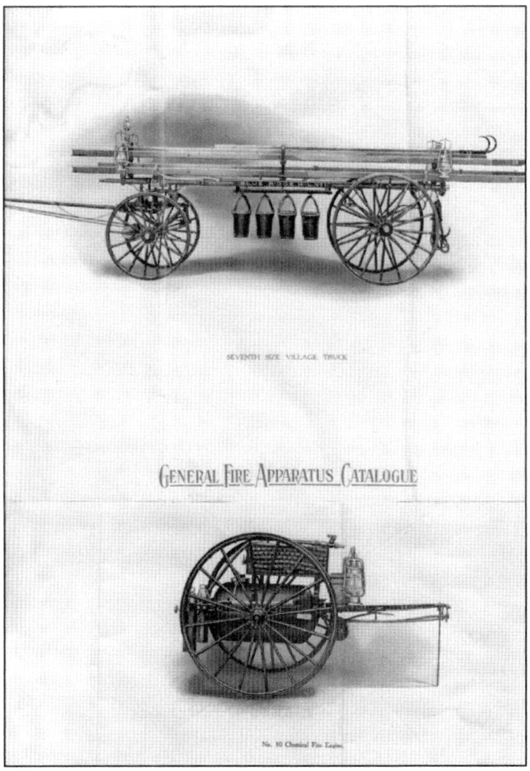

This image shows the Seventh Size-Village Truck and the Chemical Fire Engine purchased in 1909. The truck had ladder sides that were made of Oregon pine, ladder rungs made from second growth-cured ash, and one 35-foot rapid hoist rope and pulley with 12 flexible rubber buckets. The Chemical Fire Engine had a 45-gallon capacity and frame made of forged steel with a 50-foot hose. (Courtesy of Chief Thomas P. Meyers Jr.)

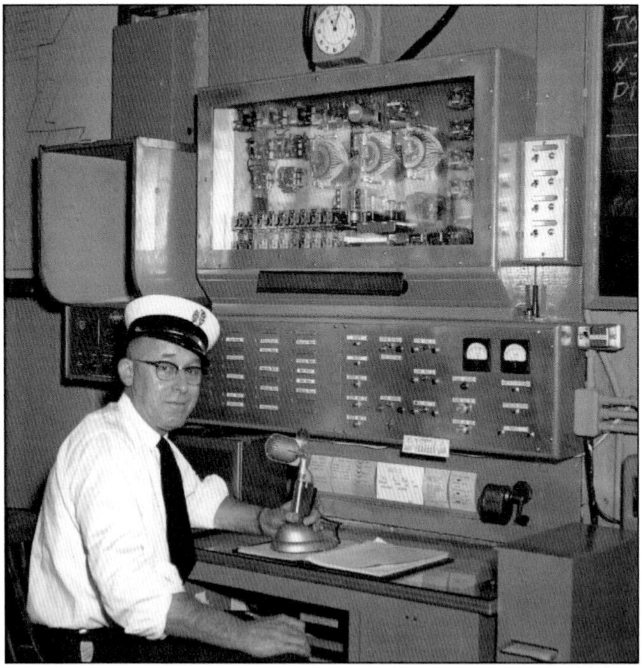

Charlie Gaylord was born on a farm in the NaAuSay Township in Kendall County in 1904. This photograph was taken by Leon Ardelean of Aurora and shows Gaylord at work. He served as fire chief for 30 years. Recalling a few memories, Gaylord said, "We would cross the river to the Bereman farm. I went to Coyne Electrical School and then worked for the Burlington Railroad. I worked at Baker Laundery for a few years. I married Miss Gladys Hildebrand, and we built a house on South River Street next to my parents. We raised our two sons there." (Courtesy of Chief Thomas P. Meyers Jr.)

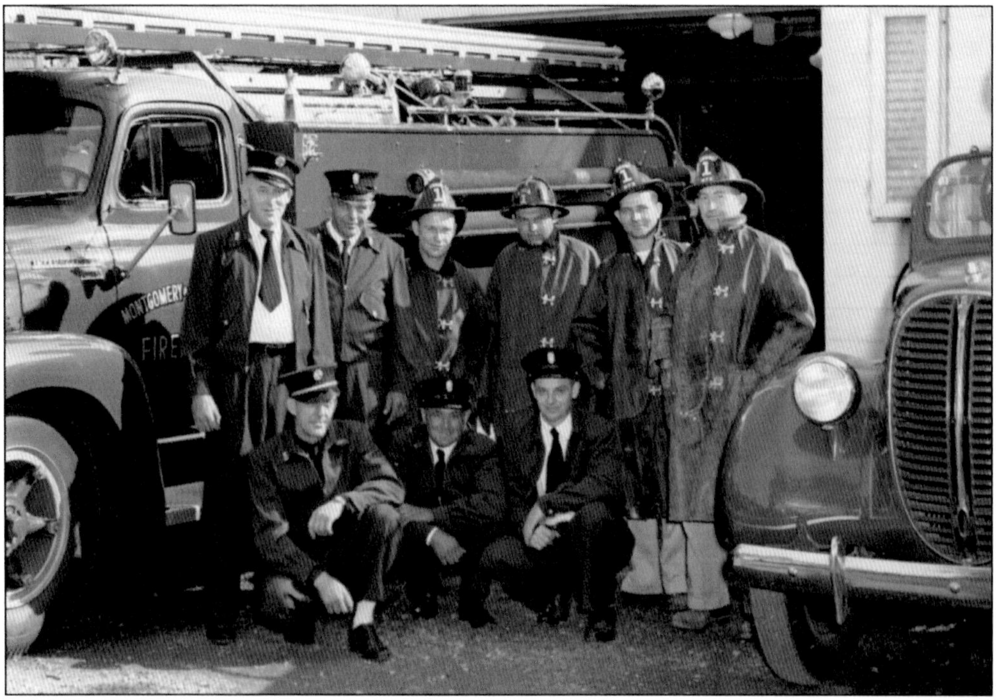

Pictured from left to right are (first row) Bob Woodrow, Alvin Paris, and Ray Kyes; (second row) Chief Gaylord, Leo Edwards, Fritz Neupert, "Blocky" Delaney, Irv Messinger, and Harry Schmidt. Chief Meyers had 52 firefighters on board in 2010, including 8 women. Jim Touvell has been with the department for 45 years. Waubonsee Community College conducts training classes for the firemen, and Delnor Hospital facilitates the paramedic trainings. (Courtesy of Chief Thomas P. Meyers Jr.)

The fire department moved across the street in 1961 to a new building, which was designed by and named for Gaylord. The area is now served by five districts, including the Montgomery Countryside Fire Protection District, the Oswego, Aurora Township, the Sugar Grove, and the Bristol Kendall Fire Protection District. (Courtesy of Montgomery Archives.)

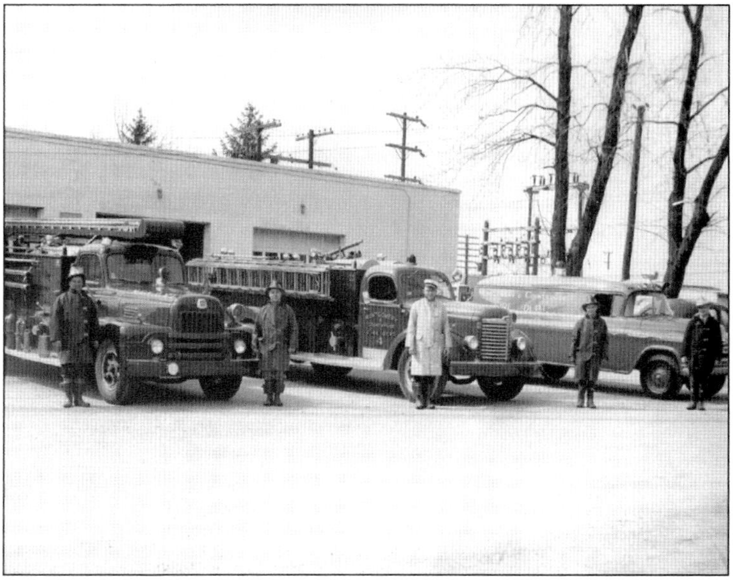

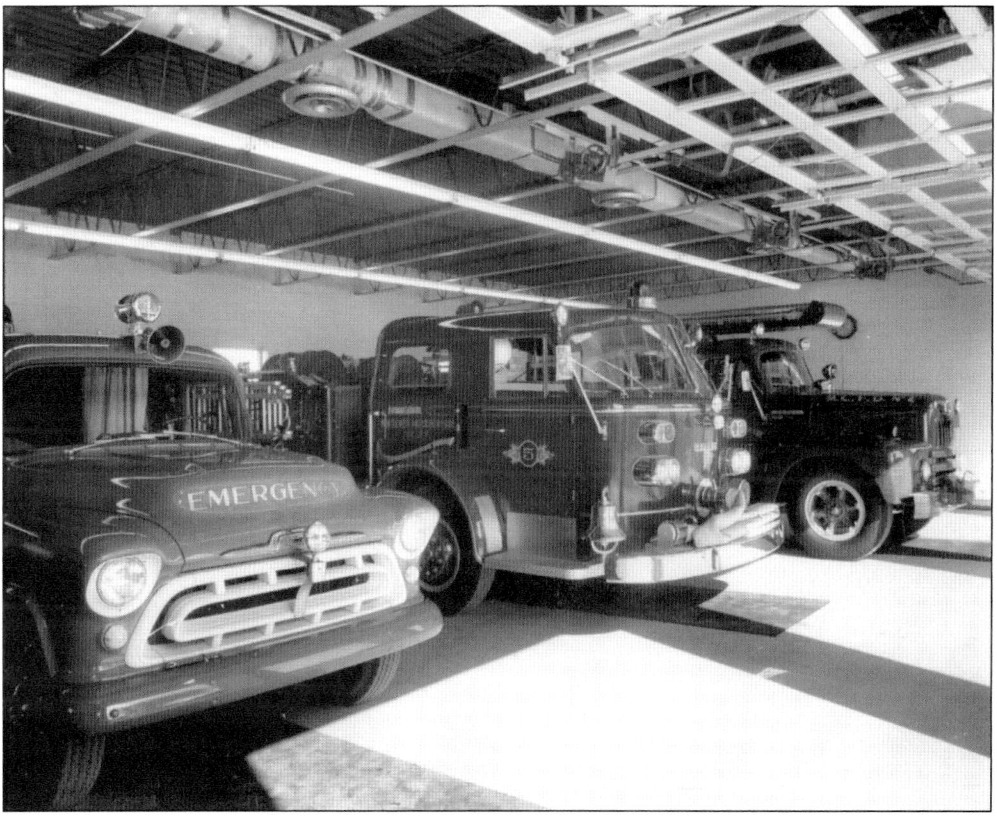

The grand opening of the new fire station was held in 1963 at 198 South Railroad Street. This photograph shows three trucks in their new garage facility. Chief Gaylord had said, "No one man should be indispensable in a fire department or district. The newest man is as important as the oldest." Each fire fighter was trained to drive the truck, climb ladders, and administer first aid. They were drilled to act without officers if necessary. (Courtesy of Chief Thomas P. Meyers Jr.)

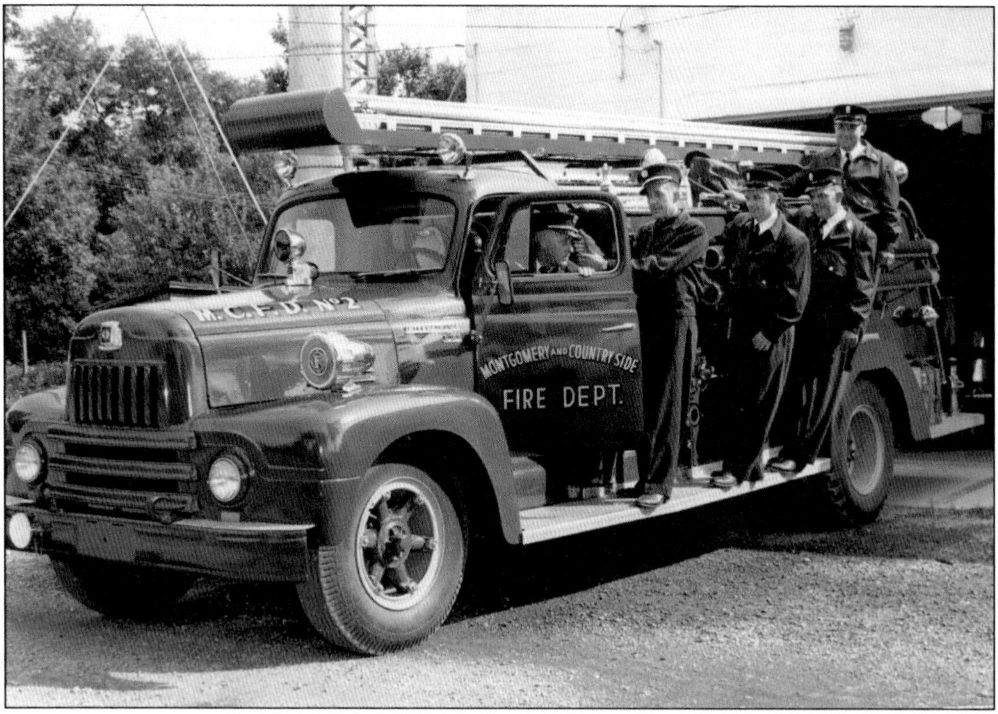

Chief Gene Kunkel and his firemen are standing on a new fire engine in this 1989 photograph. A sleigh was used on Christmas mornings to bring candy, fruits, and nuts to the residents. The members of the village board and fire department made the packages. They consisted of a pound of nuts, a pound of hard candy, an orange, an apple, and sometimes popcorn balls. The newspaper-wrapped packages were delivered to every child, widow, and shut-in. (Courtesy of Chief Thomas P. Meyers Jr.)

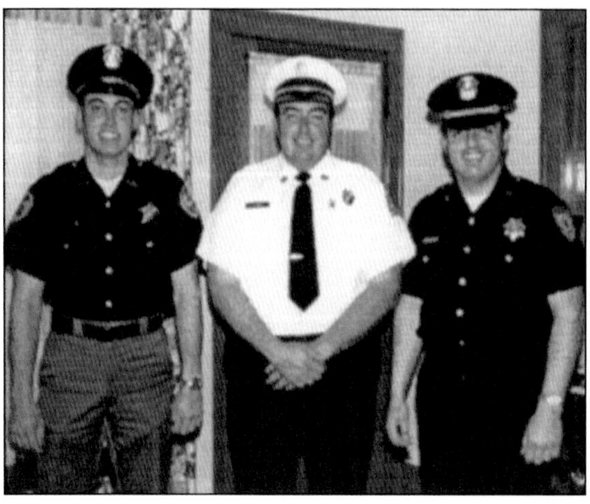

Pictured from left to right are brothers Edward J. Schmidt, Kenneth A. Schmidt, and Dennis J. Schmidt. Ed serves with the Elgin Police Department. Ken was the fire chief in the Marywood Fire Protection District in Aurora. Dennis became the chief of police in Montgomery in September 1981. In April 1974, Dennis was first hired by the Montgomery police. Dennis attended Waubonsee Community College and Aurora University in pursuit of a bachelor's degree in criminal justice. He graduated May 1983. (Courtesy of Kathy Priegel.)

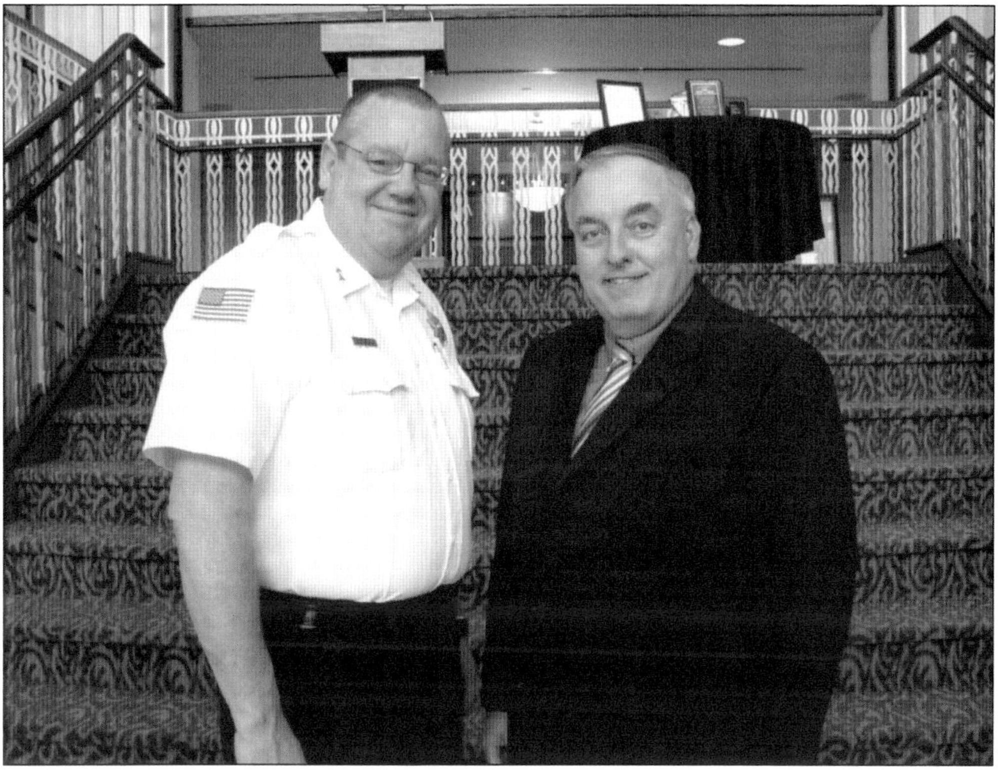

In 1882, the village board recorded, "It shall be the duty of the village constable and the police officer, if any shall be appointed, to assist the pound master to enforce ordinances." This photograph shows the Paramount Arts Center in Aurora on April 6, 2010. Pictured from left to right are the new acting chief Daniel Meyers and retired chief Dennis J. Schmidt. On November 16, 2010, village president Marilyn Michelini appointed Meyers as chief of police. Chief Meyers said, "I will serve the Village as I always have . . . with honor." (Courtesy of Kathy Priegel.)

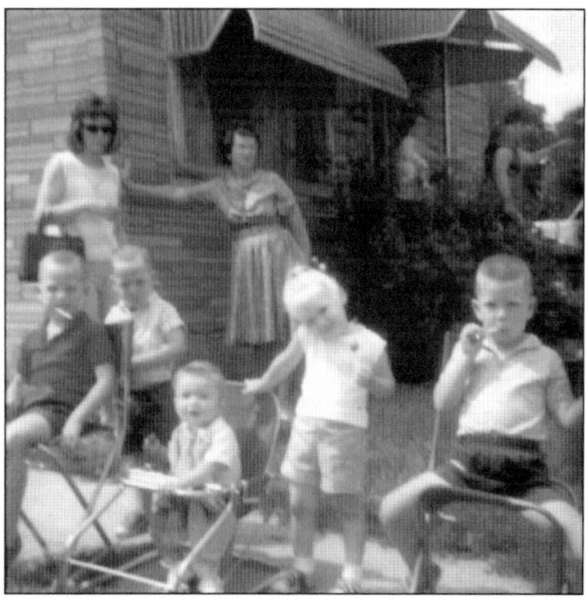

This delightful photograph shows a candid moment at the Gove home in August 1965 while the family was watching a parade. The baby in the middle is Scott Touvell, and his sister Nancy is touching his chair. When Scott was 10 years old, he died due to a brain hemorrhage. His last words were "Mommy, I love you." (Courtesy of Nancy Touvell.)

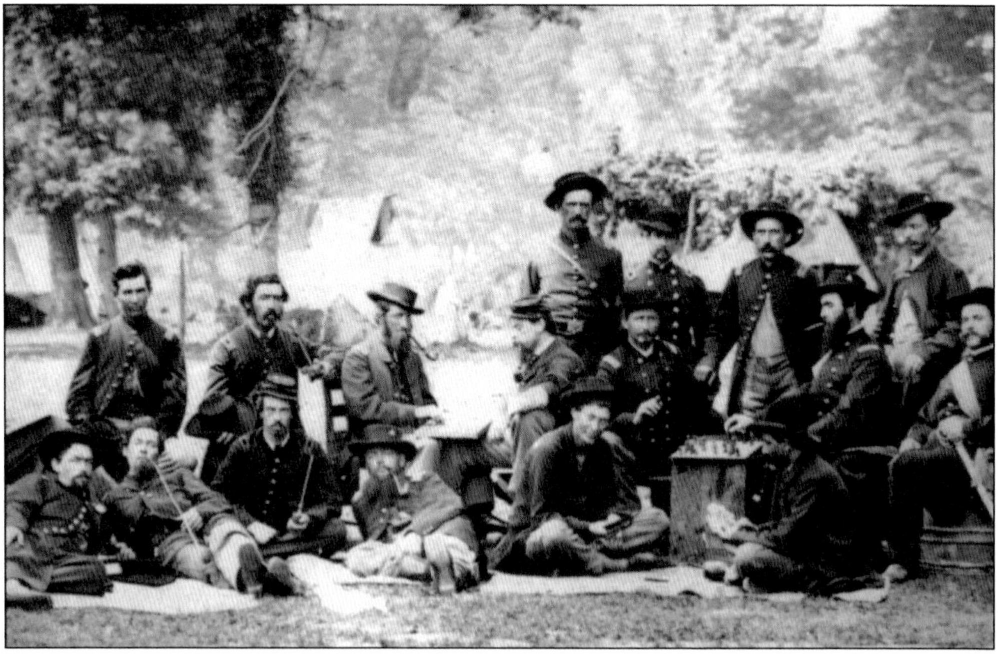

During the Civil War, Camp Hammond was organized in Montgomery on August 18, 1861, for the 36th Illinois Volunteer Infantry by virtue of General Order No. 139. Colonel Greusel became its commander. The regiment had 965 officers and enlisted men. They received Minnie and Enfield rifles along with remodeled Springfield muskets. On September 28, 1861, they left St. Louis by rail for Rolla, Missouri. Their time was taken up with "severe drill, camp-and-post guard duty, and an occasional scout." (Courtesy of Gene Michaels.)

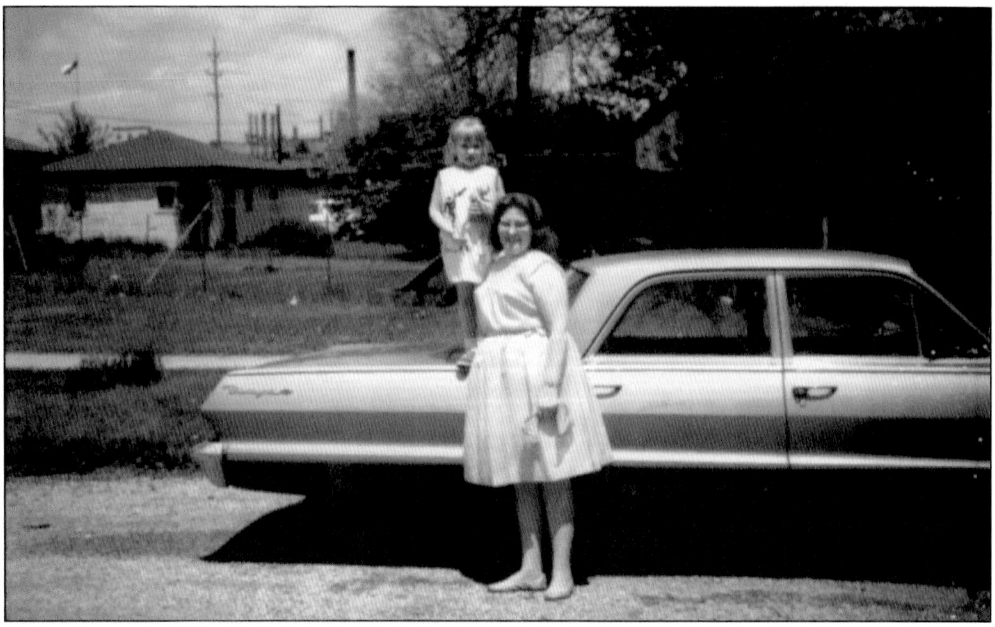

In the summer of 1966, Myrtle Hollifield Ballard poses with her daughter Kathy on North Main Street. On September 24, 1935, Ballard was born in North Carolina. She died on September 20, 1988, due to bone cancer. (Courtesy of Kathy Priegel.)

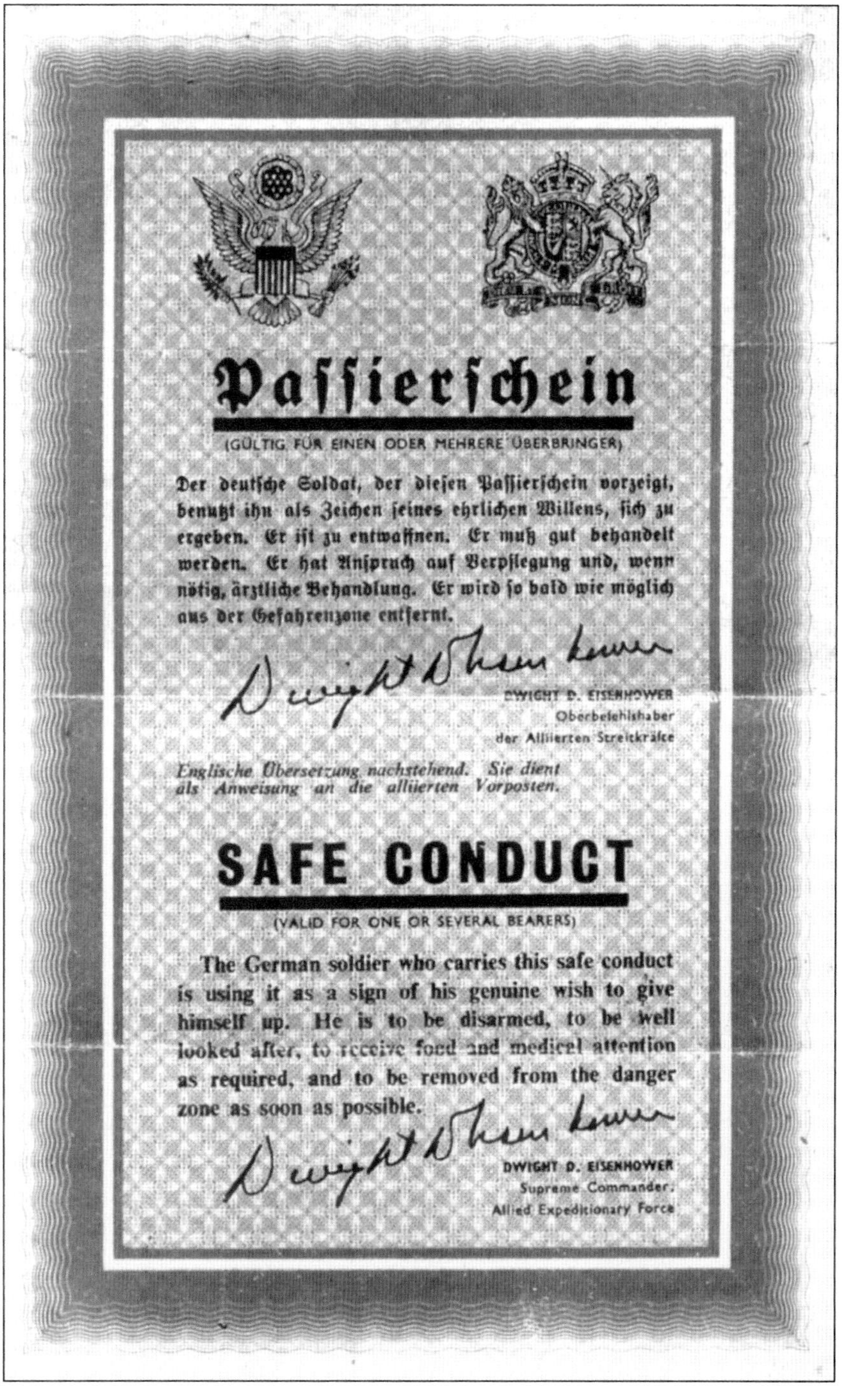

Passierschein

(GÜLTIG FÜR EINEN ODER MEHRERE ÜBERBRINGER)

Der deutsche Soldat, der diesen Passierschein vorzeigt, benutzt ihn als Zeichen seines ehrlichen Willens, sich zu ergeben. Er ist zu entwaffnen. Er muß gut behandelt werden. Er hat Anspruch auf Verpflegung und, wenn nötig, ärztliche Behandlung. Er wird so bald wie möglich aus der Gefahrenzone entfernt.

DWIGHT D. EISENHOWER
Oberbefehlshaber
der Alliierten Streitkräfte

Englische Übersetzung nachstehend. Sie dient als Anweisung an die alliierten Vorposten.

SAFE CONDUCT

(VALID FOR ONE OR SEVERAL BEARERS)

The German soldier who carries this safe conduct is using it as a sign of his genuine wish to give himself up. He is to be disarmed, to be well looked after, to receive food and medical attention as required, and to be removed from the danger zone as soon as possible.

DWIGHT D. EISENHOWER
Supreme Commander,
Allied Expeditionary Force

This is a safe conduct pass for a German soldier during World War II. The document said that a soldier "who carries this is using it as a sign of his genuine wish to give himself up. He is to be disarmed, to be well looked after, to receive food and medical attention as required, and to be removed from the danger zone as soon as possible." It was signed by Pres. Dwight D. Eisenhower, Supreme Commander, Allied Expeditionary Force. (Author's collection.)

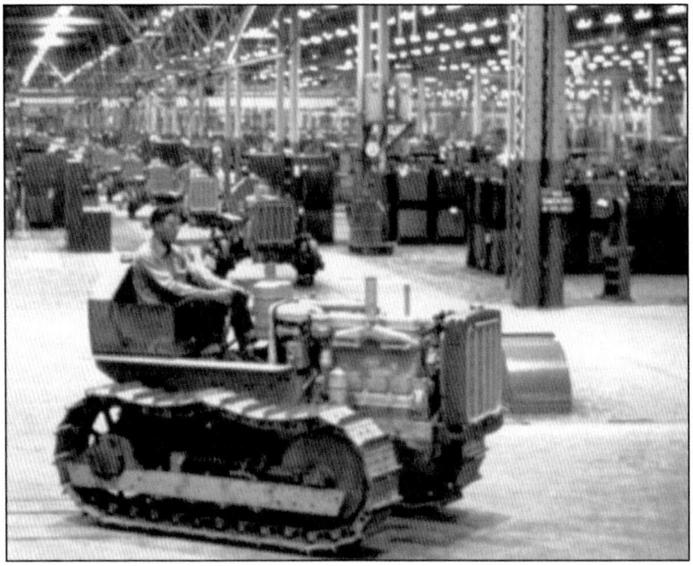

This photograph shows the first Caterpillar tractor off the assembly line at their Aurora plant on September 2, 1958. The Caterpillar plant is located along the southern border of Montgomery, spans over 370 acres, and employs more than 3,000 workers. This facility designs and manufactures wheel loaders, hydraulic excavators, compactors, and lower power-train components. (Courtesy of Rayanne Carlson and Sarah Puleo.)

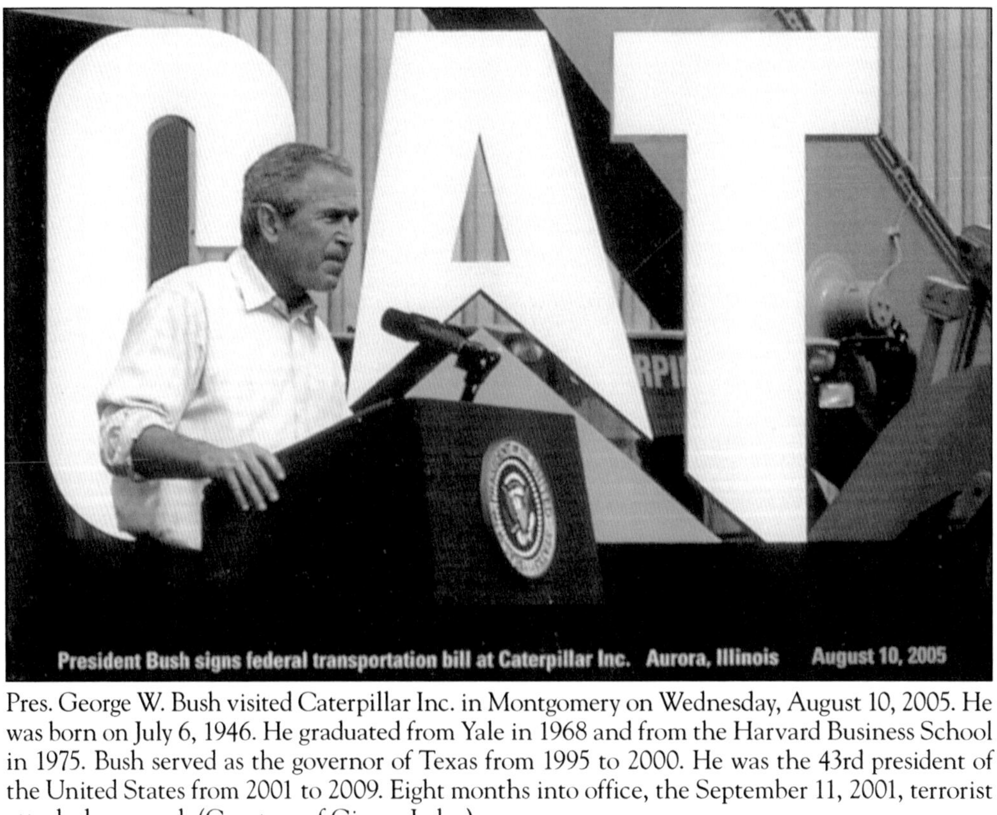

Pres. George W. Bush visited Caterpillar Inc. in Montgomery on Wednesday, August 10, 2005. He was born on July 6, 1946. He graduated from Yale in 1968 and from the Harvard Business School in 1975. Bush served as the governor of Texas from 1995 to 2000. He was the 43rd president of the United States from 2001 to 2009. Eight months into office, the September 11, 2001, terrorist attacks happened. (Courtesy of Ginger Lake.)

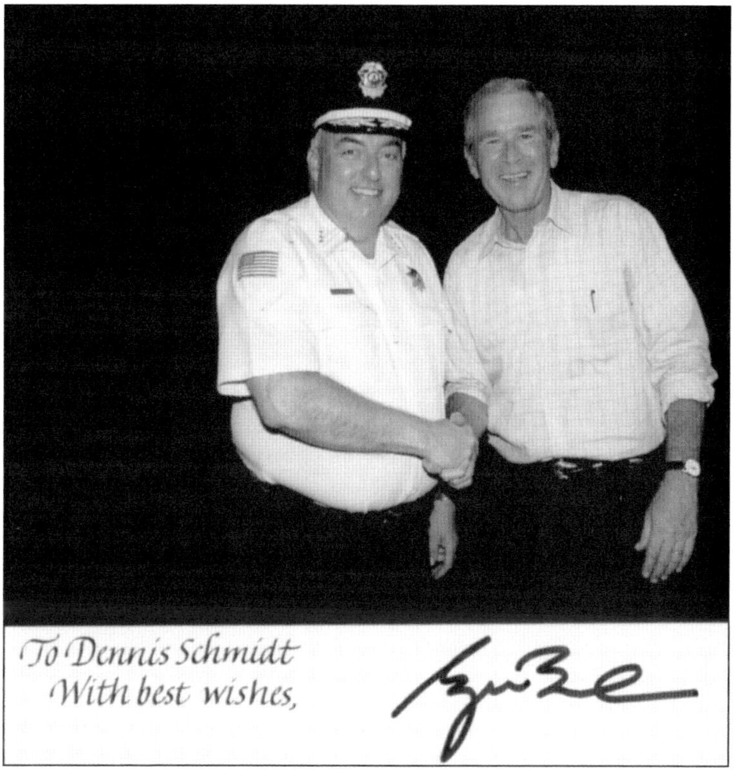

As chief of police, Dennis J. Schmidt was invited to meet President Bush during his visit to Caterpillar on August 10, 2005. Almost all police archival photographs, arrest ledgers, and documents were lost in the 1996 area flood. The documents had been stored in the basement of the old police building, which was erected on Webster and River Streets with one jail cell. The building also served as Village Hall for many years. (Courtesy of Dennis J. Schmidt.)

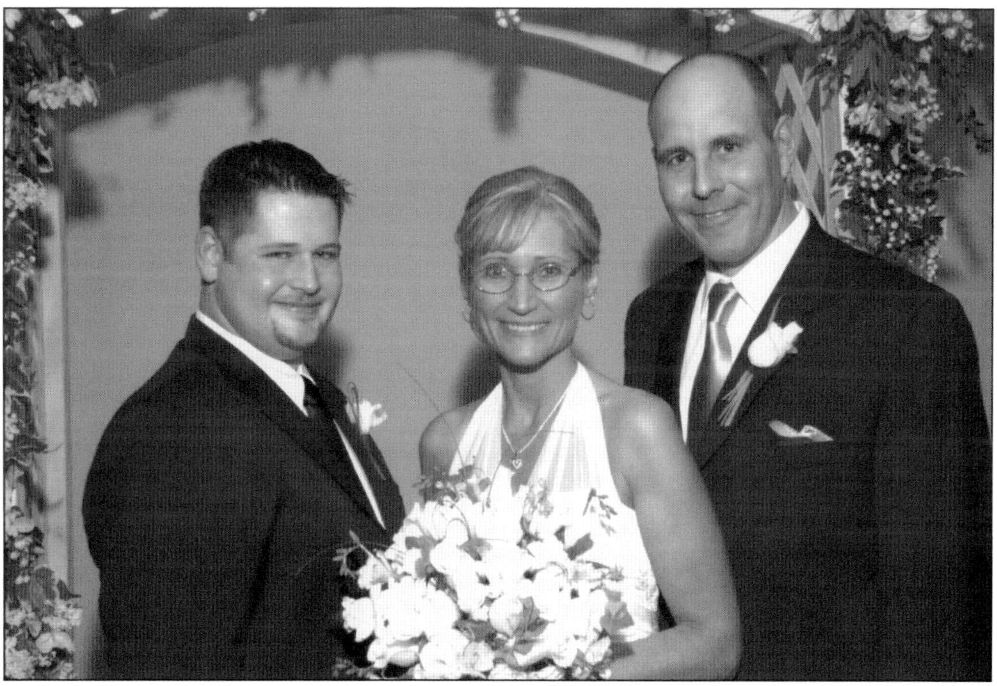

Kathy Ballard and Dave Priegel were married on February 28, 2009. This photograph shows them posing with Kathy's son Anthony Schmiesing. Kathy has served as the administrative assistant for the last two chiefs of police. (Courtesy of Kathy Priegel.)

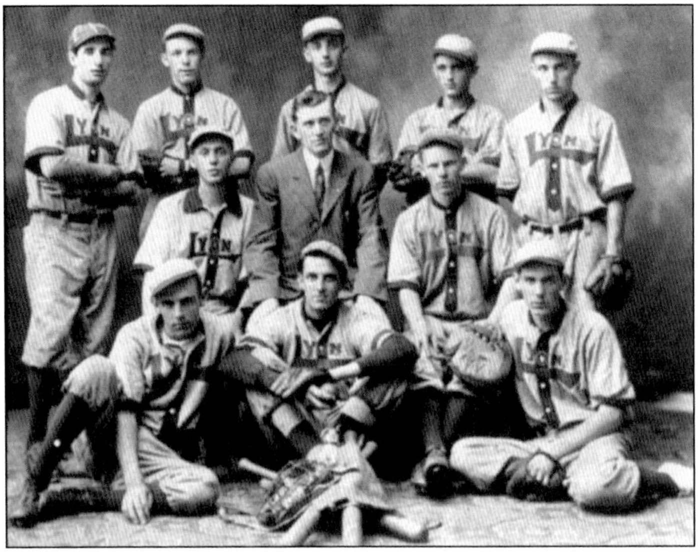

The Lyon Metal Baseball team poses for the camera. In 1928, the Lyon Metallic Manufacturing Company consolidated with their main competitor, the Durand Steel Locker Company. The new company was formed under the name of Lyon Metal Products. In 1937, the company spent $300,000 for advertising. More than 260 truckloads of finished products were handled monthly. (Courtesy of Montgomery Archives.)

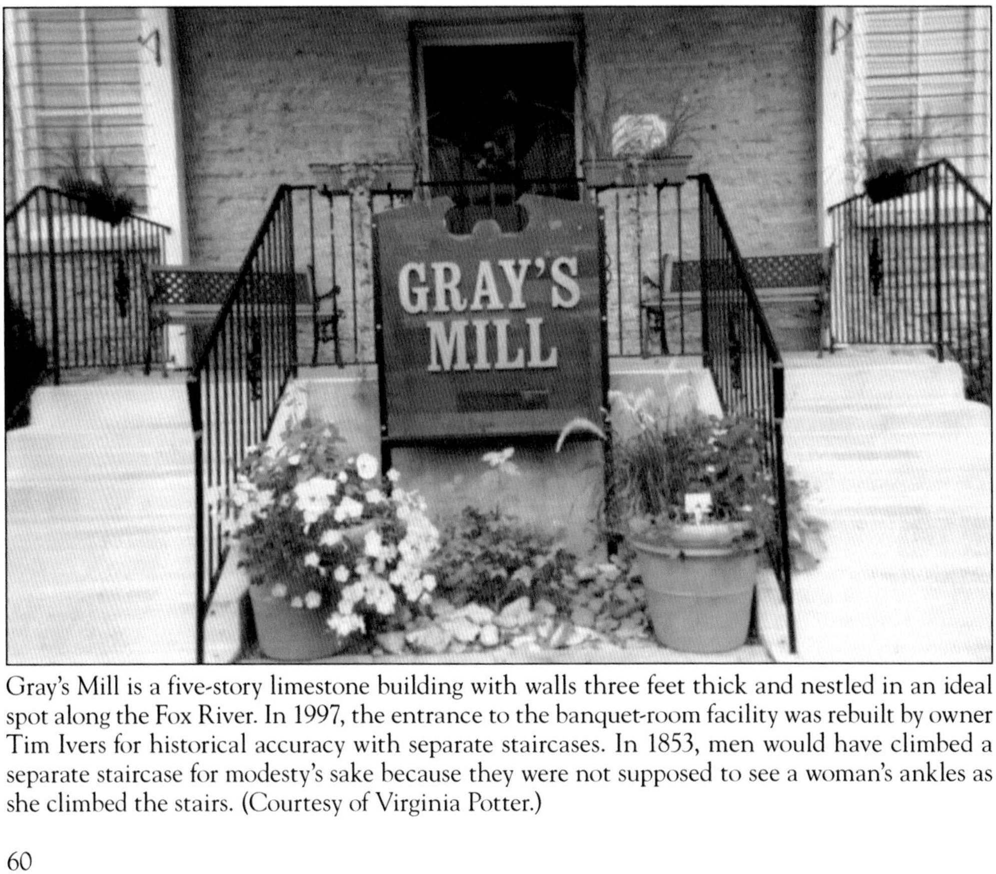

Gray's Mill is a five-story limestone building with walls three feet thick and nestled in an ideal spot along the Fox River. In 1997, the entrance to the banquet-room facility was rebuilt by owner Tim Ivers for historical accuracy with separate staircases. In 1853, men would have climbed a separate staircase for modesty's sake because they were not supposed to see a woman's ankles as she climbed the stairs. (Courtesy of Virginia Potter.)

On a beautiful summer's day in 2010, the sunlight and shadows can be seen on the side of Gray's Mill. The building is a registered national landmark, and it is one of 10 remaining in the United States. A committee from Washington rated it as the prettiest mill in the country. Instead of the typical vertical waterwheel, the mill had a five-wheel horizontal system that functioned similar to turbines. The Fox River water continues to run beneath the elevator. (Author's collection.)

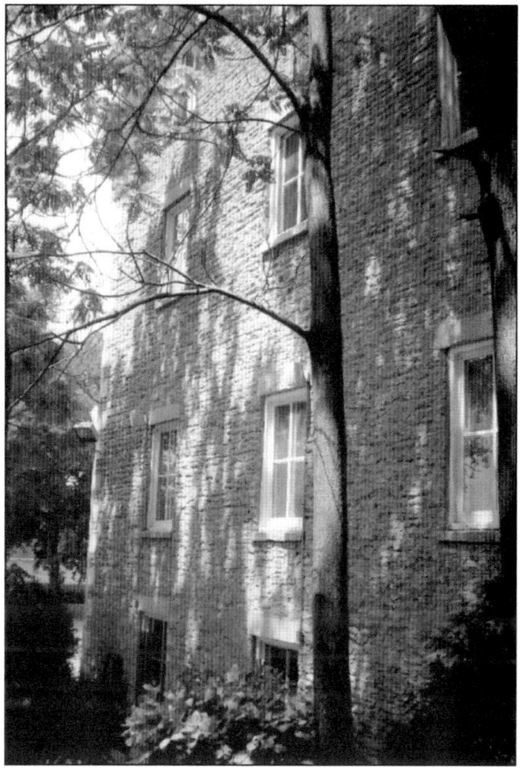

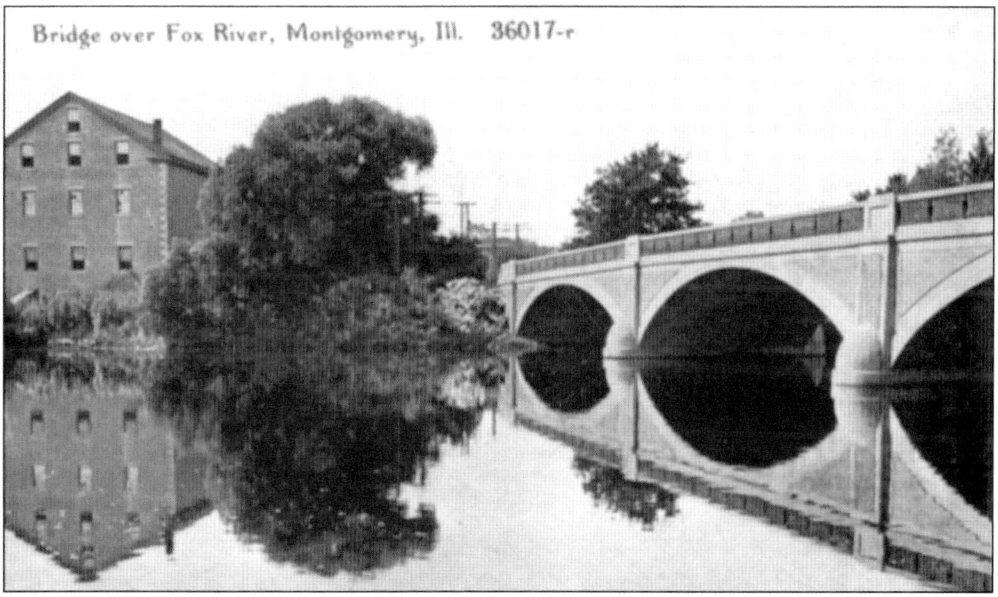

The original land sale to Daniel Samuel Gray was sealed on certificate No. 8842 on April 24, 1840. This document entitled an act that made a "provision for the sale of public lands." The deed was recorded in Volume 18, page 217, by J. Williamson at the US General Land Office. It was signed by Pres. John Tyler, who was sworn in at the Indian Queen Hotel in Washington, DC, on April 6, 1841. The event followed the death of Pres. William Henry Harrison on April 4, 1841. (Courtesy of Virginia Potter.)

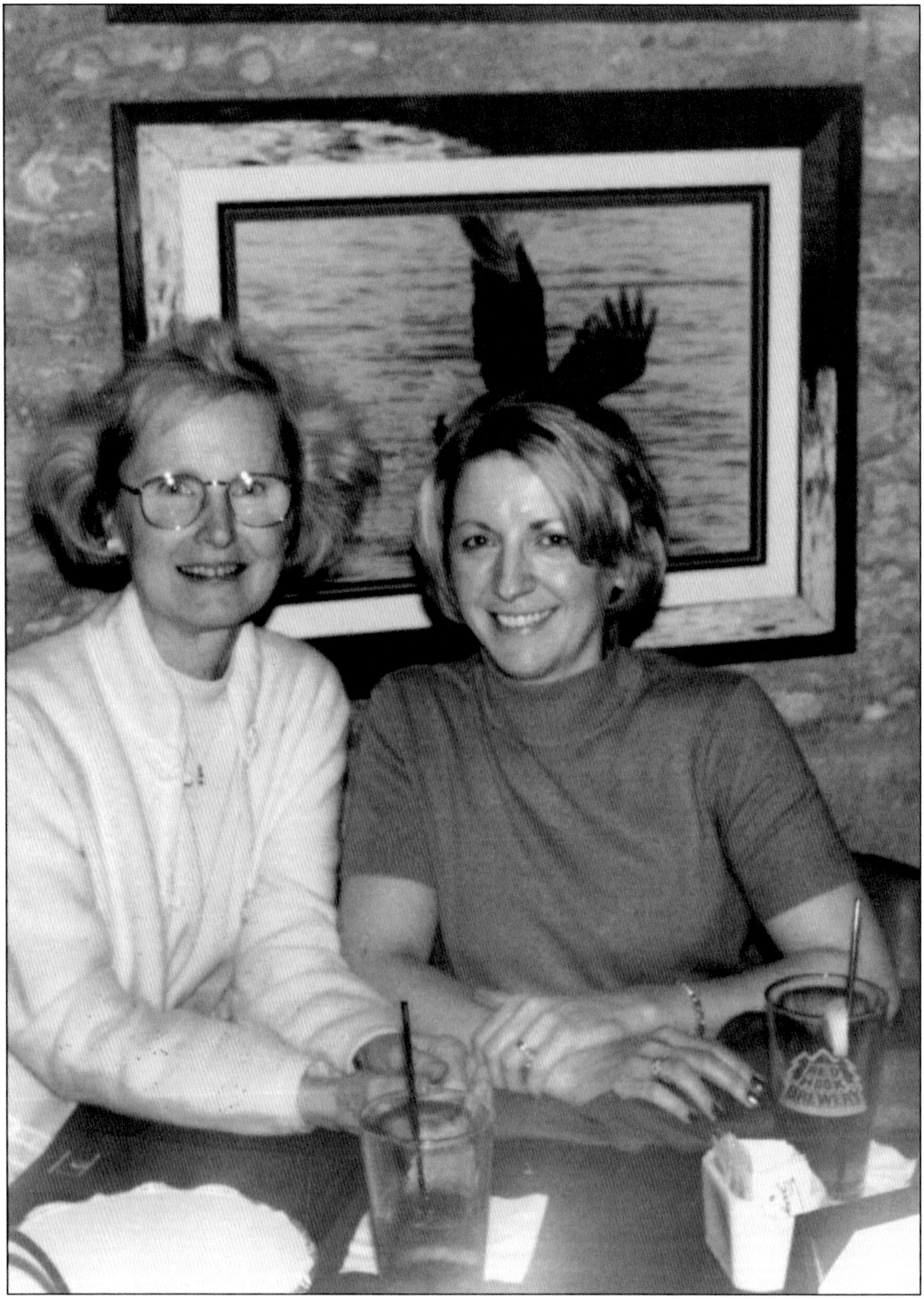

Taken on Valentine's Day in 2004, this photograph shows Jo Fredell Higgins and Lynette Hoover DeYoung enjoying lunch at Jason's at Gray's Mill Restaurant. Lynette is married to Earl. They have one daughter, Allison. The wooden rosettes around the windows were from the county courthouse in Douglas, where Abraham Lincoln practiced law. Gray's Mill was listed in the National Register of Historic Places on December 17, 1979. (Author's collection.)

Five

Quiet Homes and First Beginnings

Give me odorous at sunrise a garden of beautiful flowers where I can walk undisturbed.

—Walt Whitman

Those who lived in Southern Illinois in 1809 had traveled mostly from Kentucky, Virginia, and Pennsylvania. When Illinois obtained statehood on December 3, 1818, there were 40,000 residents. There were only a few schools for reading, writing, and arithmetic in this unsettled wilderness. There was one school for surveying and bookkeeping. The lawyers and professional men came from abroad. Preachers of the gospel had no formal training except in the study of the Holy Scriptures. Such a thing as regular commerce was nearly unknown. By 1833, the population had grown to 150,000. Slavery had been outlawed.

The open prairie was compared to a "sea of grass." Daniel Samuel Gray's frame house was on Jefferson Street. It also served as a tavern when Gray held one of the first liquor licenses. In 1840, there was a tavern sign that read, "This gate hangs high and hinders none. Refresh and pay and travel on."

The federal surveyors arrived in 1837 and completed the work for Aurora Township in 1839. Each township was designed as 36 square miles and composed of 36 sections that were one square mile each. Between 1870 and 1900, there were 15 different species of fish in the Fox River. Those included Atlantic salmon, chinnok salmon, rainbow trout, and shad.

The Village of Montgomery has been a community that fosters graceful living and family relationships. Village life creates a song of domestic harmonies alongside the flowing Fox River. As resident Kathy Priegel said, "Anyone on the block would leave lawn chairs out and neighbors would come by, sit for a while, and share the news of the day. All were welcome." Overhead, the sapphire sky would blanket the homes as children said their night prayers and adults tucked them in. The animals in the barns would close their eyes as the owls and wrens peacefully slept. As Isaac Bashevis Singer has written, "Among the undergrowth and wild mushrooms . . . They sang a song which is heard only by those who know that everything lives and nothing in time is ever lost."

Indian history and pioneer accomplishments tell us of our past while we look forward in anticipation to the future. The Village celebrated its 175th anniversary in 2010 amid celebrations, concerts, lectures, and remembrances.

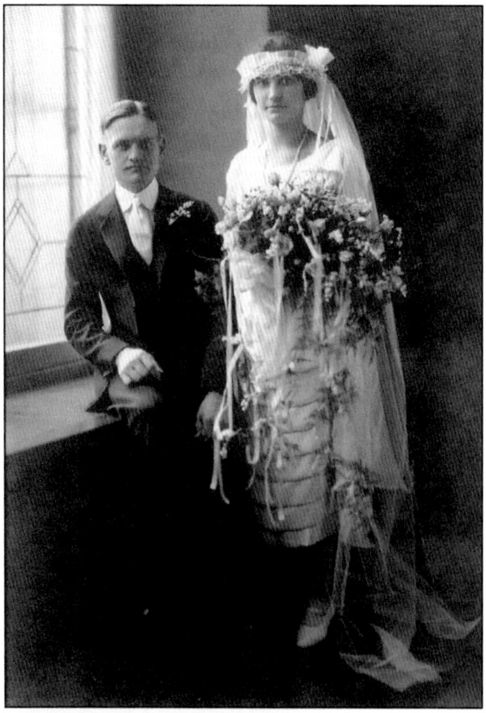

What a stunning wedding photograph! Felix Michaels and May Dewald were married in September 1925. Felix was born in 1894 and passed away in 1975. May was born in 1896 and passed away in 1955. They were parents to Elizabeth, Paul, and Gene Michaels. Felix owned the Michaels Grocery Store located at 109 Main Street for decades. (Courtesy of Joan and Gene Michaels.)

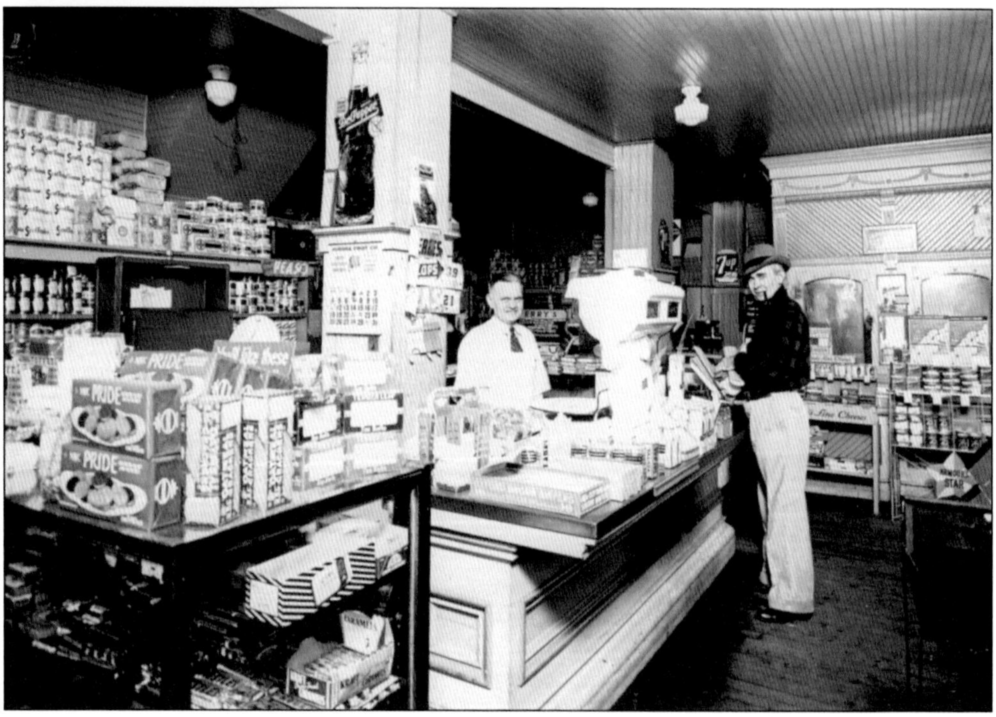

This photograph shows Felix Michaels with customer Cameron Jones in 1930. The meat cooler on the right was originally cooled by ice and was later converted to a refrigerator. Gene Michaels was the second generation of the family to operate the store. Before retirement in 1995, Gene offered "good merchandise, fair prices, and good treatment of customers." (Courtesy of Gene Michaels.)

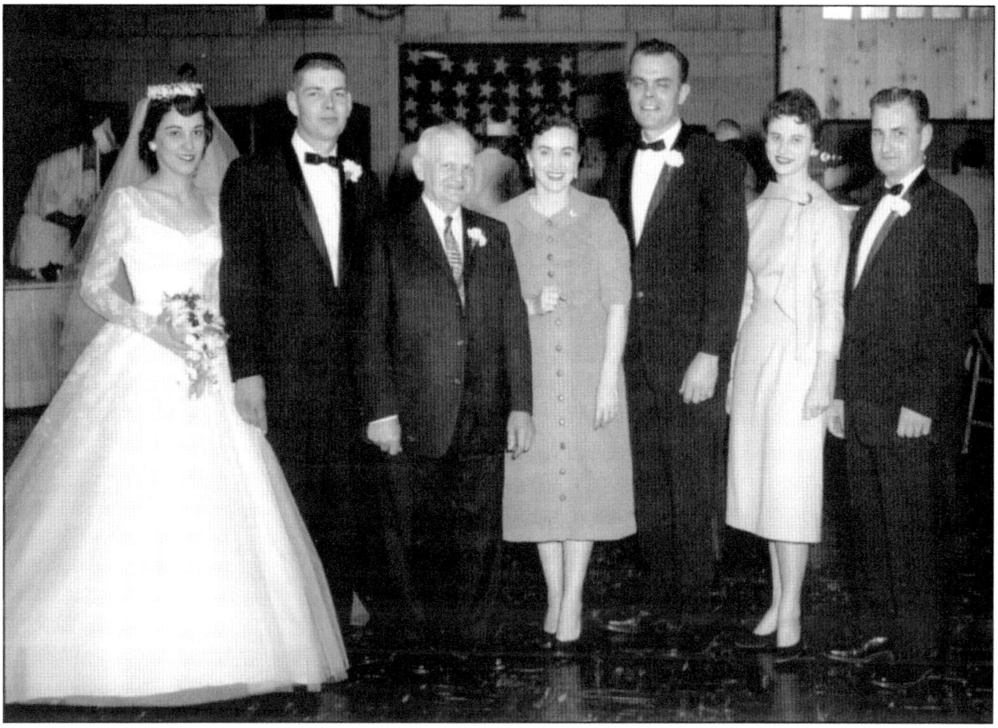

Pictured from left to right are Joan Michaels, Gene Michaels, Felix Michaels, Elizabeth Michaels Fletcher, Bill Fletcher, Gerry Michaels, and Paul Michaels. Pastor Bruno Daukas of St. Nicholas Church in Aurora performed the ceremony on November 27, 1958. The wedding reception was held at the Montgomery VFW Hall. The couple enjoyed a honeymoon to New Orleans. (Courtesy of Joan and Gene Michaels.)

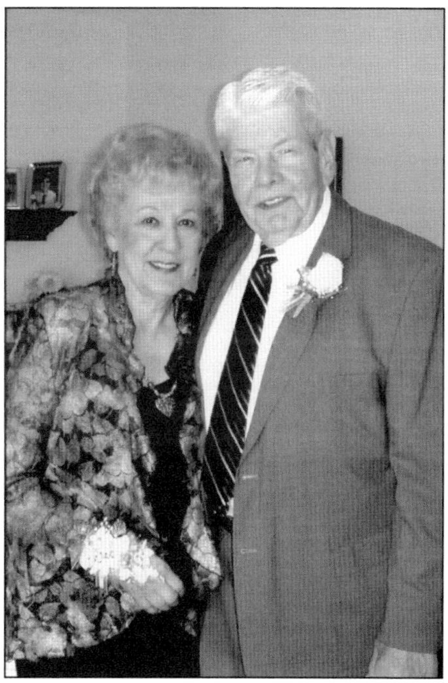

Shown celebrating their 50th wedding anniversary are Joan and Gene Michaels. They hosted family and close friends at Long Island Sound after Mass and a special blessing at St. Peter's Church. They have four children Sheila, Rich, Tom, and Dan, and their eight grandchildren joined them on this special occasion. (Courtesy of Joan and Gene Michaels.)

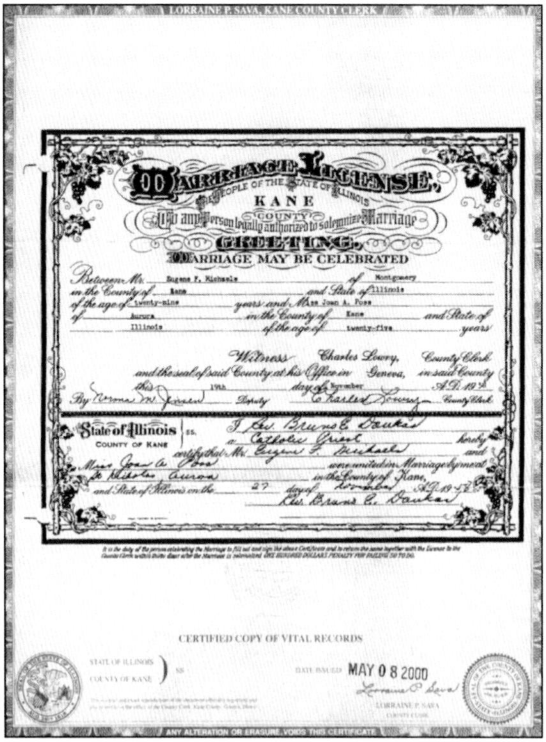

LORRAINE P. SAVA, KANE COUNTY CLERK

MARRIAGE LICENSE,

THE PEOPLE OF THE STATE OF ILLINOIS

KANE

COUNTY

To any Person legally authorized to solemnize Marriage

GREETING,

MARRIAGE MAY BE CELEBRATED

Between Mr. Eugene F. Michaels of Montgomery in the County of Kane and State of Illinois of the age of twenty-nine years and Miss Joan A. Foss of Aurora in the County of Kane and State of Illinois of the age of twenty-five years

Witness Charles Lowry, County Clerk and the seal of said County at his Office in Geneva, in said County this 19th day of November A.D. 19

By Norma M. Jensen Deputy Charles Lowry County Clerk

State of Illinois } ss.
COUNTY OF KANE

I Rev. Bruno E. Daukas a Catholic Priest hereby certify that Mr. Eugene F. Michaels and Miss Joan A. Foss were united in Marriage by me at St. Nicholas Aurora in the County of Kane, and State of Illinois on the 27 day of November A.D. 1958

Rev. Bruno E. Daukas

CERTIFIED COPY OF VITAL RECORDS

STATE OF ILLINOIS } SS
COUNTY OF KANE

DATE ISSUED MAY 0 8 2000

Lorraine P. Sava
LORRAINE P. SAVA
COUNTY CLERK

ANY ALTERATION OR ERASURE VOIDS THIS CERTIFICATE

Here is the marriage license certificate for Joan and Gene Michaels. The Illinois State Board of Health issues marriage licenses and returns them to the county clerk's office. The witnesses were Paul Michaels and Jean Truskenski, and the document was labeled as No. 85683 and filed on November 20, 1958 by the county clerk Charles Lowry. (Courtesy of Joan and Gene Michaels.)

The VFW Auxiliary Post No. 7452 was organized in 1946. Within the year, the post purchased a lot at 121 North Street where they built a 40-foot, cement-block building. Six years later, they built the banquet hall and later purchased a land to the north of the building for a parking lot. (Courtesy of Montgomery Archives.)

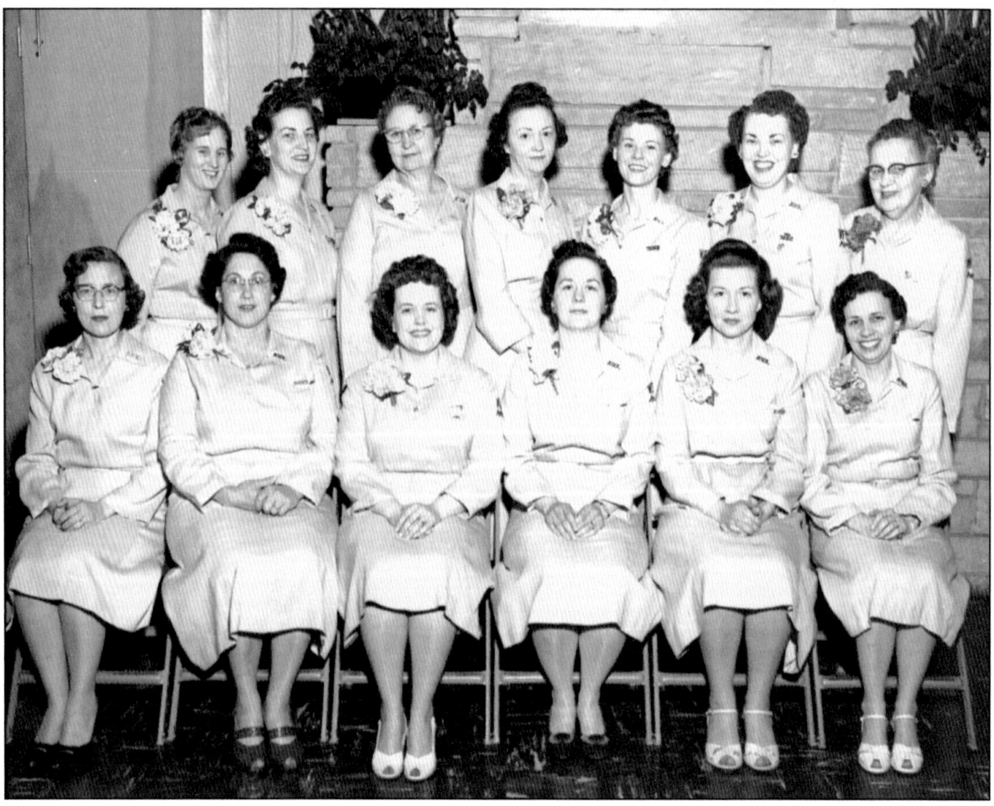

Beautiful bride Clarice Gove Pessina is pictured on her wedding day in 1925 when she was 17 years old. Clarice was born in 1908 and was a sister to Clyde Gove. Her husband, William Passina, was a truck driver for a local department store. William was the son of George Passina, who emigrated from Italy around 1889. According to the 1930 census, Clarice and William lived in Aurora and had two children, William and Caryl. (Courtesy of Montgomery Archives.)

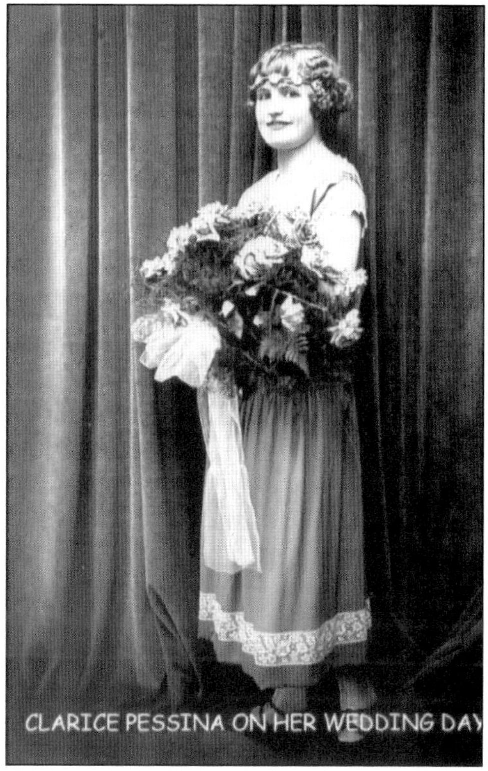

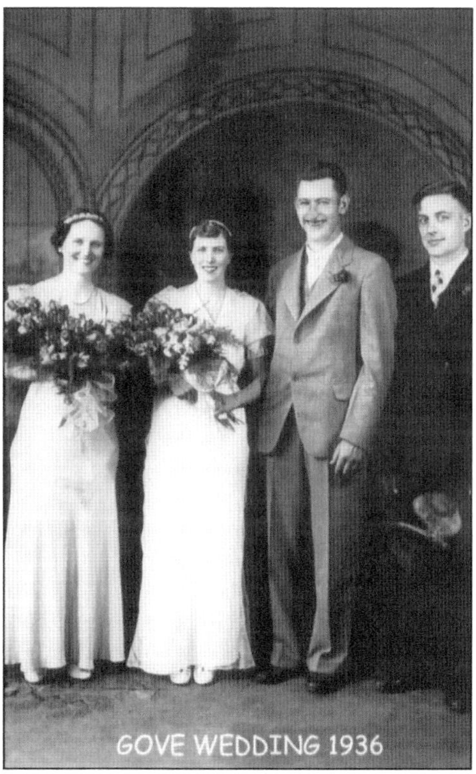

Clyde Gove's wedding day was on June 19, 1936. From 1947 to 1967, Clyde and Helen Watson Gove owned their home, which is now the restored Settler's Cottage. They had four children, Betty, Dorothy, Richard, and an infant daughter who died. Helen wrote the weekly Montgomery news column for the *Aurora Beacon-News*. (Courtesy of Montgomery Archives.)

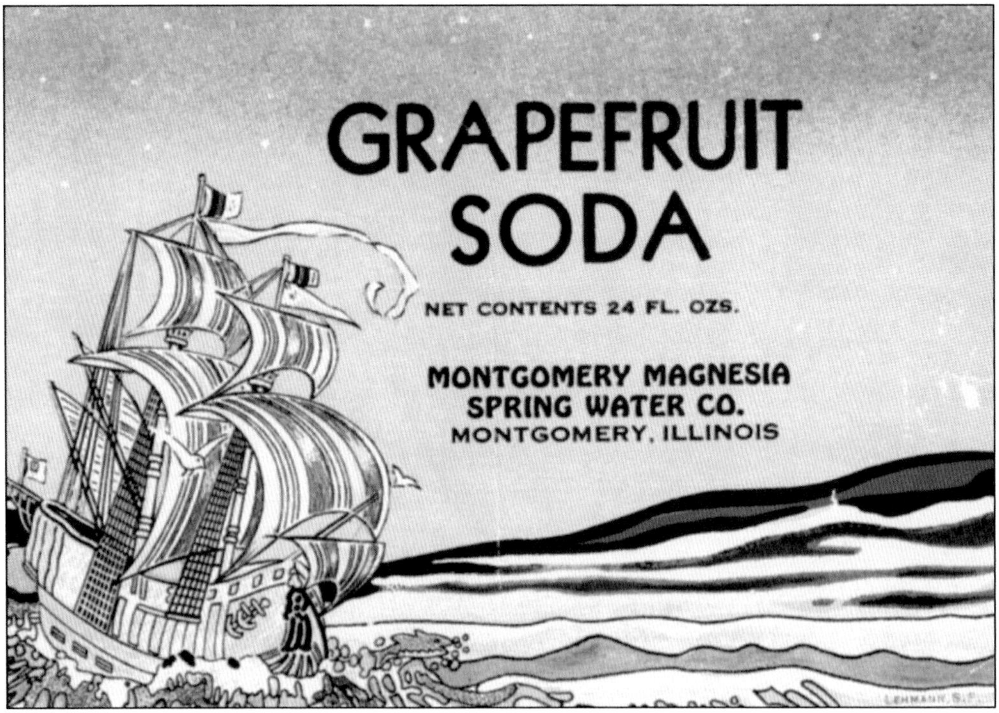

The Montgomery Magnesia Spring Water Company began in 1890 near Mill and Pearl Streets. In 1900, the business was taken over by Gottlieb Klink. Its spring-water product was shipped to the Otis Hinckley & George J. Schmitt Plant in Chicago that had opened in 1888. Klink expanded the business to manufacture soda pop, which was sold at his store just south of Gray's Mill. Flavors included lemon sour, orange cider, and birch beer. School children would try and find empty discarded bottles to exchange it for a fresh bottle of soda. (Courtesy of Wilma Beyer Hauer.)

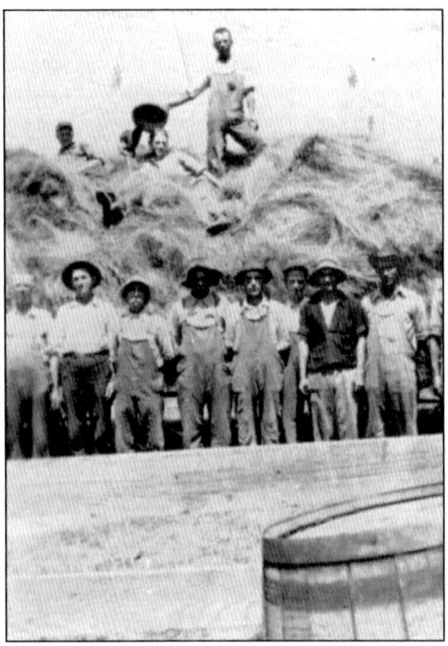

This 1910 photograph shows James Richard Mosley wearing a hat in the sheep yards at the far left. The Burlington Northern Railroad owned the Montgomery Stock Yards along Route 31. The sheep yards were the last stop for livestock before they reached the Chicago Stockyards. In the 1960s, the yards handled 225,000 sheep and 100,000 head of cattle each year, which meant more than $25 million worth of livestock annually. The number of full-time employees ranged from 25 to 50, depending on the season. The yards had six barns and a residence to house travelers. (Courtesy of Barbara Peck.)

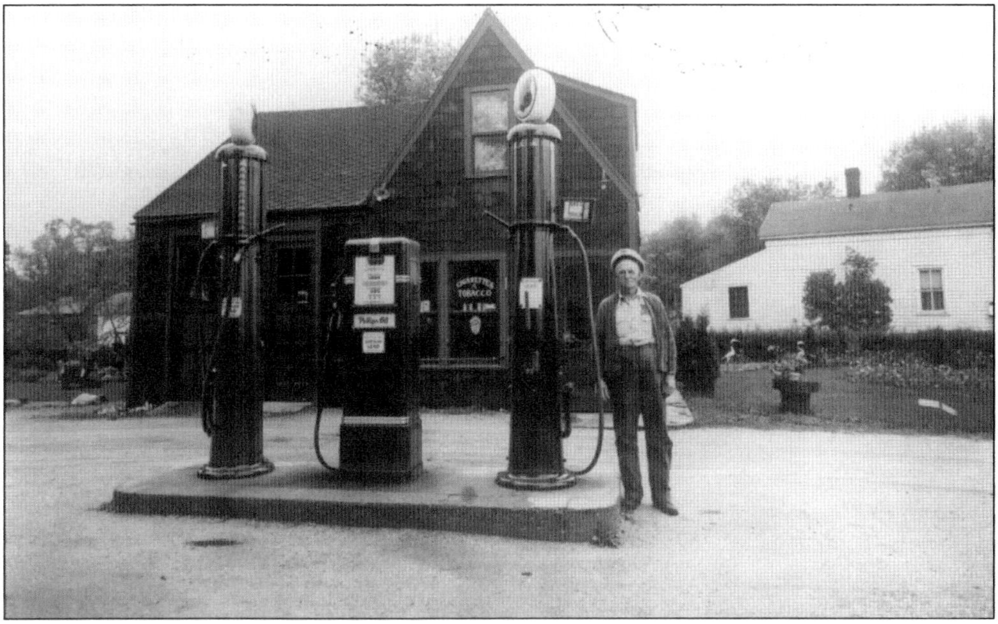

James Richard Mosley was born on May 29, 1875. He worked at the sheep yards prior to building this Phillips 66 gas station. He was the grandfather of the Mosley, Colwell, and Weber children. He died on September 21, 1951. (Courtesy of Barbara Peck.)

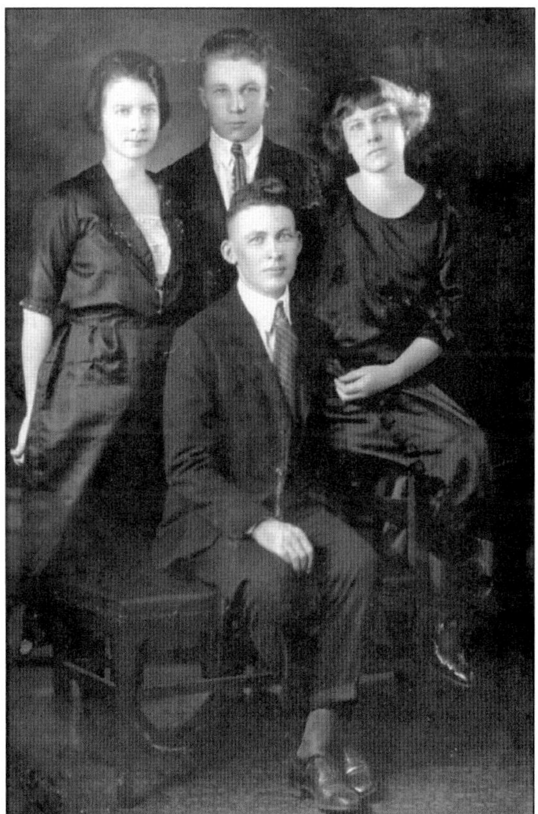

Pictured in 1922, from left to right are Ellen, Richard, Cora, and William Ira Mosley. They were the children of Richard and Maggie Mosley. As Sadie Parrott Lewis wrote, "For a hushed and lingering presence fills the vastness with a friendship." (Courtesy of Barbara Peck.)

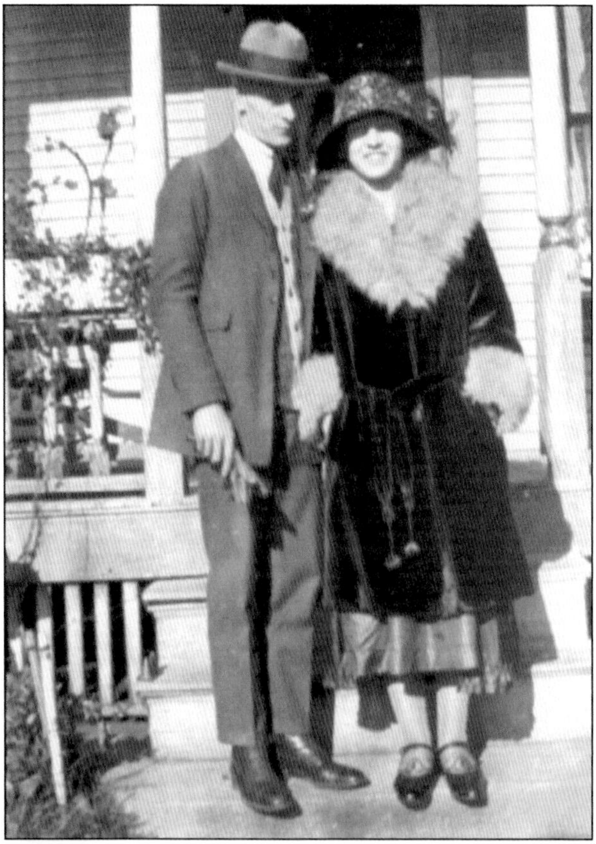

John and Cora Mosley Weber married on December 6, 1923. They had four children, Nina, Margaret, Glen, and Annie. John worked at Lyon Metal and was a volunteer fireman. He had the fire department telephone in his home. (Courtesy of Barbara Peck.)

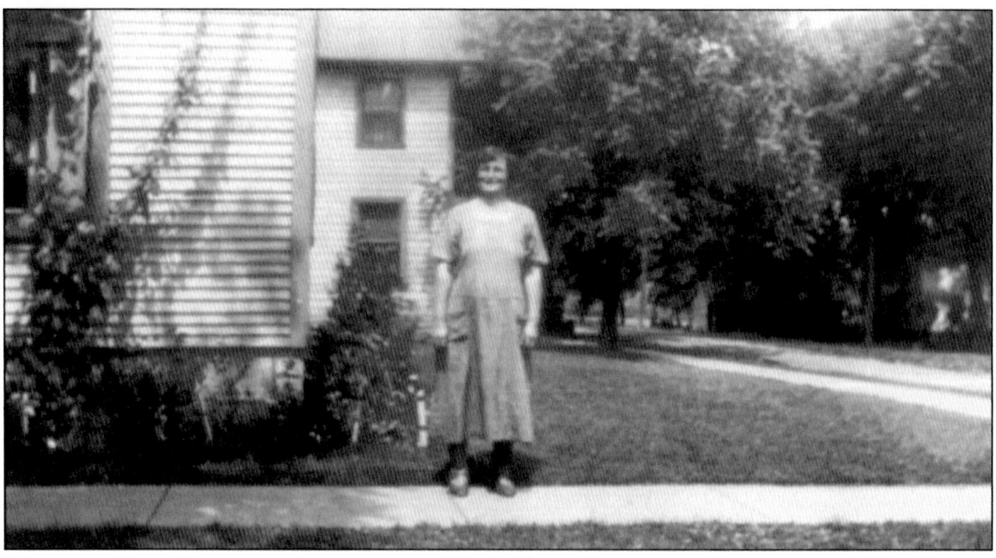

Margaret Alvira Doran was the youngest of 12 children. Her parents, Lawrence and Ellen Doran, emigrated from Ireland on May 1, 1857. Lawrence worked as a well driller, and he spoke French, Gaelic, and English. Maggie was a hardworking, thrifty person, and she took over running the gas station and the milk depot when her husband was ill with heart trouble. The gas station was located at the corner of Webster and River Streets. (Courtesy of Barbara Peck.)

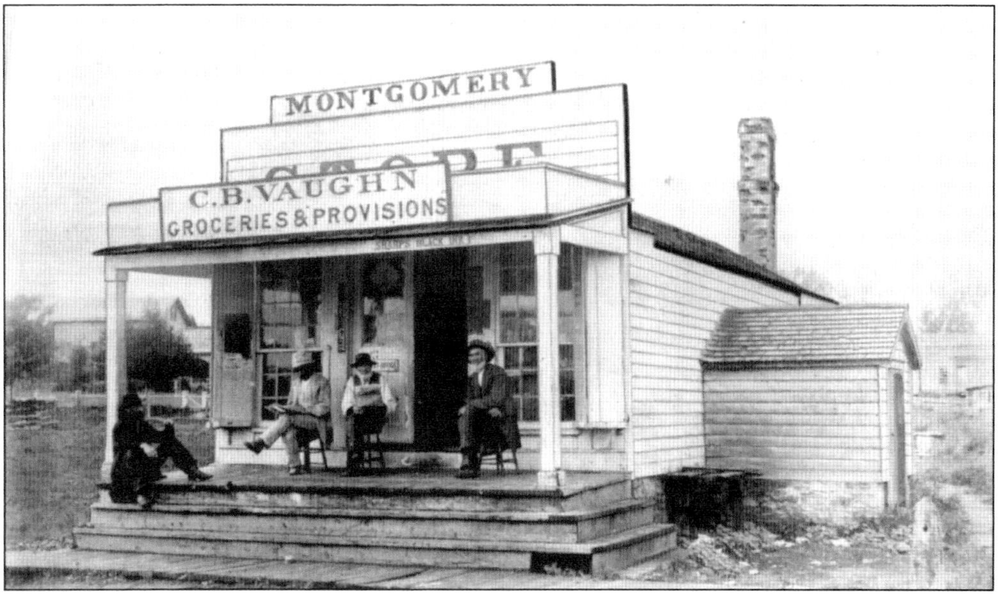

In 1870, the C.B. Vaughn General Store was situated at the west end of Montgomery Bridge. Pictured from left to right are Mr. Barnhart, James Apps, C.B., and Alonzo Filkins. The village store was also the post office. In the basement of the store, there was a spring-fed well where butter was stored because ice was not available. (Courtesy of Paul Straits/Montgomery Archives.)

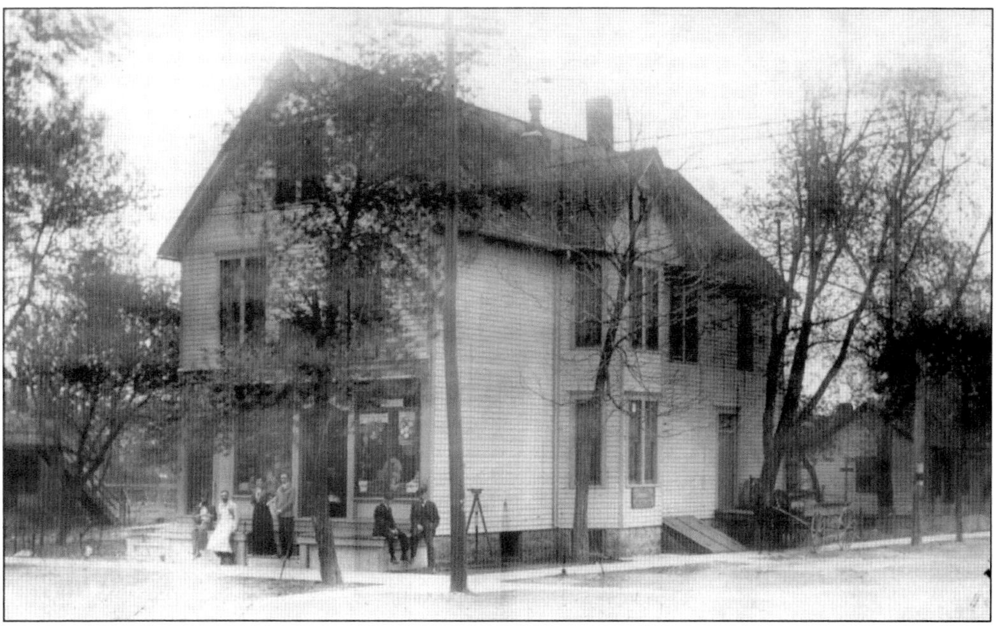

This 1885 photograph shows the Esser's Grocery Store on the corner of Webster and Main Streets. The Queen Anne-style building was designed by Millgate in 1880. Carrie and William Beher are on the steps. Later, Carrie and William owned the grocery store on the corner of Railroad and Webster Streets. The store also housed the post office. The Michaels family bought it in 1925. (Courtesy of Paul Straits.)

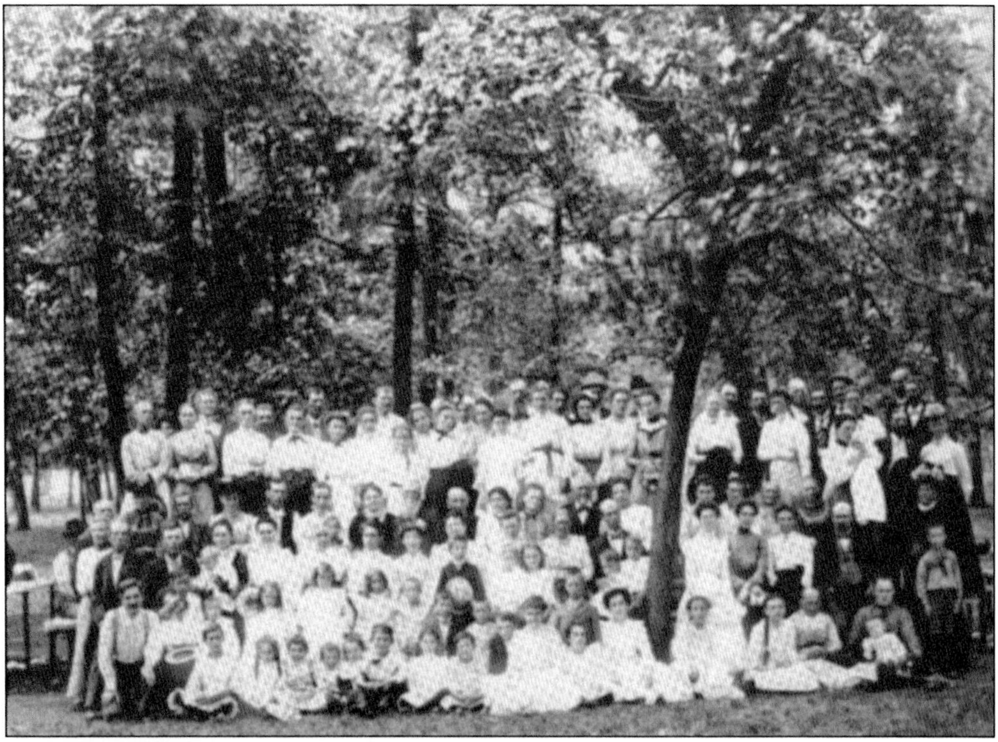

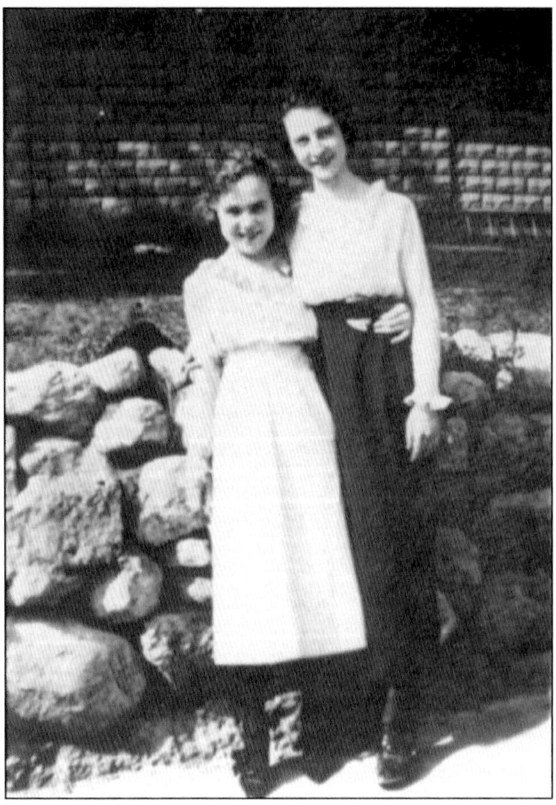

Members of the Keck family gathered in 1901 for a reunion at Riverview Park. The elevation of Montgomery is only 610 feet, making it the lowest site in Kane County. One early source listed the length of the Fox River as 220 miles. It flows southward, and overflows into the Illinois River at Ottawa. The river's drainage basin is 130 miles in length and averages 20 miles in width, which covers an area of 2,697 square miles, of which 1,080 square miles lie in Wisconsin. (Courtesy of Montgomery Archives.)

Schoolmates Bessie Carpenter and Ellen Mosley smile sweetly in front of the Keck School, around 1910. (Courtesy of Barbara Peck.)

This 1946 photograph shows Frank C. Schaefer, who had emigrated from Germany. Schaefer's greenhouse was established in 1926. Did hollyhocks flourish along the greenhouse row? (Courtesy of John Schaefer.)

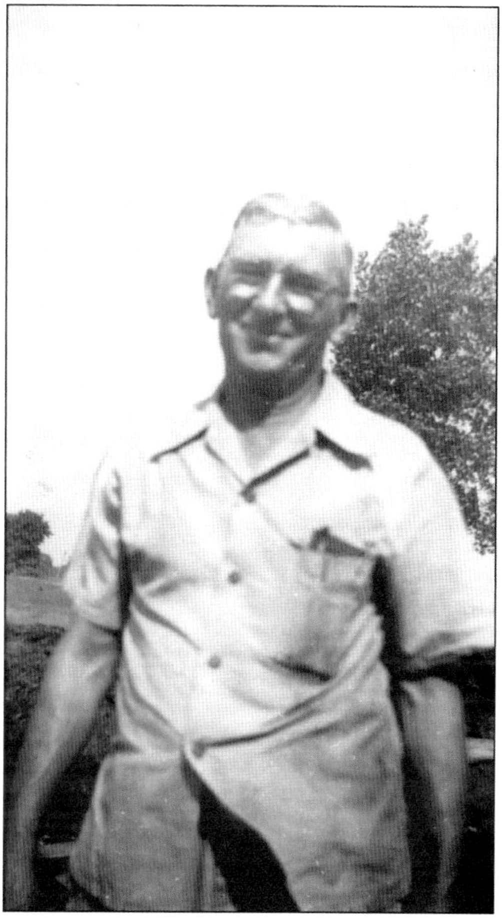

An early 1950 photograph shows Dorothy Monkmier, Esther Dehiltz, Ione Wood, Pearl Erwin, and Lucille O'Malley in front of the greenhouse. Frank C. Schaefer arrived from Germany almost penniless. He began to do greenhouse work for Judge Newhall in Aurora. The judge saw Schaefer's talent and loaned him money to start the Aurora Greenhouse Company with a partner in 1907. The company later became Schaefer's Greenhouse. (Courtesy of John Schaefer.)

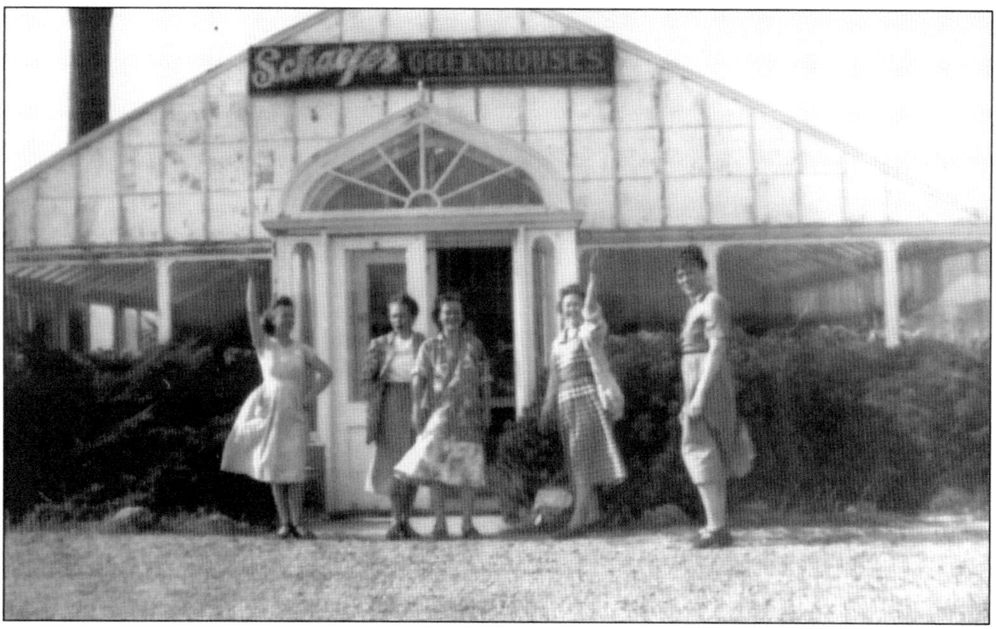

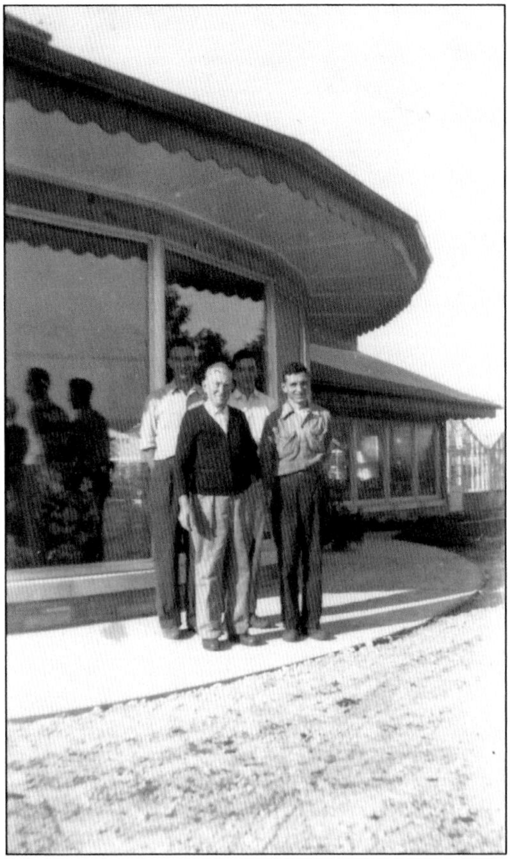

This photograph shows the Schaefer family standing at the newly remodeled front entrance of the greenhouse in the early 1950s. Pictured from left to right are (first row) Frank C. Schaefer and Edward Schaefer; (second row) Eric Schaefer and Frank W. Schaefer. Eric Schaefer celebrated his 100th birthday on November 17, 2009, and he passed away on March 29, 2010. Today, four generations of the Schaefer family are working at the greenhouse. (Courtesy of John Schaefer.)

This photograph shows a view of Schaefer's Greenhouse in 1926. Frank C. Schaefer had started the greenhouse business with a small potting shed, one boiler, and two greenhouses. (Courtesy of John Schaefer.)

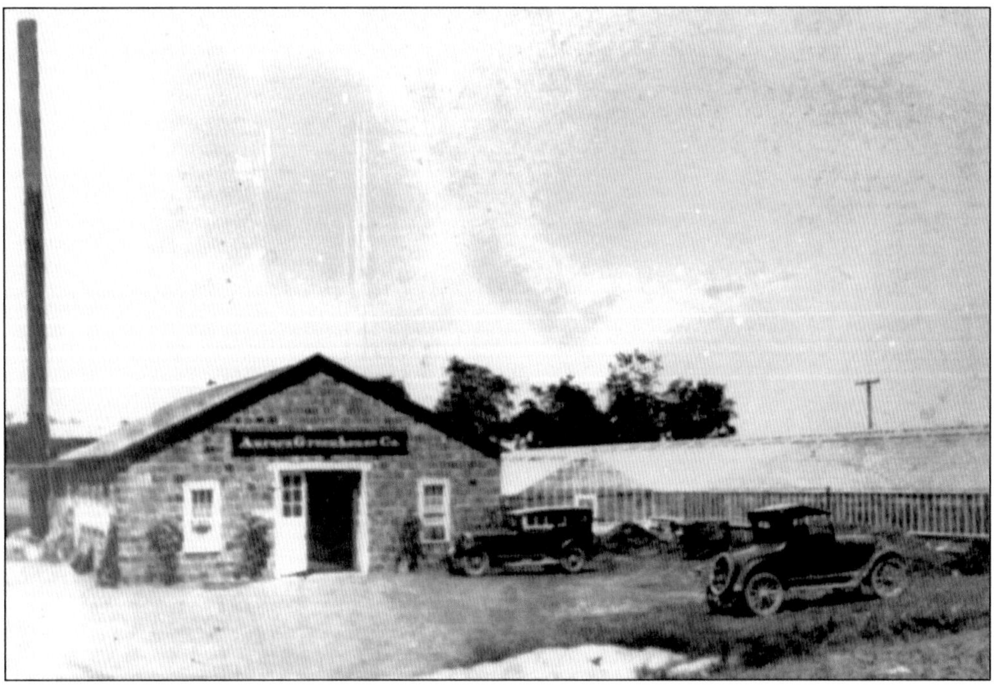

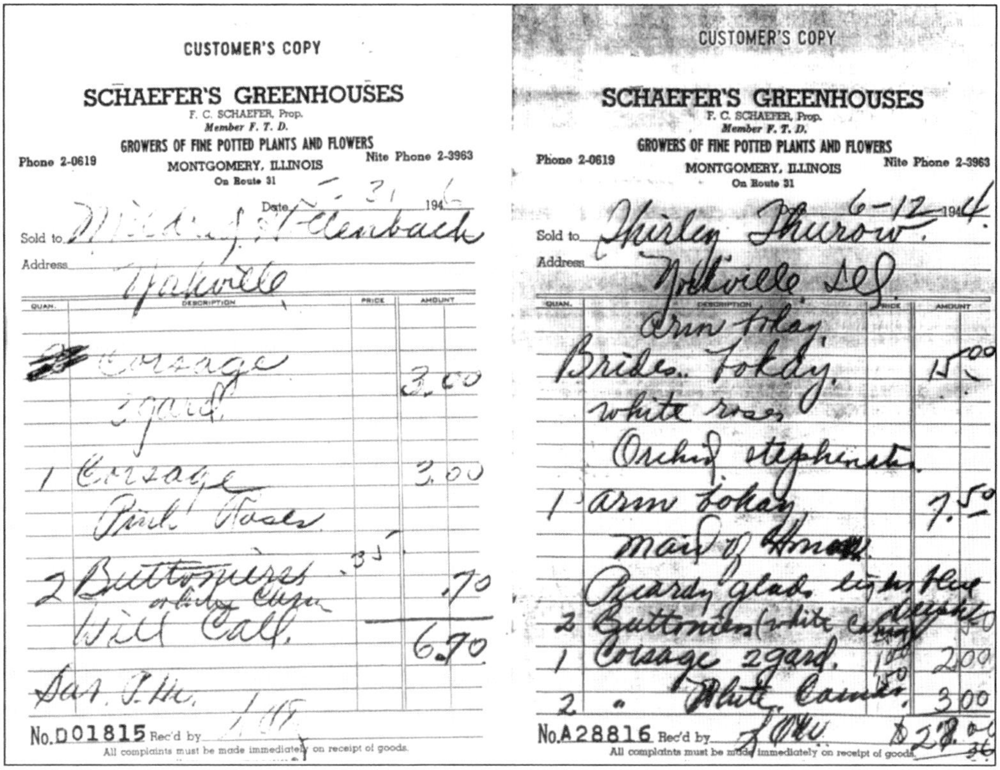

Schaefer's Greenhouse is the premier florist in the Fox Valley area, and quality is their hallmark along with excellent service. This 1946 invoice on the left priced a pink-rose corsage at $3 and a gardenia corsage at $3. Dated on June 12, 1944, the bill on the right priced a bride's "bokay" (bouquet) of white roses at $15, the maid of honor's bouquet at $7.50, and two gardenia corsages at $2 each. (Courtesy of Kendall County Historical Society.)

Tragedy struck Schaefer's Greenhouse twice in three years. On July 18, 1996, there was a heavy flood and 16.91 inches of rain submerged the greenhouse buildings under six feet of water. Because of the flood damage, the 35 greenhouses needed $1 million in repairs. On June 15, 1999, a fire broke out and burned the electrical wires housed in the ceiling. The towering flames and thick smoke were tamed by 18 fire departments. (Courtesy of John Schaefer.)

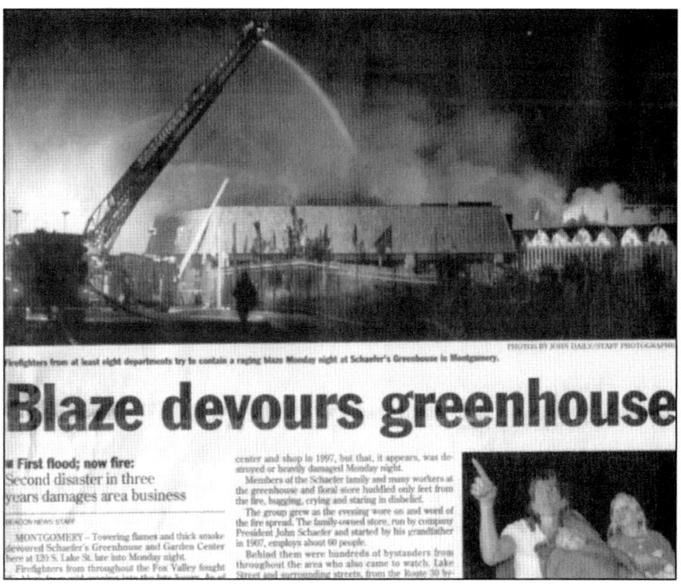
PHOTOS BY JOHN DAILY/STAFF PHOTOGRAPHER

Firefighters from at least eight departments try to contain a raging blaze Monday night at Schaefer's Greenhouse in Montgomery.

Blaze devours greenhouse

First flood; now fire: Second disaster in three years damages area business

BEACON NEWS STAFF

MONTGOMERY – Towering flames and thick smoke devoured Schaefer's Greenhouse and Garden Center here at 120 S. Lake St. late into Monday night.

Firefighters from throughout the Fox Valley fought

center and shop in 1997, but that, it appears, was destroyed or heavily damaged Monday night.

Members of the Schaefer family and many workers at the greenhouse and floral store huddled only feet from the fire, hugging, crying and staring in disbelief.

The group grew as the evening wore on and word of the fire spread. The family-owned store, run by company President John Schaefer and started by his grandfather in 1907, employs about 60 people.

Behind them were hundreds of bystanders from throughout the area who also came to watch. Lake Street and surrounding streets, from the Route 30 by-

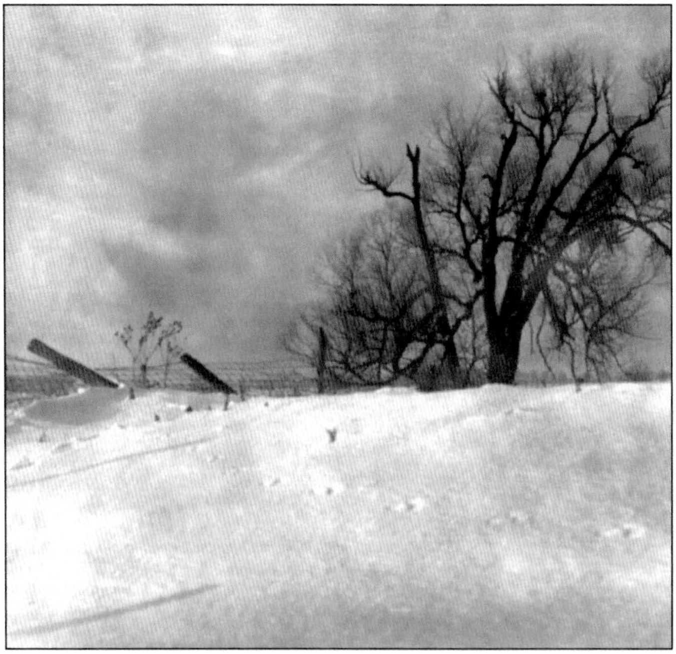

This photograph shows a stark winter scene along the barren fields of Montgomery. In the mid-1800s, land could not be purchased until it was surveyed and authorized for sale by the government. Payments were made in gold at the rate of $1.25 per acre, and it was payable to the Chicago Land Office. By 1942, it became illegal for anyone to possess gold money. (Courtesy of Montgomery Archives.)

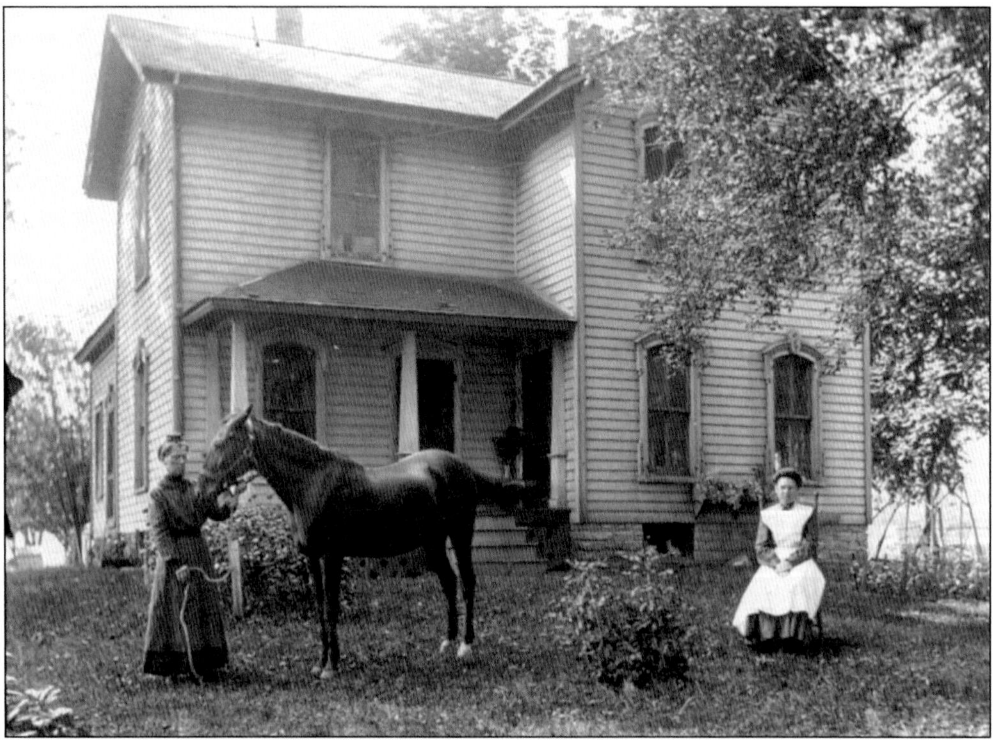

This photograph shows the family farm on Aucutt Road. Mrs. Perkins is seated on the right and her sister Patricia is holding a horse named Felicia. In 1830, accounts of the fertile prairies brought a wave of immigration to Illinois. A popular song in those days said, "Move your family West, if good health you would enjoy / And cross at Dixon's ferry in the State of Illinois." In the same year, Abraham Lincoln arrived with his parents to Illinois. (Courtesy of Cecil Piggott Jr.)

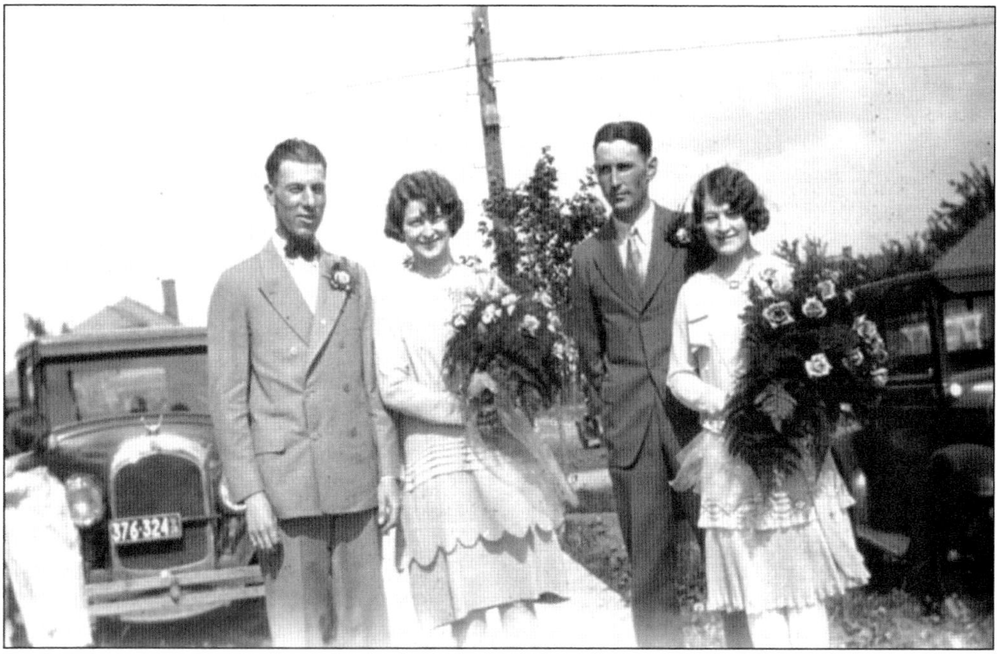

Cecil Piggott Sr. and Catherine "Katie" Haskell were married at Fourth Street Methodist Church in Aurora on June 18, 1928. Cecil was a special agent for the Burlington Railroad, and Katie was a telephone operator for the train depot. Cecil held the rank of captain for the railroad and died on November 8, 1974. Catherine died on June 6, 1985. (Courtesy of Cecil Piggott Jr.)

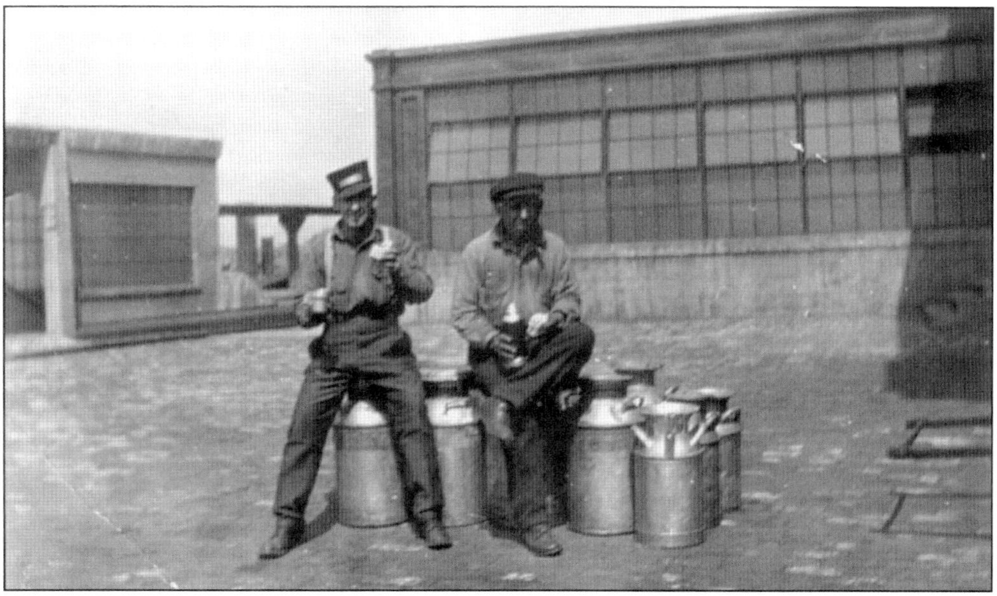

This photograph shows John Arthur Haskell and Henry "Nye" Haskell in the 1900s as baggage men at the Burlington Depot in Aurora. Nye was born on March 18, 1869, and he would treat farm animals in exchange for room and board. His flyer advertised, "He is the man who puts your horses' and mules' teeth in shape so they can masticate their food." Nye kept a matched set of Colt 44s in a velvet case. He also had a pair of loaded dice that always rolled 7s. He died on May 13, 1961. (Courtesy of Cecil Piggott Jr.)

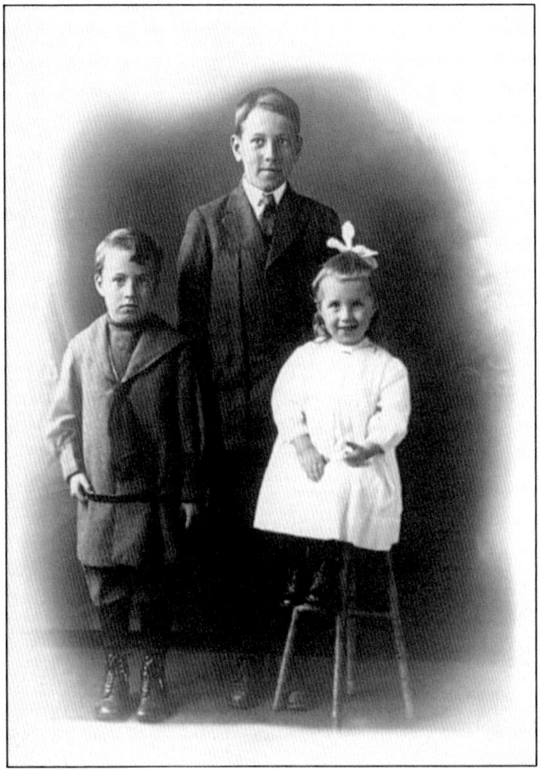

This 1912 photograph shows Cecil Piggott Sr., age 11, his brother Harold, age 5, and sister Doretha, age 2. During this time, life was serene in Montgomery, punctuated only by the occasional train whistle or the whispered wings of the nightingale. (Courtesy of Cecil Piggott Jr.)

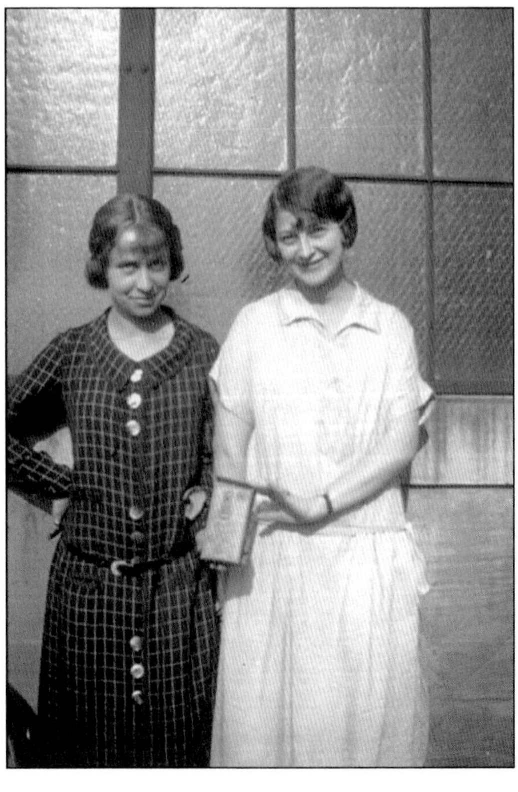

Catherine "Katie" Haskell Piggott and her friend Gert Sonles are shown on a workday at the Burlington Railroad office. It was a romantic era during the 1920s. During this time, the correct dress for women included four-buttoned shirts, hand-sewn gloves, brown taupe hosiery, coats made of tweedy material, satin blouses, and wool suits. Tea hour included chocolate fudge, charlotte russe, white plum pudding, malt cocoa, tea, and coffee. (Courtesy of Cecil Piggott Jr.)

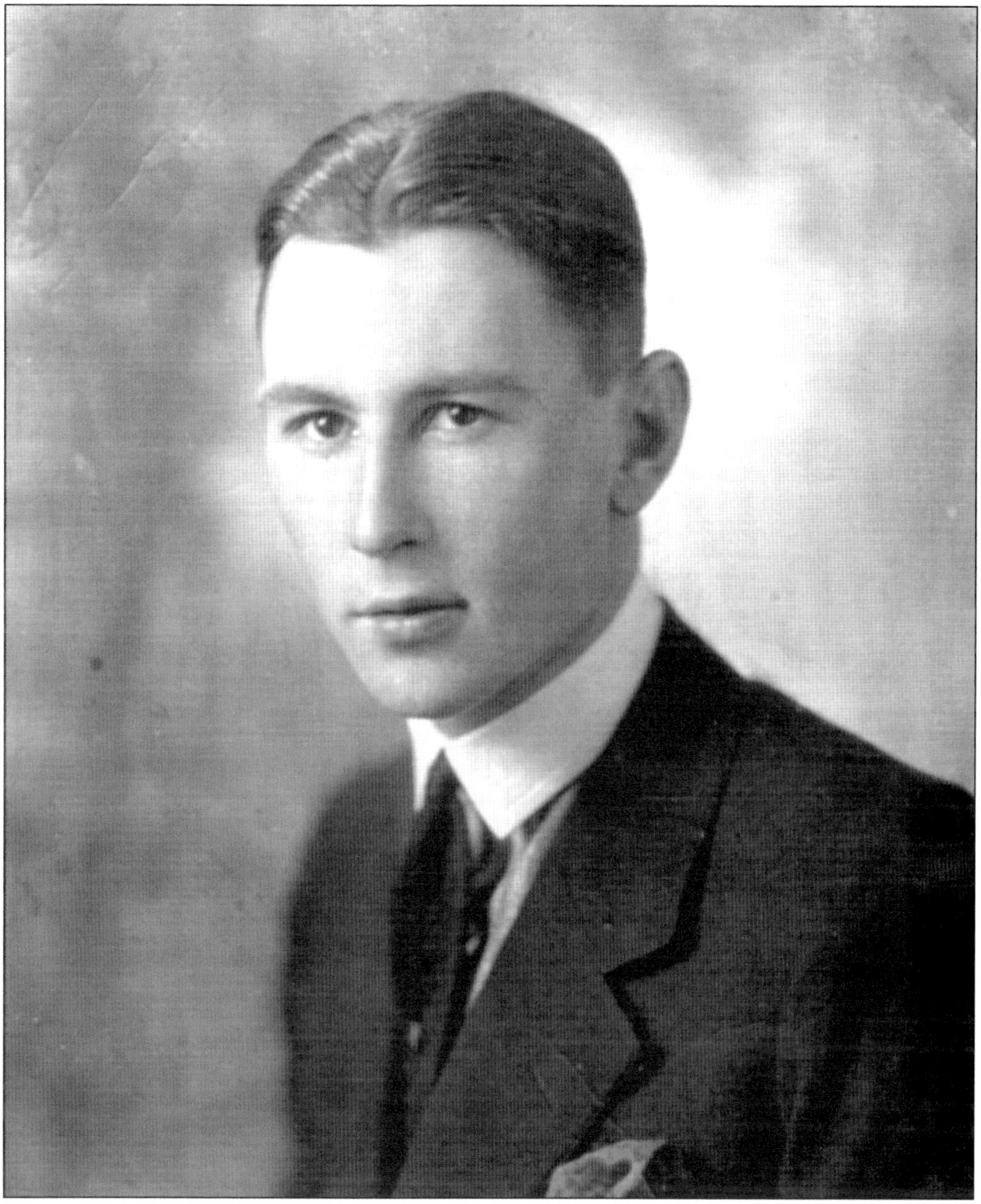

This portrait shows a young Ed Geddes who was best friends with Cecil Piggott Sr. Ed was the best man at Cecil's wedding. Both were special agents assigned to the Mendota-to-Burlington railway lines during the Depression. In 1932, Ed took one side of the train and Cecil took the other. They were looking for tramps or vagrants. Cecil heard two shots and ran to the other side of the train. Ed was on the ground mortally wounded and died. He was only 30 years old. (Courtesy of Cecil Piggott Jr.)

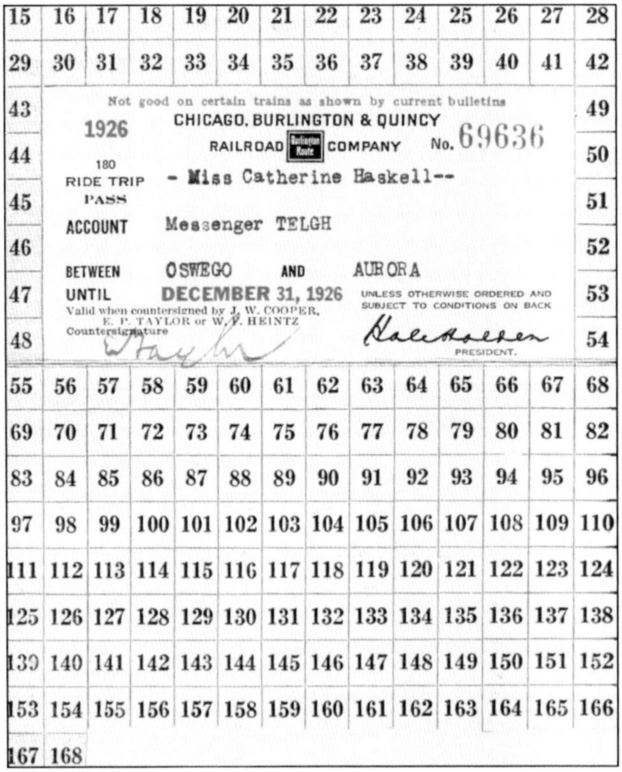

This trip-punch card belonged to Catherine Haskell Piggott and enabled her to receive free rides. Notice the date of December 31, 1926. Her husband, Cecil Piggott Sr., retired from the Chicago, Burlington & Quincy Railroad Company. One evening, Catherine played cards with the Burtness couple and had a perfect pinochle hand: double aces all around. The newspaper reported that she gave "an exultant shout" with the rarely held hand. (Courtesy of Cecil Piggott Jr.)

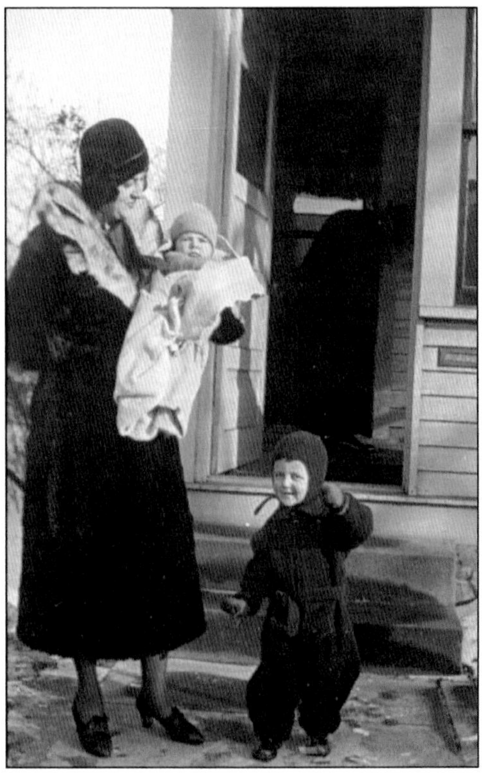

Shown is Catherine "Katie" Haskell Piggott with her sons Frank (in her arms) and Cecil Jr. (standing). Frank was born on September 4, 1932, and Cecil was born on May 26, 1930. Cecil Sr. later wrote a congratulatory letter to teacher Grace M. Nicholson on May 22, 1949. He was aboard the USS *Coral Sea*, which was anchored off Augusta, Sicily. In the letter, he wrote, "I'm a member of the radio gang onboard the largest warship in the world. She carries near 4,500 men." (Courtesy of Cecil Piggott Jr.)

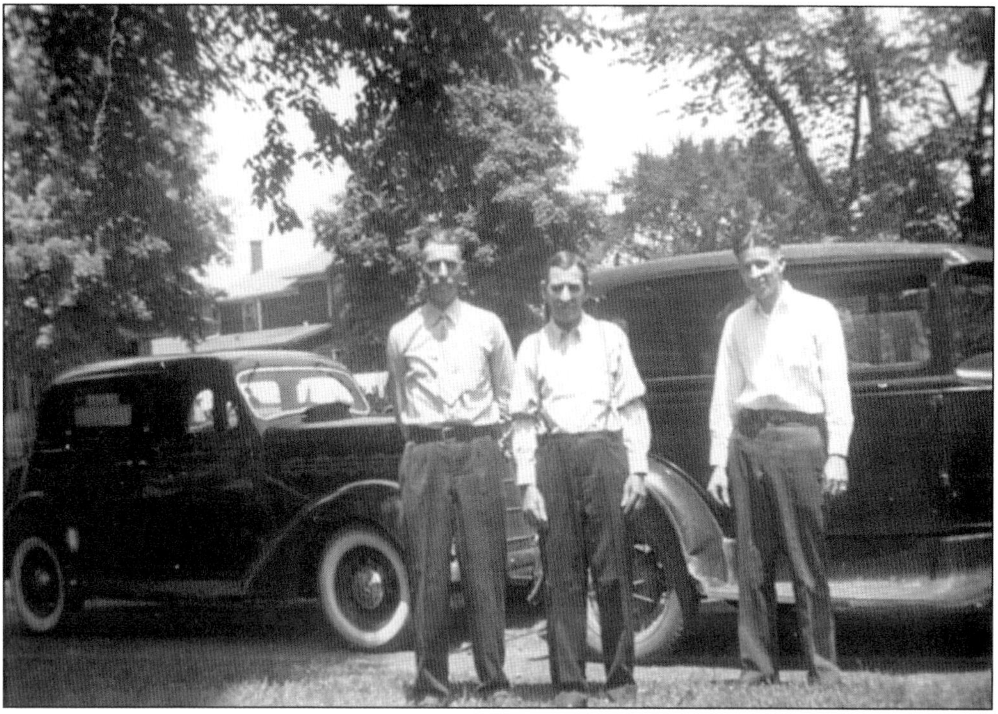

In June 1941, Cecil Piggott Sr., John Arthur, and Frank Piggott pose after visiting their great-aunt Alice Edwards Jones. (Courtesy of Cecil Piggott Jr.)

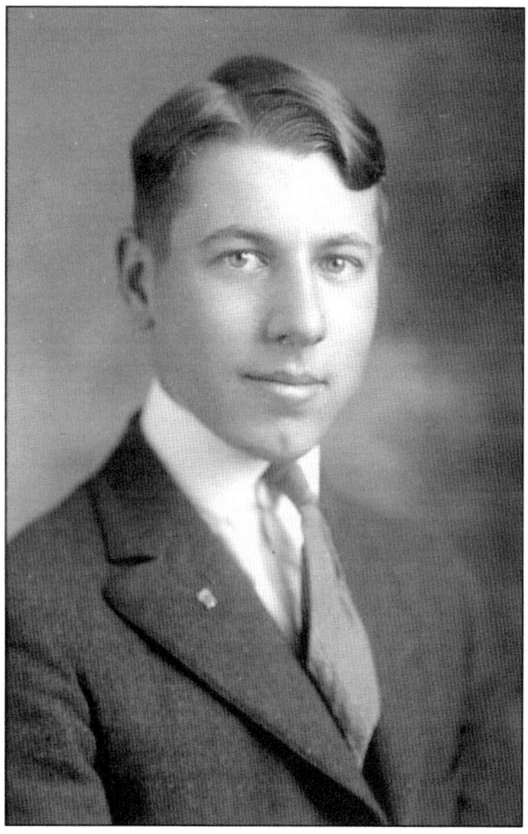

Cecil Piggott Sr. grew popcorn for the family, and then he began to sell it to 25 different accounts. He grew, processed, and packaged the popcorn. He bought the seeds from Noble Popcorn. He named his company C.P. Popcorn, and it was in business for 50 years. In 1963, a fire destroyed two of his barns, one filled with hay and the other with popcorn. The fire caused $15,000 of damage. At the company's height, there were 85 accounts and four delivery routes in 1975. In 1987, the family sold the business for $5,000 to Wayne Wilheim. (Courtesy of Cecil Piggott Jr.)

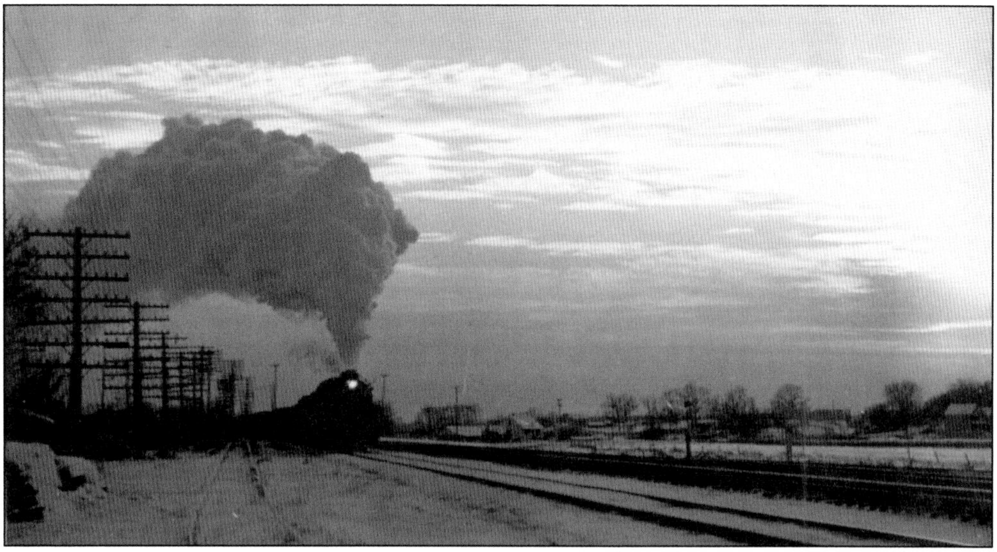

The darkening sky welcomed this steam engine passing by Montgomery. The train was owned by the Chicago, Burlington & Quincy Railroad (CB&Q). From 1866 until 1922, the train depot stood at LaSalle and New York Streets in Aurora. On February 12, 1849, a charter for the Aurora Branch Railroad had been granted, and the construction of the road cost $125,868.77. By 1855, the line had grown and became CB&Q. During the early 20th century, cadastral maps showed that CB&Q was not a major landholder in Montgomery. (Courtesy of Montgomery Archives.)

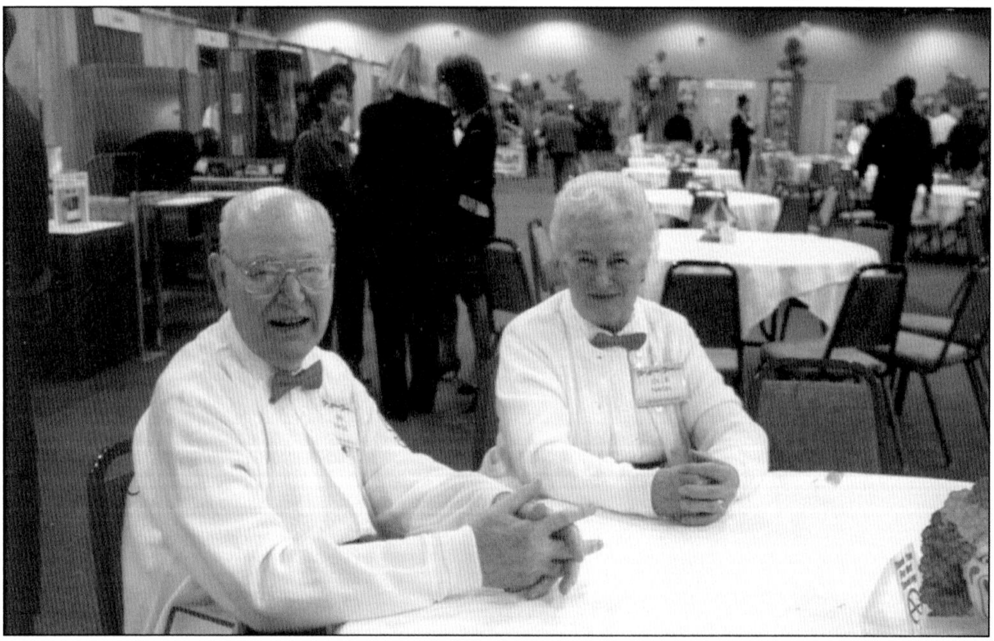

Erwin and Ollie Nagel are shown enjoying a Fox River Foods-business event. The company beginnings trace back to 1948, when Erwin Nagel purchased the Aurora Meat Locker Plant. On November 24, 1956, the company opened its doors to a new level of food service distribution. There were six full-time employees and three part-time employees. Today, there are 497 employees. Erwin and Ollie married on July 6, 1940, and had two children, Ken and Bonnie. (Courtesy of Ken Nagel.)

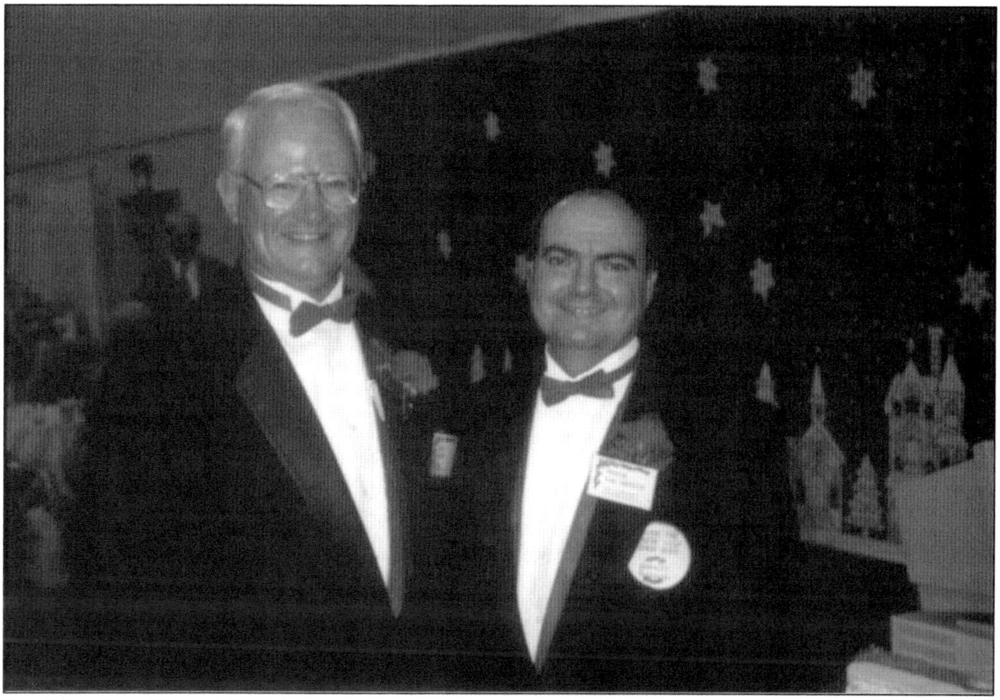

Ken Nagel and Frank Karabetsos are shown in a recent photograph at a business event. In 1956, Fox River Foods had annual sales of $267,000. Today, the annual sales figure is $340 million. The facility can house food in a 326,000-square-foot storage, which is equivalent to seven acres under one roof. In 2008, Fox River Foods won the Excellence in Distribution Award held by the International Foodservice Manufacturers Association. Today, they serve over 7,000 customers. At their annual food show at Pheasant Run Resort in St. Charles, Illinois, 300 vendors attract as many as 2,000 attendees each year. (Courtesy of Ken Nagel.)

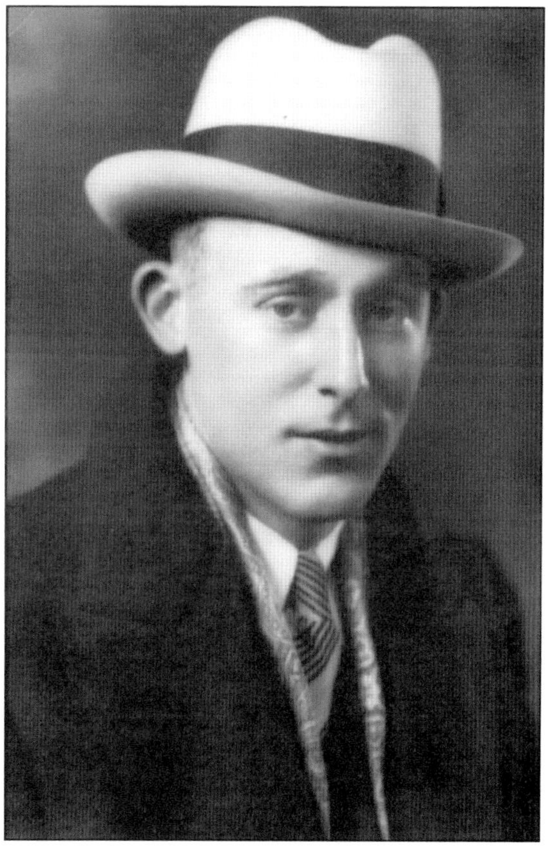

This 1940 photograph shows a stylish Charlie Gaylord. As Shakespeare wrote in *Richard II*, "The setting sun, and music at close, / As the last taste of sweets, is sweetest last, / Writ in remembrance, more than things long past." (Courtesy of Montgomery Archives.)

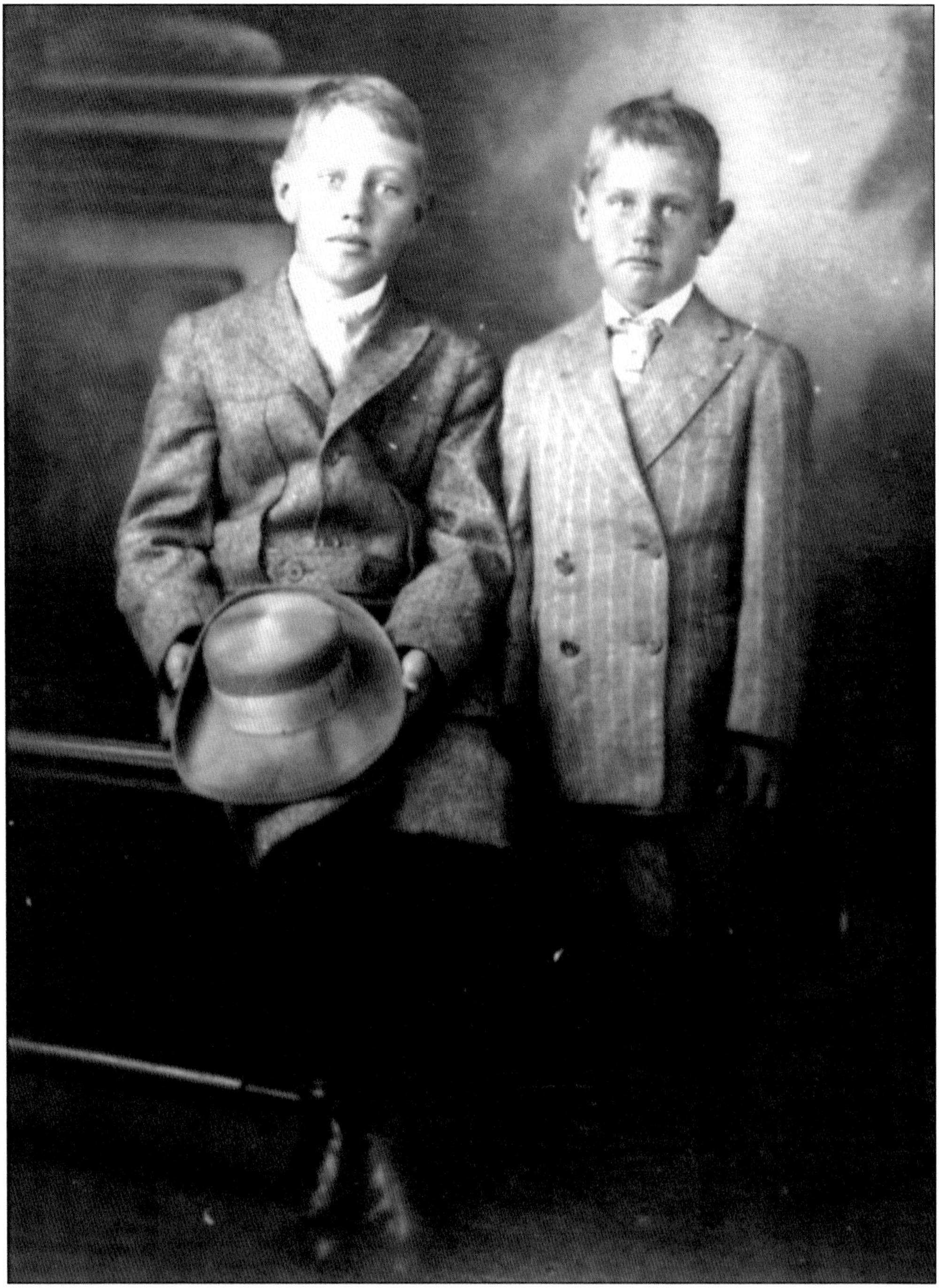

Shown are Harold Skow and his friend. Harold was born in 1904. His parents, Theodore and Christine Skow, had emigrated from Denmark, and the family lived near Elmer's Dog House. One day, Harold and his friend decided to play under the Montgomery Bridge instead of going straight home after school. They were having a fine time until Harold heard his mother driving the horse and buggy onto the bridge. She scampered down under the bridge and gave him a whipping. He never forgot to go straight home from school after that. (Courtesy of Ione Martin.)

Six

The Muslin Graces of Settler's Cottage

Forget not that the earth delights to feel your bare feet and the winds long to play with your hair.

—Kahlil Gibran

Clara Cecelia Dietsch Mosley and William Ira Mosley bought a little cottage that was 100 years old for $700. The quaint college was located at 209 Clinton Street. Their first child, Barbara, was born in 1932. Patricia was born in 1933; Alice, in 1935; William Jr., in 1940; Jeannie, in 1942; and Kathleen, in 1944. The youngest child, Marie, was born in 1949, which was after they moved to 216 Madison Street. William was born on September 5, 1901, and died on January 18, 1960. Clara was born on January 23, 1912. William operated a coal yard and ice business on Webster Street, which was west of the railroad tracks. The Depression had a firm grip on all businesses in Montgomery. When his suppliers insisted on payment, he was forced out of business. During these times, bankruptcy did not exist, forcing William to make weekly payments until all his bills were paid.

The cottage had one large bedroom upstairs. There was a potbelly stove and sewing machine in the all-purpose room on the first floor. When the cottage was first built, there was no electricity or telephone. When the Mosley family lived there, they had those amenities plus indoor plumbing. There was a gas stove on four legs with a side oven. The usual breakfast was steaming bowls of oatmeal, which was cooked overnight in a pot and heated by the back burner. Recalling a few of her childhood memories, Patricia Mosley Torrence said, "On the big, round oak table that was covered in oilcloth, we ate, did dishes, and our homework. We cut out paper dolls, worked jigsaw puzzles, and listened as mother read to us. Daddy kept chickens and rabbits in backyard cages and butchered them for meals. There was a sauerkraut crock on the back porch. We had a big garden and canned many foods for each winter."

This home, now called Settler's Cottage, is located at 198 North River Street. It is the oldest remaining structure in the village and was originally owned by Daniel Samuel Gray, who was the founder of Montgomery. The Historic Preservation Commission has worked since 2003 to restore this historical home. The cottage had a grand reopening on August 14, 2010. Funds for the restoration of the Settler's Cottage came from grants and donations. Members of the commission include chair Jeanette Lee, Patricia Mosley Torrence, Ken Eggert, John Aman, Tom Yakaitis, Gene Michaels, staff liaison Debbie Buchanan, executive assistant to village manager Anne Marie Gaura. The commission also planned monthly historical events and presentations.

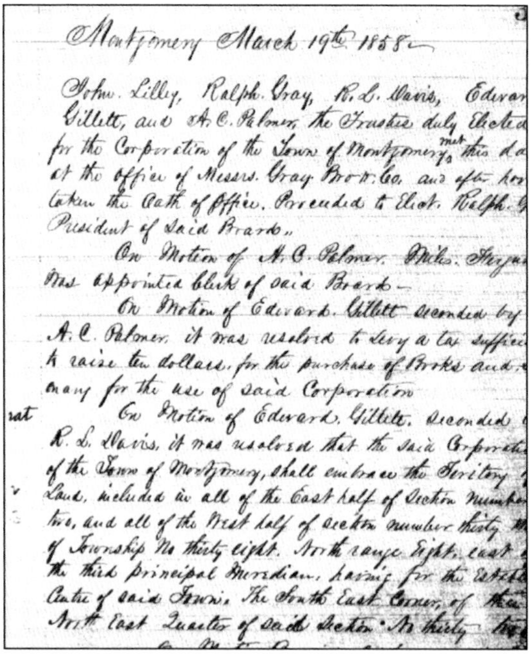

Montgomery March 19th 1858

John. Lilley, Ralph. Gray, R. L. Davis, Edwar
Gillett, and A. C. Palmer, the Trustee duly Elected
for the Corporation of the Town of Montgomery met this da
at the office of Messrs. Gray Bro & Co. and after hav
taken the Oath of office. Proceeded to Elect. Ralph. G
President of Said Board.

On Motion of A. C. Palmer. Miles. [illegible]
was appointed Clerk of said Board—

On Motion of Edward. Gillett seconded by
A. C. Palmer. it was resolved to levy a tax suffic
to raise ten dollars. for the purchase of Books and
[illegible] for the use of said Corporation

On Motion of Edward. Gillett. Seconded
R. L. Davis. it was resolved that the said Corporati
of the Town of Montgomery, shall embrace the Territory
Land. included in all of the East half of Section Numbe
two, and all of the West half of section number thirty
of Township No thirty eight. North range Eight. east
the third principal Meridian. having for the [illegible]
Centre of said Town. The South East Corner, of the
North East Quarter of said Section. No thirty two

This handwritten page in lovely script contains recorded notes for a meeting on March 19, 1858. The note read, "Board met at the mill office. Mr. Smith was paid $18 for use of mill office for one year. Adam Phye was paid $1.50 for surveying services on River Street. The poll tax was fixed at $2 in money." Another recorded entry on May 5, 1882, stated, "It shall not be lawful for any horse, colt, sheep, goat, or bull to suffer or permit them to run at large within the limits of village at any time . . . The fines are not less than $1.00 nor more than $5.00." (Courtesy of Helen Prester.)

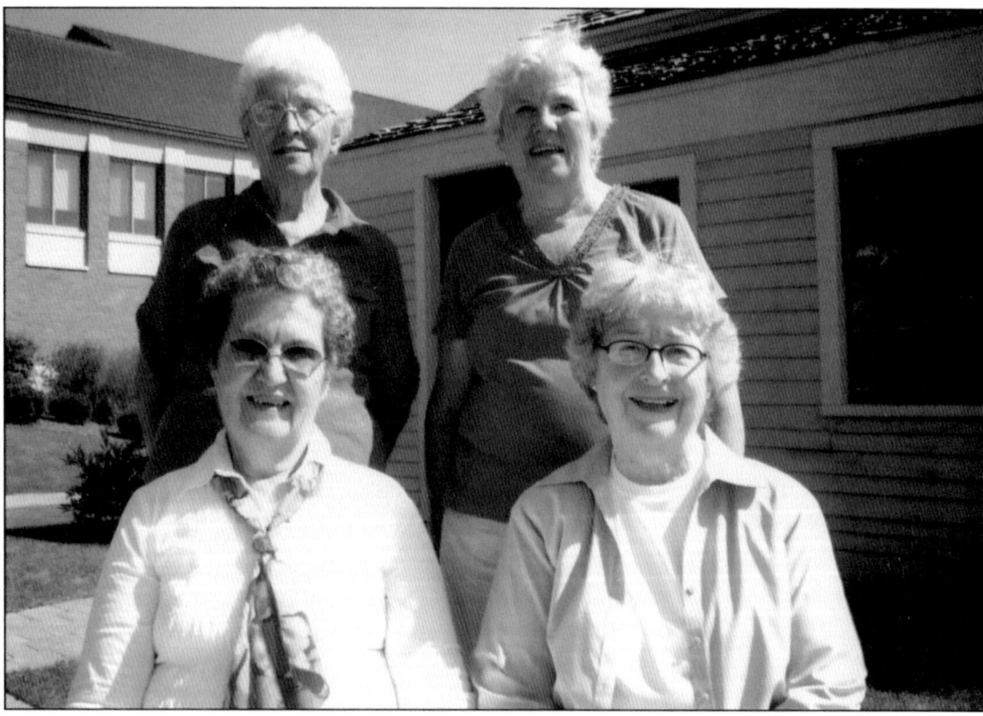

On a very steamy, 90-degree day in July 2010, four Mosley sisters pose in front of the house where they grew up. Pictured from left to right are (first row) Barbara Mosley Peck and Patricia Mosely Torrence; (second row) Alice Mosley Seidelman and Jeannie Mosley Wollenweber. Altogether, the four sisters have 36 children, 84 grandchildren, and 32 great-grandchildren. Their mother, Clara, had 52 grandchildren when she died on March 29, 1977. They recalled liking fried-fruit pies as children. (Author's collection.)

Pictured from left to right are family members Jim Strejc, Frank Strejc Sr., Anne Strejc, Bob Strejc, Clarence Strejc, Adeline Strejc and Frank Strejc Jr. The surname "Strejc" was Czechoslovakian, and their grandfather changed it to Straits. Clarence was born on March 4, 1919. Bob was born on June 6, 1930. (Courtesy of Paul Straits/ Vesco Reprographic.)

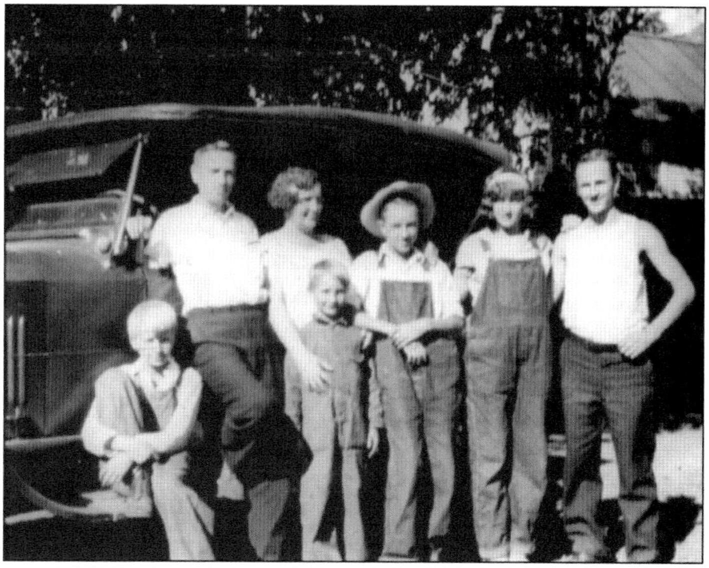

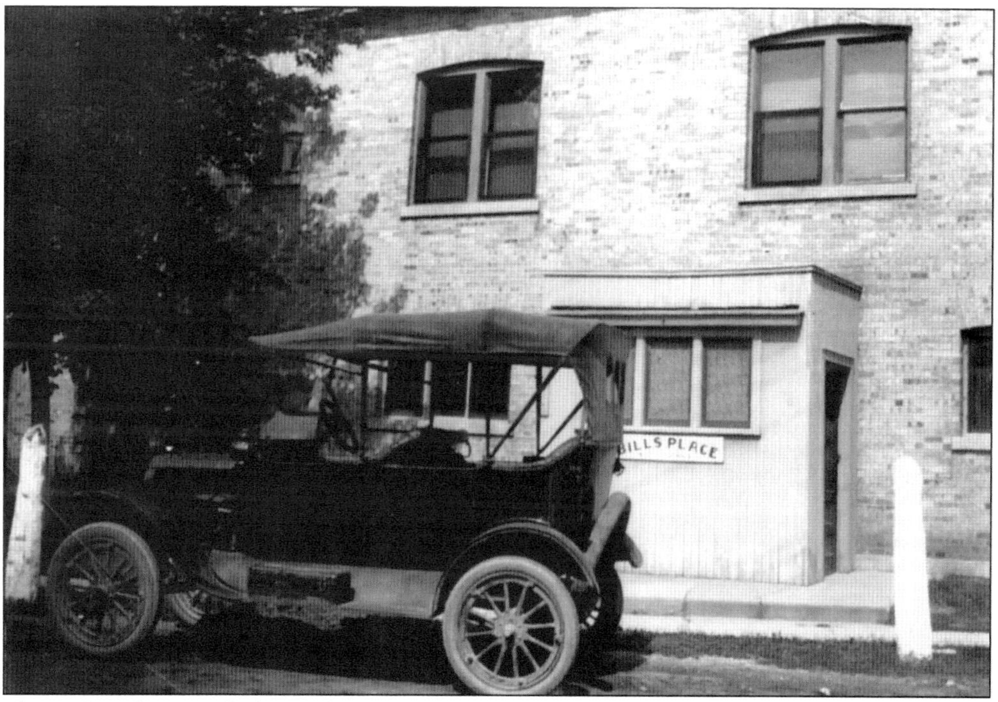

This 1930s photograph shows the entrance to Bill's Place Tavern. The tavern is located on the corner of Webster and Mill Streets. In 1907, Montgomery authorized the Aurora Brewing Company to construct and operate a saloon on the northwest corner of River and Mill Streets. The Mill Tavern, with Mike Grass as its proprietor, was built on the site of the old cottage-cheese plant, which had burned down earlier. (Courtesy of Paul Straits/Alice Sutcliff.)

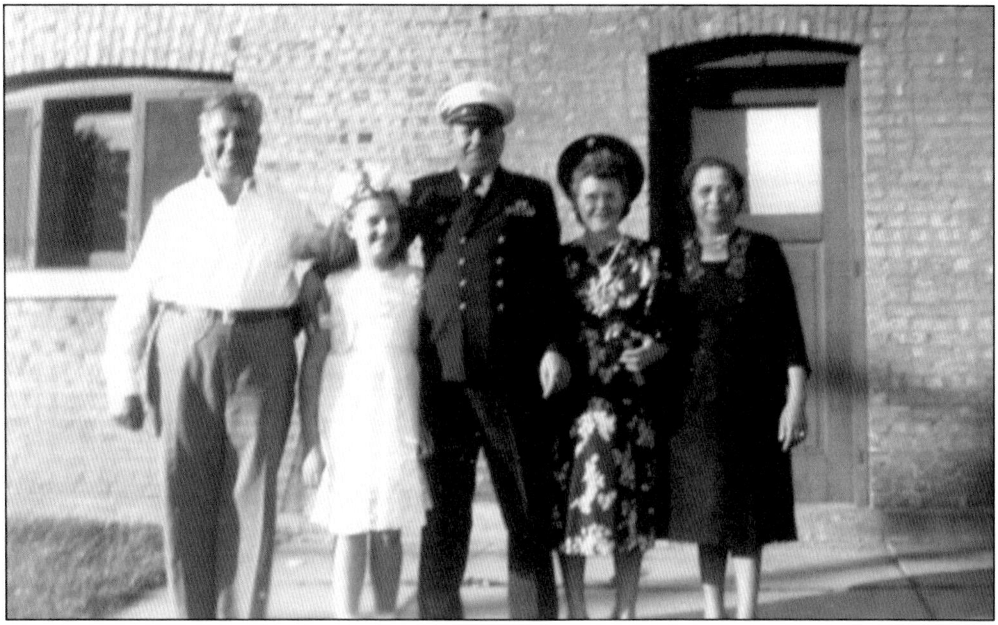

This photograph shows Alex Pocus and Sophie Pocus in the center with unidentified friends in 1950. They operated The Mill Tavern from 1944 until 1956, when Alex passed away. Sophie passed away in 1957. Their daughter Alice took over the business in 1958. In the late 1940s, Alice remembers when neighbors would come with a bucket and fill it with beer for 25¢. (Courtesy of Alice Sutcliff/Montgomery Archives.)

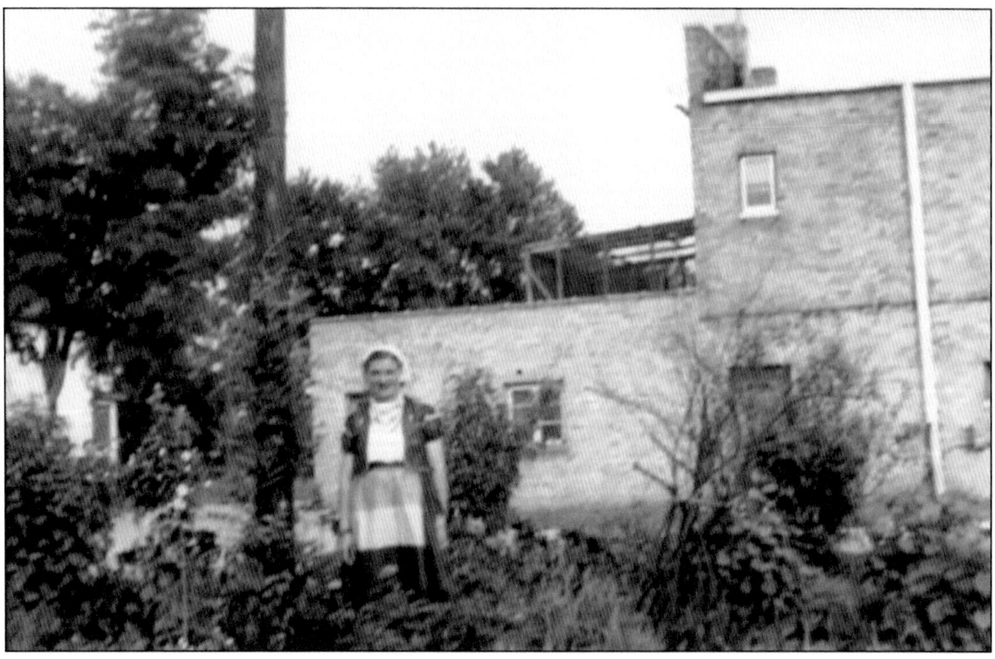

Alice Pocus poses by The Mill Tavern in 1951. She graduated from St. Peter's Catholic School that year and continued her studies at West Aurora High School. Her third husband, Lester Sutcliff, died in 1995. Many customers helped The Mill after the 1996 flood, which caused the basement to be submerged under water for three days. (Courtesy of Alice Pocus Sutcliff.)

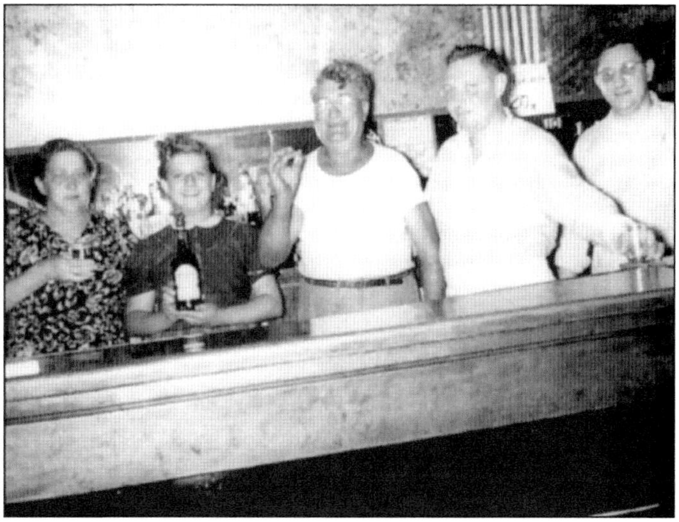

In this 1952 photograph, Sophie Pocus, Alice Pocus, Alex Pocus, Barney Poss, and cousin Frank Zalagenus pose at The Mill Tavern. The Mill had a full-service kitchen that served chicken, fish, Italian beef, hamburgers, and pizza. In 1970, as her children were growing up, Sophie discontinued the full-serve kitchen and began serving East Side Café pizza. In 1979, the liquor store was added. (Courtesy of Alice Pocus Sutcliff.)

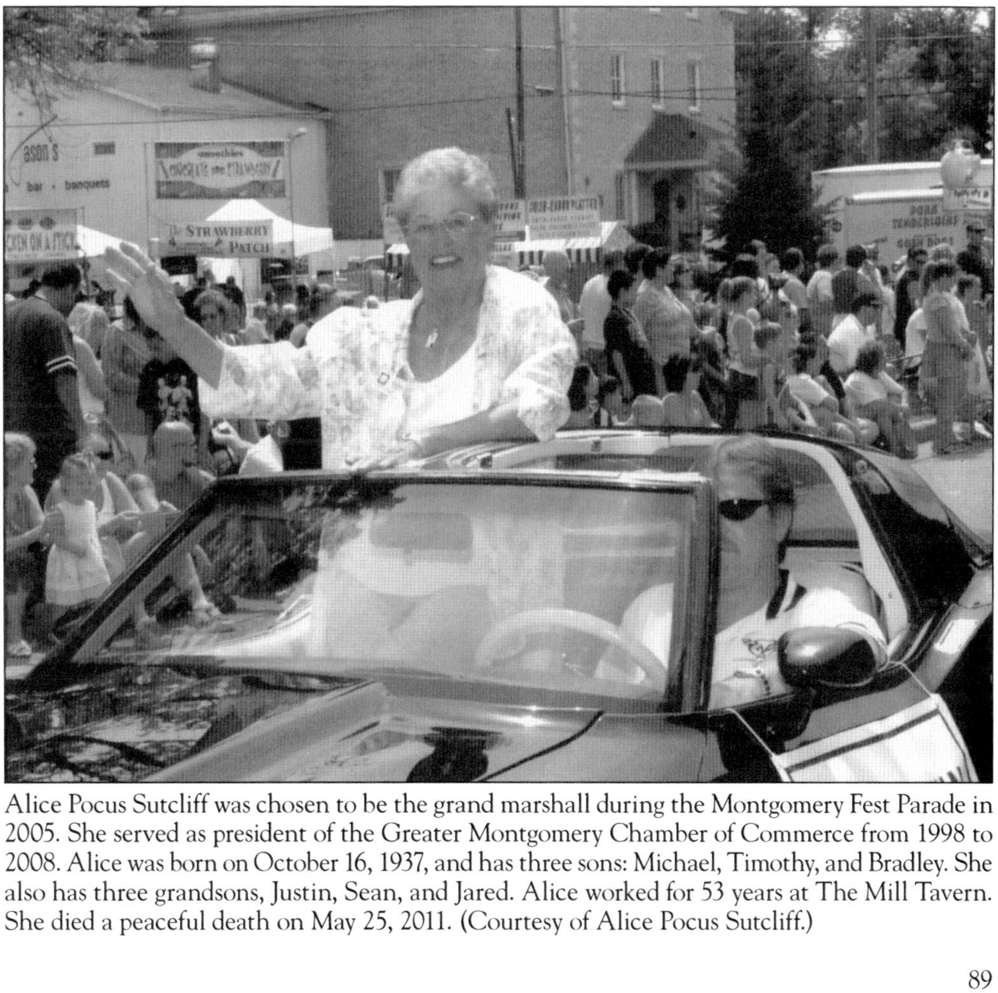

Alice Pocus Sutcliff was chosen to be the grand marshall during the Montgomery Fest Parade in 2005. She served as president of the Greater Montgomery Chamber of Commerce from 1998 to 2008. Alice was born on October 16, 1937, and has three sons: Michael, Timothy, and Bradley. She also has three grandsons, Justin, Sean, and Jared. Alice worked for 53 years at The Mill Tavern. She died a peaceful death on May 25, 2011. (Courtesy of Alice Pocus Sutcliff.)

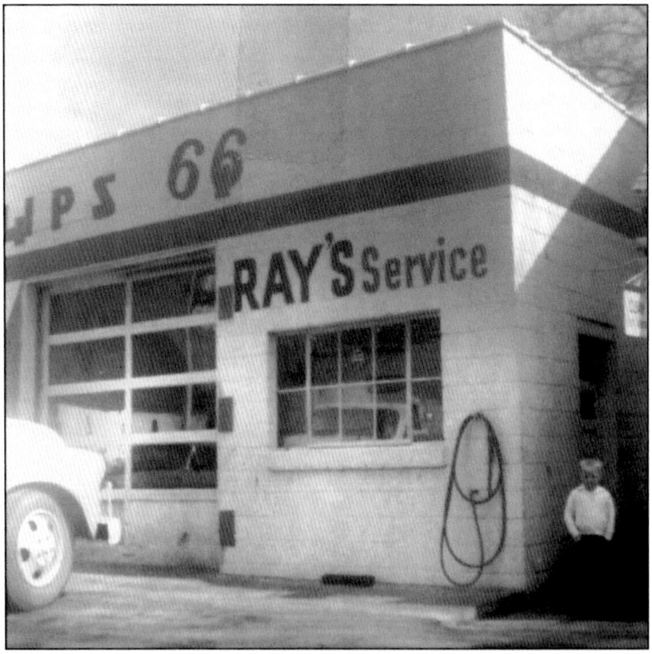

The gas station was located on the corner of Webster and River Streets, and was owned by Ray "Slick" Carlson from 1960 to 1963. His wife, Goldie Hornyan Carlson, was his bookkeeper. They raised four children, Rayanne, Mickey, Diane, and Steve. The small boy in the photograph is his son Steve, who was three years old. Ray was born on July 14, 1929, and passed away on September 23, 1999. (Courtesy of Goldie and Rayanne Carlson.)

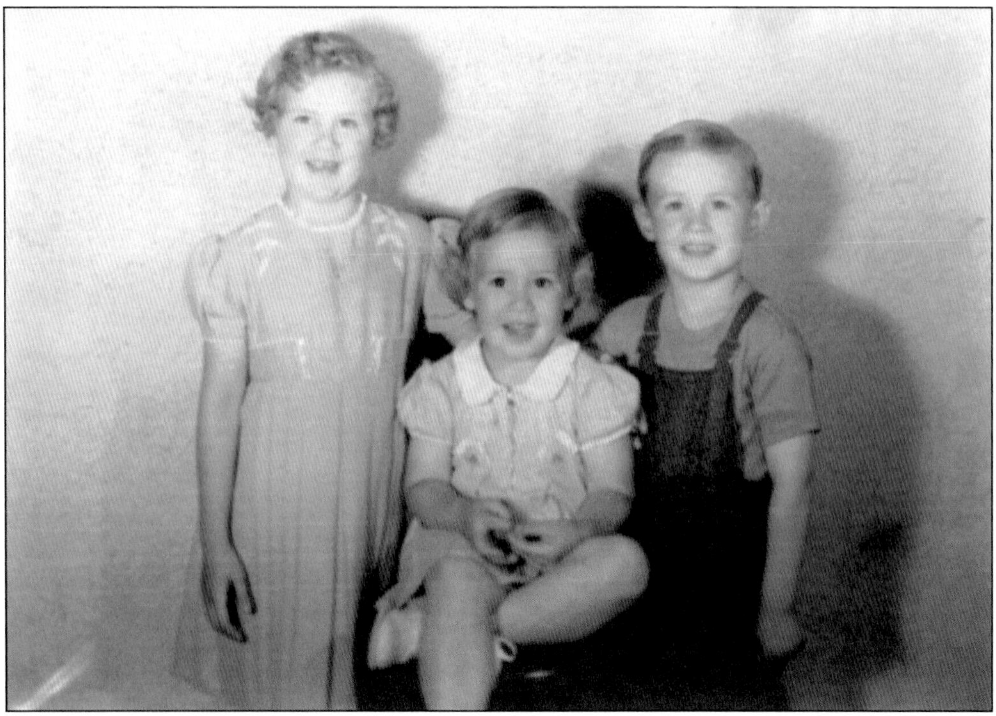

Pictured from left to right are Lorene, Juanita, and Richard "Shorty" Dickson in Bristol in 1940. Their parents were Simon and Thelma Wedemaier Dickson. Simon came from the parish of Half Morton in Dumfriesshire, Scotland. Four generations of the Dickson family farmed the land beginning in 1863 by means of yoked oxen and primitive plows. The main crop during this time was wheat, which had to be laboriously hauled to Chicago with oxen. The trip took five days, and the profits were not large. (Courtesy of Shorty Dickson.)

Simon and Thelma Wademaier Dickson pose for the camera in 1980. They were married for 55 years until he passed away on August 21, 1991. Thelma passed away on July 11, 1994. Simon's great-grandfather had purchased a tract of 200 acres in the Bristol Township. He operated this homestead until 1893, when he became the owner of the family's present farm that had 170 acres in Bristol. Simon's skilled hand of husbandry produced bountiful crops from his land. In political faith, Mr. Dickson was a stalwart Republican. (Courtesy of Shorty Dickson.)

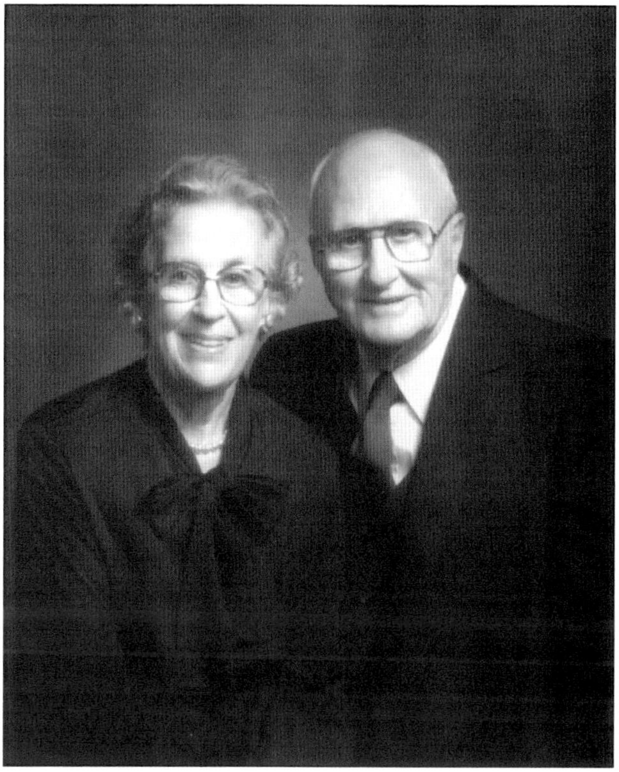

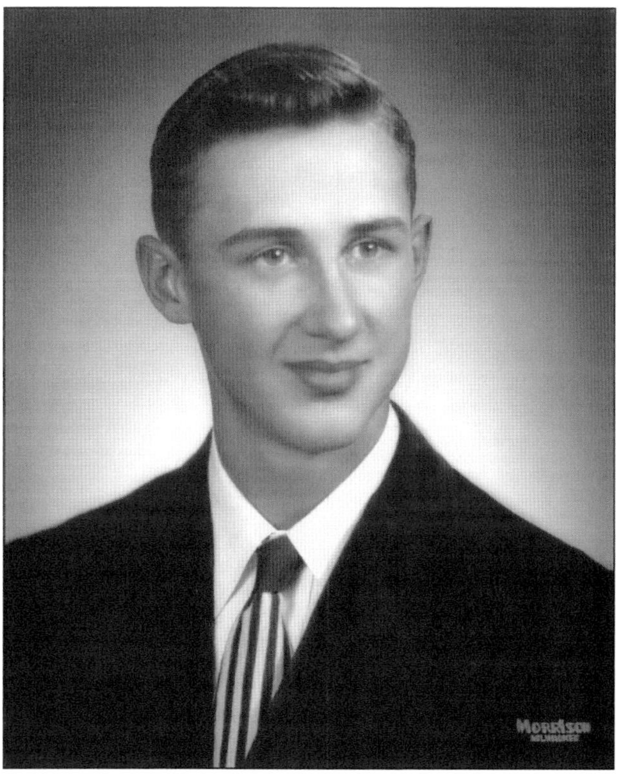

Richard "Shorty" Dickson was born on September 21, 1936. Richard's nickname derived from his father, Simon, who first called his baby son "Shorty." This 1953 photograph was Shorty's graduation portrait from Yorkville High School. He graduated from the University of Illinois with a degree in agricultural science. Shorty taught in Hebron, Illinois, before returning to Bristol, where he worked in the insurance industry for the next 40 years. (Courtesy of Shorty Dickson.)

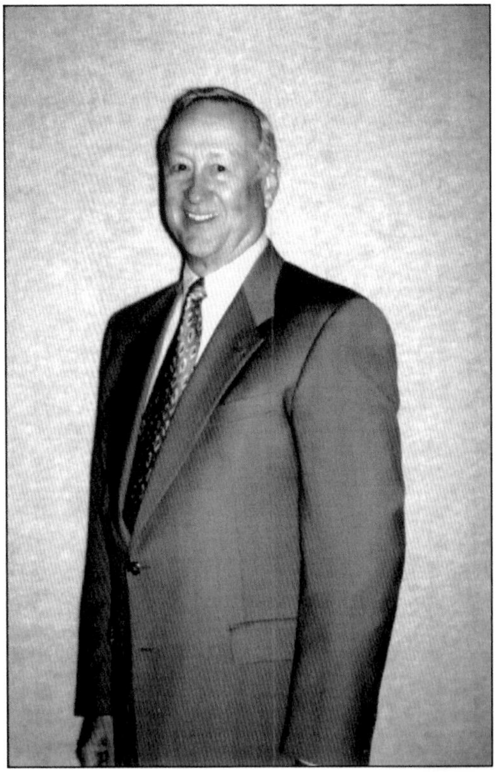

This 2000 photograph shows Richard "Shorty" Dickson at a community event. He is a trustee of the Bristol Kendall Fire Department and the Oak Grove Cemetery Board, where his father also served as a trustee for 50 years. He is also on the board of Trinity United Methodist Church and Kane County Mutual Insurance Company. For the past 36 years, Shorty has served on the board of trustees for Waubonsee Community College. In a 1914 county history, his father, Simon, was said to have "an untarnished name and an unsullied reputation." This is also true of Shorty. (Courtesy of Shorty Dickson.)

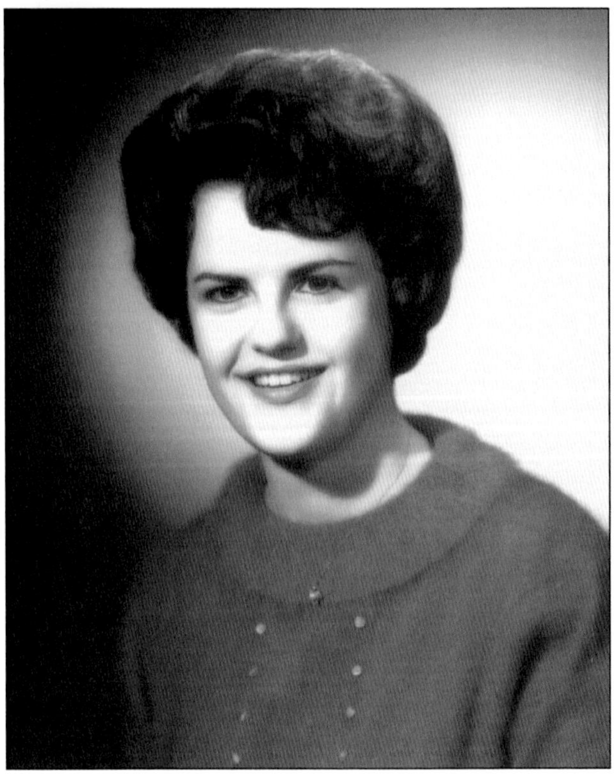

Anita Kingsbury and Richard "Shorty" Dickson married on November 26, 1966, and raised three children, Joan, Matthew, and Wesley. They have four grandchildren, Courtney, Daniel, Rachel, and Kari Ellen. Anita attended West Aurora High School and Texas Christian University. Anita died on January 16, 1996, of pancreatic cancer. (Courtesy of Shorty Dickson.)

On September 26, 1998, Richard "Shorty" Dickson and Marian Braund were married at the First Lutheran Church in Plano, Illinois. After an Alaskan-cruise honeymoon, they settled on the Dickson family's farm property. Marian was born on September 11, 1939, in Elroy, Wisconsin. She first married Allen R. Lee. Later, they were transferred to the Montgomery area by Caterpillar Inc. Lee passed away on October 12, 1985. (Courtesy of Shorty and Marian Dickson.)

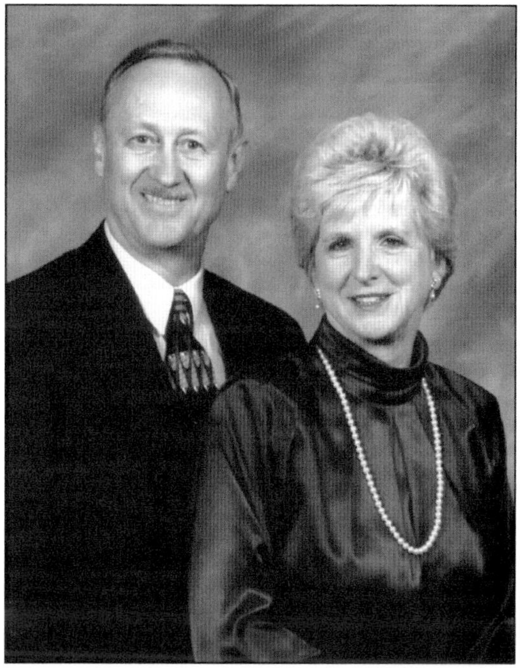

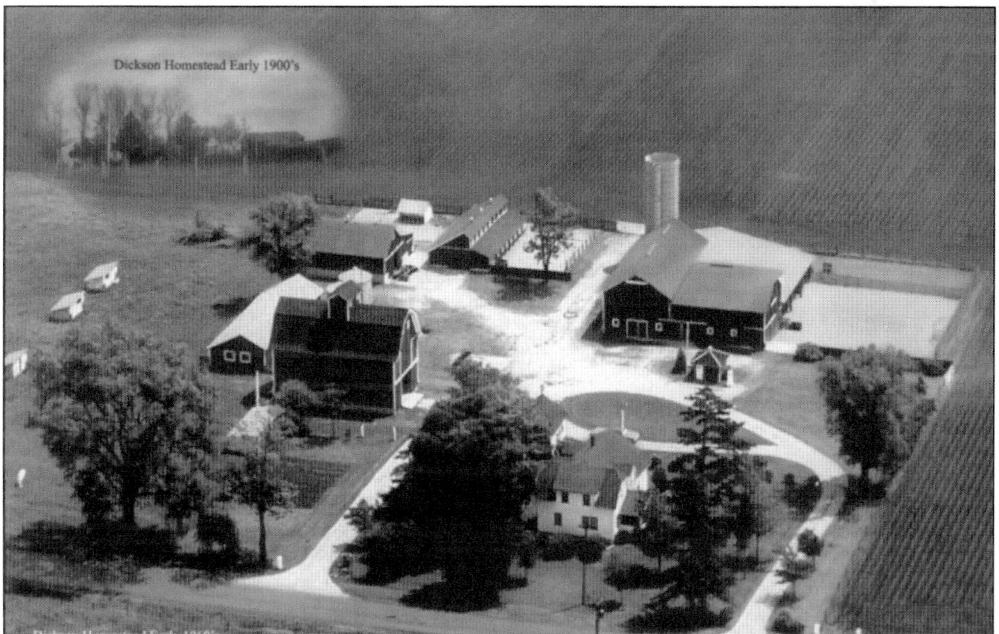

The inset image in the upper-left corner shows the Dickson homestead in the early 1900s. The aerial photograph was taken in the early 1960s. Today, this 4.5-acre farm is preserved as the Dickson-Murst Farm, and sponsors public educational events there. In 1870, an agricultural schedule listed the farm's production as worth $1,200.00. The animals were valued at $1,500.00. From 1869 to 1870, the farm produced 160 bushels of spring wheat, 900 bushels of Indian corn, 1,000 bushels of oats, 30 bushels of Irish potatoes, 500 pounds of butter, and 20 tons of hay. In 2009, the farm was recognized with the Governor's Hometown Award. (Courtesy of Shorty Dickson.)

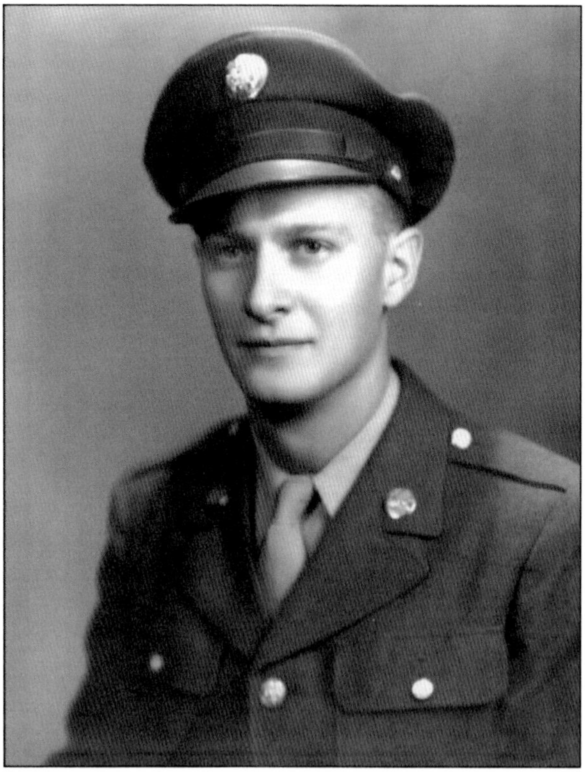

Pfc. Clarence Ted Christian was born on May 7, 1920. He was the son of Clarence and Myrtle Hoganson Christian. In 1943, he was drafted from Kendall County and had a three-month training at Fort Bragg. His serial number on his dog tags was 36749365. Clarence received the American Campaign Medal, the European–African–Middle Eastern Theater Ribbon with two Bronze Battle Stars, the Good Conduct Medal, and World War II Victory Medal for his wartime service. He received an honorable discharge on January 23, 1946. (Courtesy of Diane Christian.)

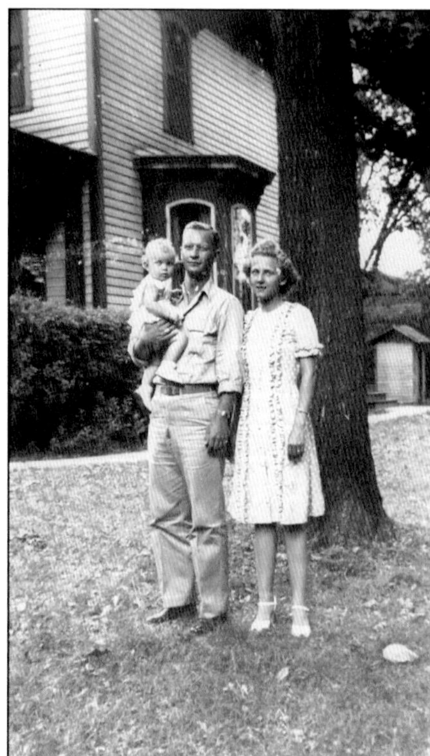

This 1944 photograph shows Clarence Ted Christian holding daughter Ruth Ann with his wife, Elaine. He served in the Army and was assigned to the 787th Field Artillery Battalion in 1943. Recalling his memories from his time in the service, he said, "Training was extremely vigorous. I remember a 19-mile hike at night in the rain with pack on." After 1946, he wrote a letter that read, "Home, family, new house, vacations to 50 states, and daughter Diane Marie." On September 3, 2007, he passed a quiet death at the age of 87. Elaine Christian now resides at Jennings Terrace in Aurora. (Courtesy of Diane Christian.)

Seven

Charming Chautauqua on the Fox River

The Chautauqua debate was held on the great question of equal suffrage. The Reverend Miss Gertrude Von Petzold of London and Senator Shirley Billiland of Iowa presented arguments on both sides.

—1910 Chautauqua Program

It was August 1903. Harriet C. Waterhouse, who was the superintendent at Book's Classical School in Chicago, was preparing to teach courses on Descartes, elocution, literature, and physical culture at the first Chautauqua on the Fox River in Montgomery. The Iroquois word chautauqua means "two moccasins tied together" or "jumping fish." To attend the lectures, the price was $2 per season or 25¢ per day.

Accommodations included a free dressing room for the ladies where "water, soap, and towels will be liberally provided." A dining hall and lunch counter was facilitated by a competent caterer who served the meals at 25¢ each. Iced tea, coffee, pure lemonade, and ice cream were available at tents or lunch tables at home prices. The sanitary arrangements had proper attention, and the buildings were kept scrupulously clean. In 1910, the Eighth Annual Aurora Chautauqua Assembly was held at the Fox River Park, and its program described the park as "one of the most picturesque points along the Fox River with an abundance of grass, flowers, and vines, and it is richly shaded by beautiful forest trees." On the grounds, there were two flowing wells that belonged to the Montgomery Magnesia Spring Water Company. The electric car line brought over 2,000 daily passengers to the park.

The park had opened on November 7, 1899. Goddard's String Band provided the music for dancing that day. After closing for the winter months, the park reopened in the early spring of 1900. There was a three-arch entrance, the train station, dance and refreshment halls, the bandstand, a children's playground, and a baseball diamond.

That summer, the final segment of the Aurora and Geneva Railway was completed from Aurora to Elgin. This opened up more direct streetcar connections to Riverview Park. Theodore Howard, mayor of Aurora, described the park and said, "This beautiful spot is to be a prohibition park, and if anyone drinks liquor here, he will have to bring it in his clothes. It will be a credit to Aurora and Montgomery." Travelers could take the interurban line of the Aurora, Elgin & Chicago Railway. In 1907, a steel auditorium was built with the latest design for proper acoustic properties. The streets of the tenting section were supplied with incandescent lights, and at night, the grounds were "brilliantly lighted with artistically designed electrical arc lamps, which produced a fairyland effect."

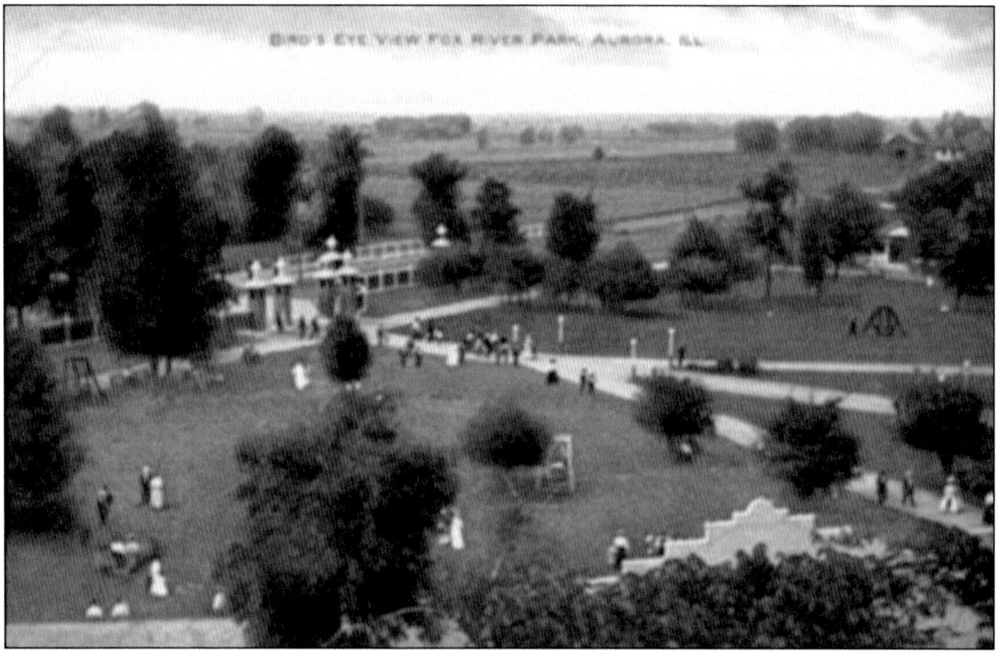

The halcyon days of Riverview Park began on November 7, 1899. Montgomery was decorated with hundreds of American flags. More than 500 citizens attended the dedication. The weather was ideal, and many people went on a picnic. Some men went clamming in the Fox River, which was an enjoyable pastime. The clamshells were sold to a button factory in Aurora. (Courtesy of Montgomery Archives.)

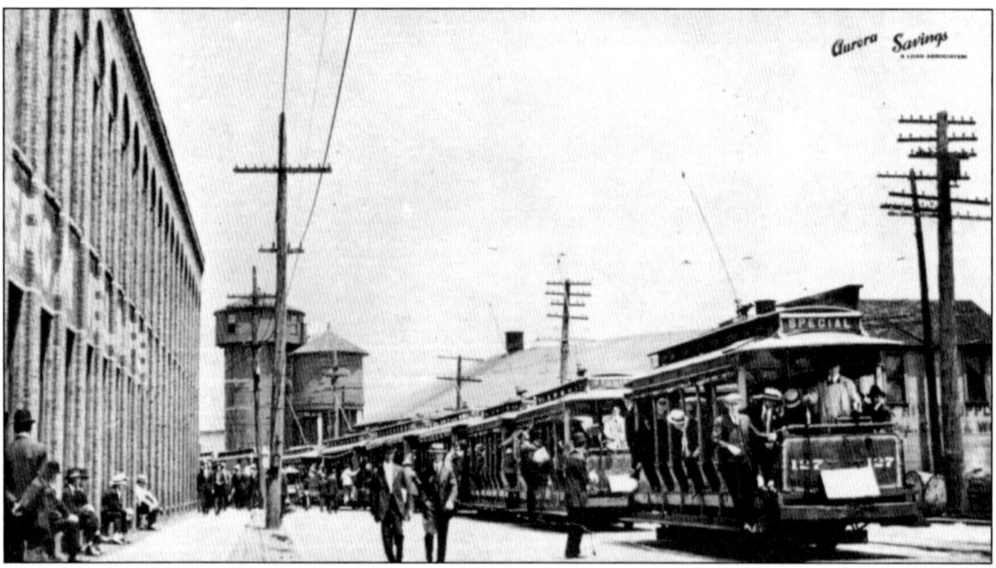

The Chautauqua was organized on high grounds, and these assemblies were one of the great moral and educational forces in the country at that time. These events wanted to inspire its attendees by providing a guide, pathway, and a "lamp to the feet of thousands." In Aurora, this streetcar took passengers to Riverview Park. It was there that the annual Chautauqua was held. (Courtesy of Dave Chrestenson.)

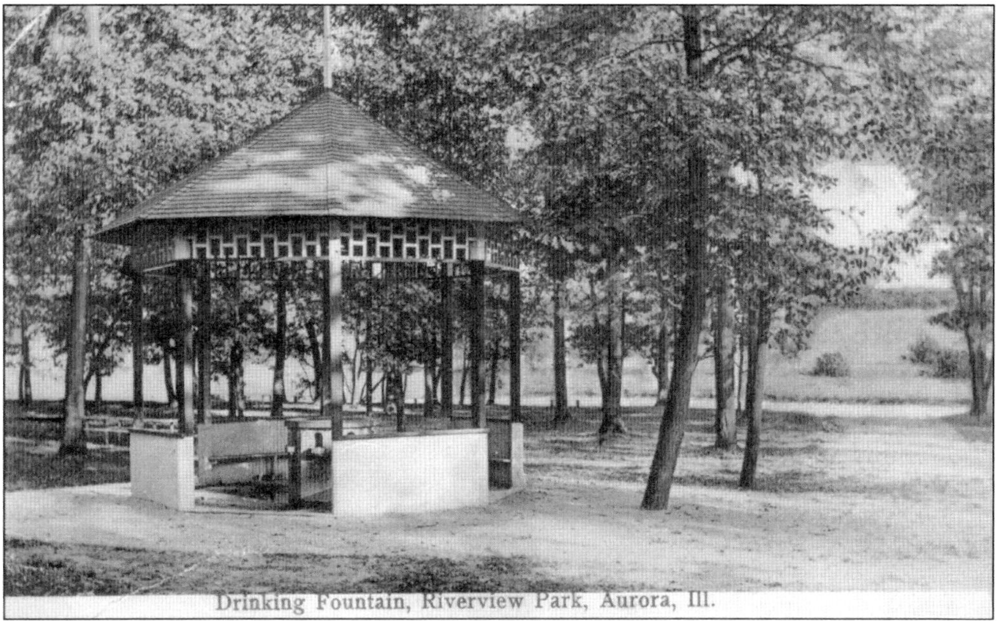

Shown is the drinking fountain at Riverview Park. Women wore long skirts and fashionable hats. Gentlemen wore suits and straw hats. This was the golden age of postcards. Millions were printed in Europe and sold in the United States for one penny. Postage for government postcards cost 1¢ each, but privately printed cards required postage that was the 2¢ letter-rate postage. This image was made into a postcard by Aurora Federal Savings and Loan Association. (Courtesy of Dave Chrestenson.)

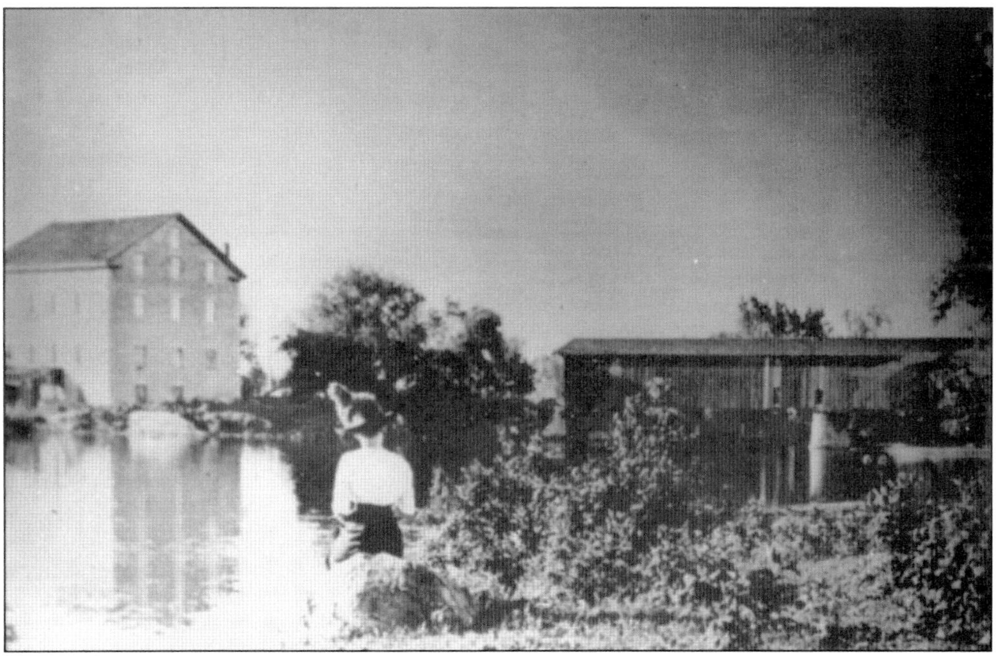

What a lovely day along the Fox River. This photograph was taken on March 25, 1916. The breeze is gentle, and the sun smiles just beyond the horizon. The woman sits with her notebook on the riverbank as she watches the old bridge and mill. (Courtesy of Montgomery Archives.)

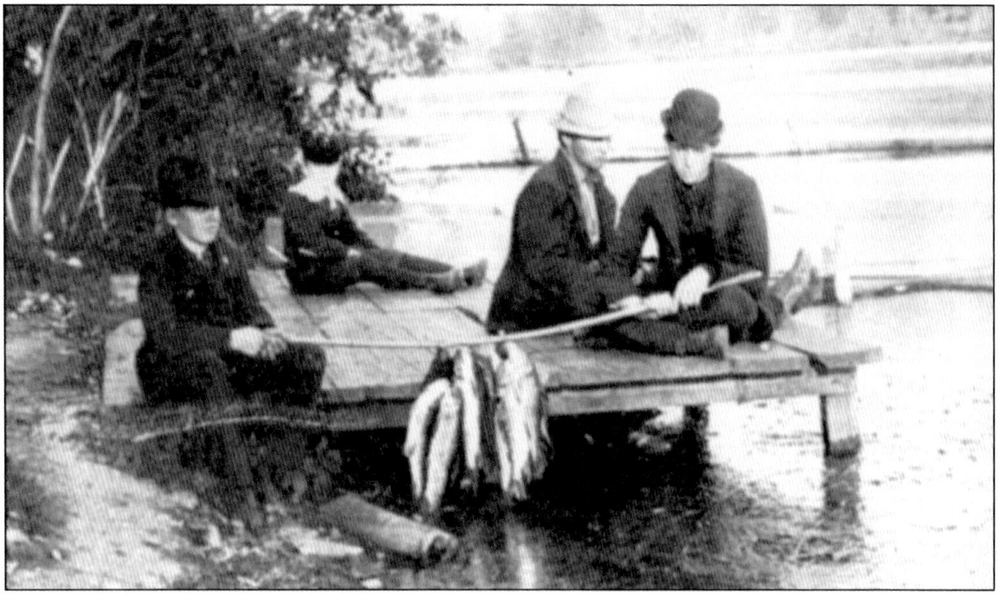

This unidentified group is relaxing and fishing by the Fox River in 1915. (Courtesy of Montgomery Archives.)

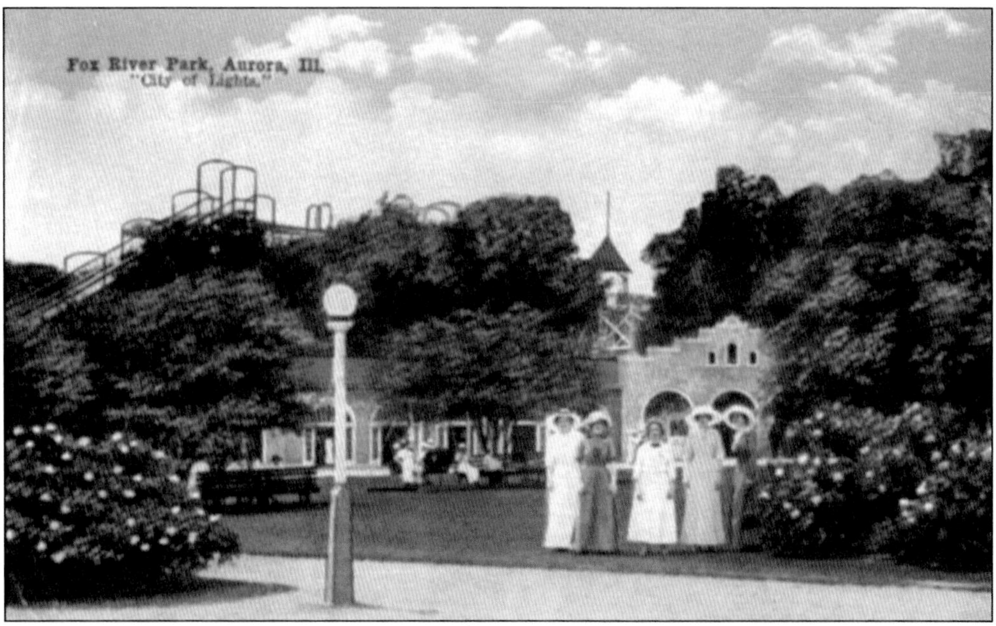

The Riverview Penny Arcade showed many pictures of Charlie Chaplin and other movie stars. Ice cream cones, Cracker Jacks, candy, pop, and other treats were bought on premises. At the bandstand, a hat contest was held where girls and women would go up on stage and try the hats on. Whoever looked the best in a particular hat won that accessory. (Courtesy of Montgomery Archives.)

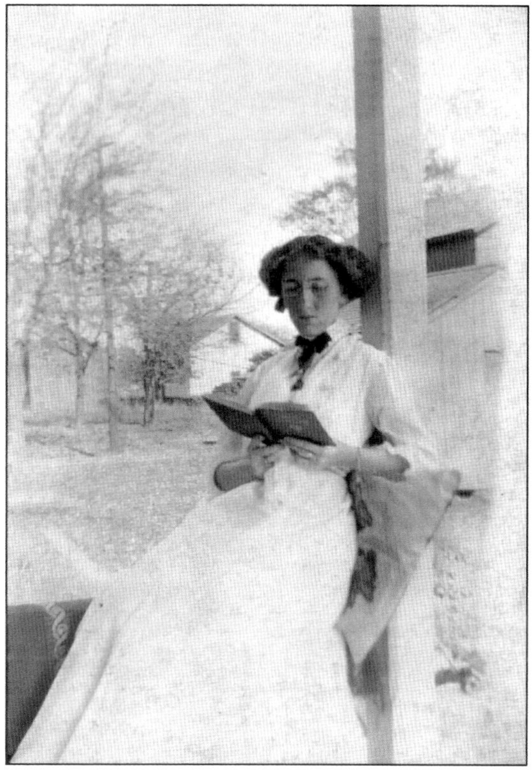

Elizabeth Cordelia Smith LaDew is pictured in 1877. (Courtesy of Ron LaDew.)

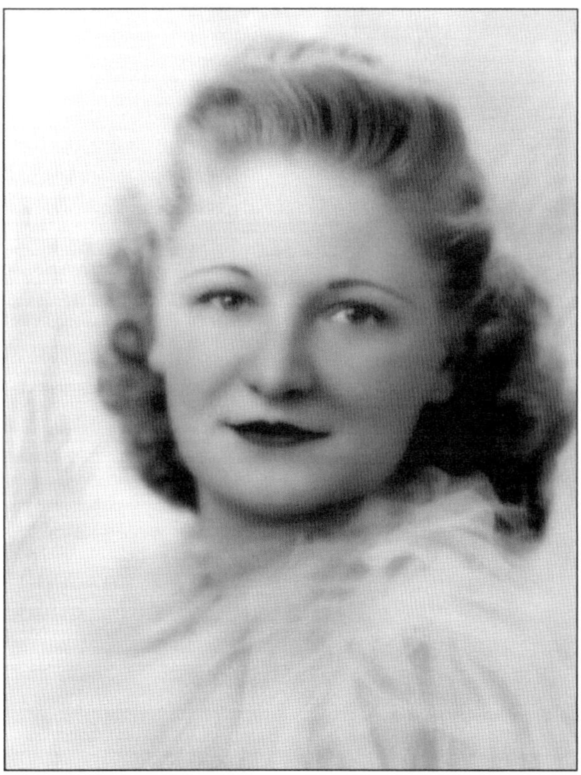

Anne Kumpic posed for this stunning portrait in 1942. She wed Stanley King on March 17, 1951. Originally from Lithuania, Anne was a homemaker and lived close to the Fox River in Montgomery. (Courtesy of Cindy King Adams.)

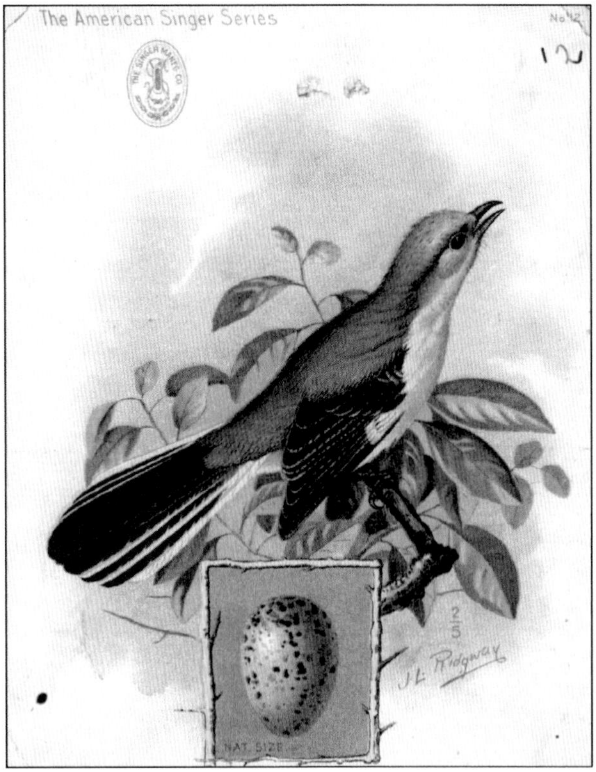

Did a mockingbird greet the King family one summer morning? With a beautiful form and easy motions, he is rapid and graceful. Perpetually animated with a playful caprice and a look full of intelligence, the mockingbird inhabits milder regions of America, making a nest in a thicket or a bunch of low bushes. His flood of song can be heard across the Fox River. (Author's collection.)

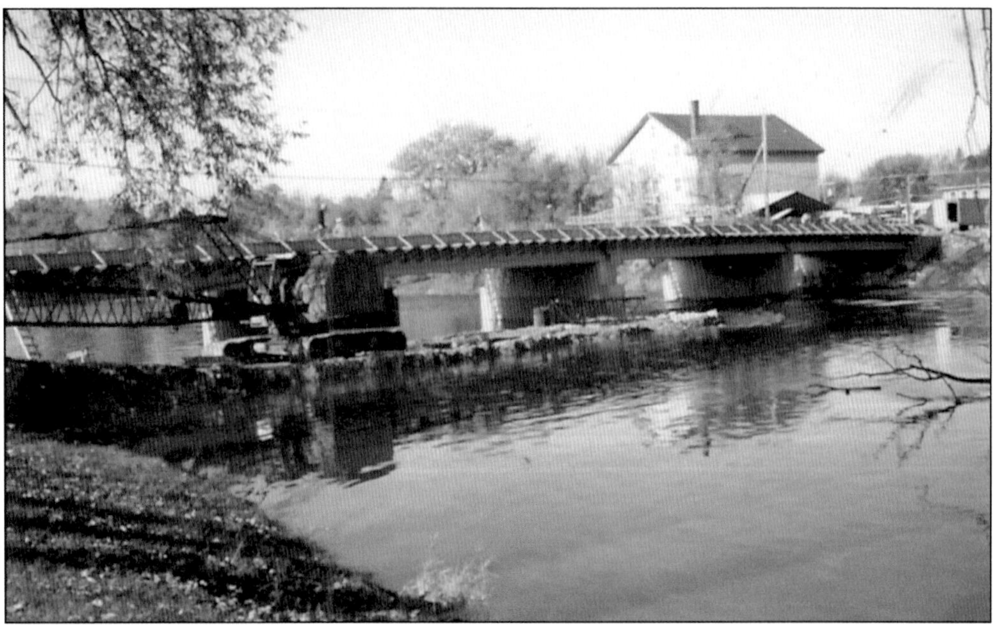

Montgomery's new dam on the Fox River is pictured in 1984. In 1969, the dam was built for flood control and navigation as part of the Stratton Project's dam system, which was designed to keep the river navigable from the Wisconsin border to the confluence with the Illinois River. The dam is owned by the Illinois Department of Natural Resources and measures 7 feet high and 325 feet long. (Courtesy of Cindy King Adams.)

Cindy King Adams and her son David Jr. strike a delightful pose in 1988. David was born on February 1, 1985. He attended the Grace M. Nicholson School, Washington Junior High, and West Aurora High School. David joined the Army in 2006. (Courtesy of Cindy King Adams.)

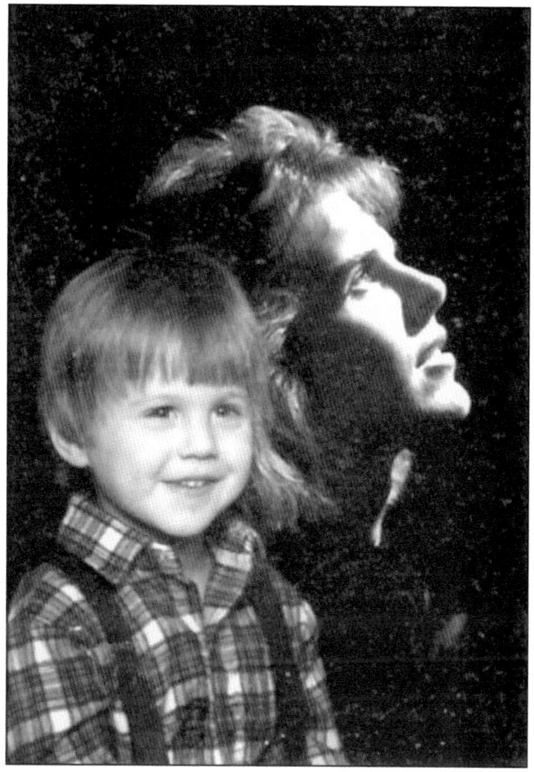

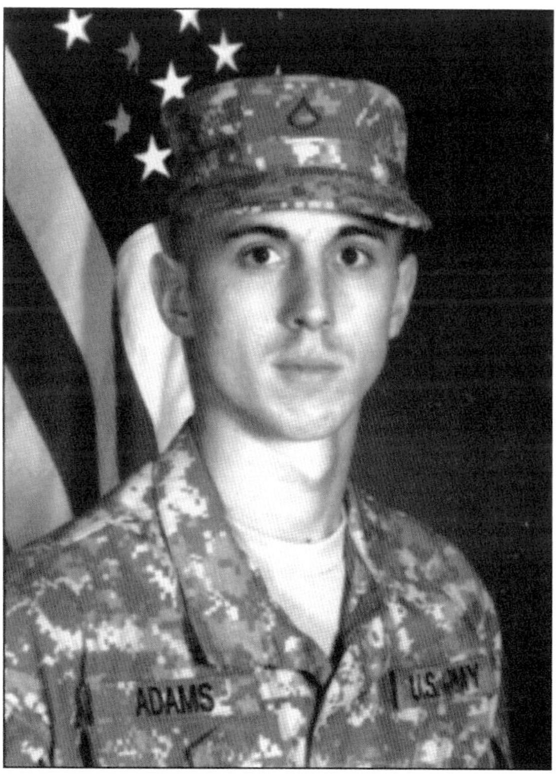

Pfc. David Adams Jr. served in Iraq in 2008 and is now stationed at Fort Bliss, Colorado. (Courtesy of Cindy King Adams.)

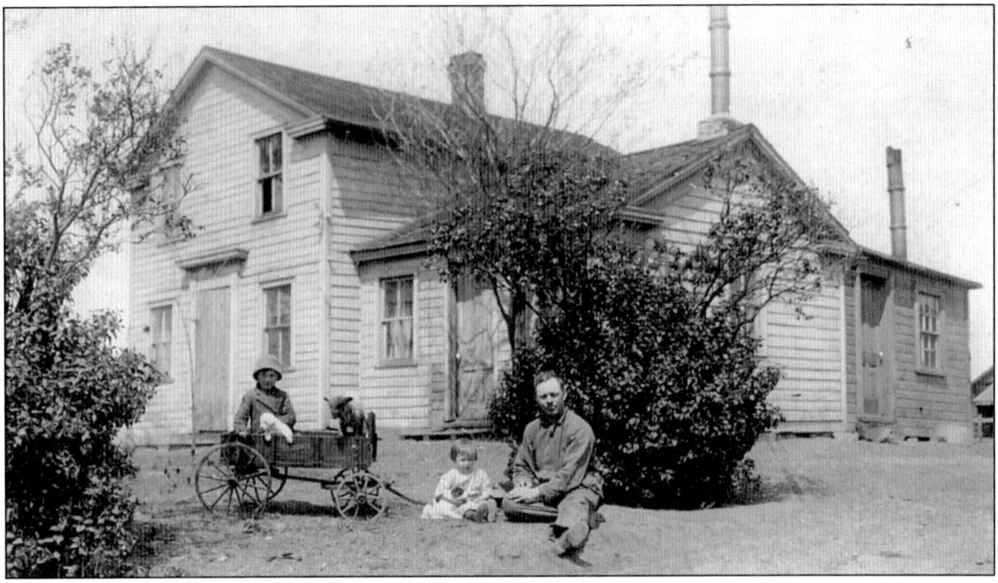

This photograph shows the Martner family farm that was located on Baseline Road in 1912. Pictured from left to right are Clyde Martner, the family dog Ralph, their lamb Snuggy, Gladys Martner, and Charles J. Martner. The farm was sold during the Depression. As Thomas Jefferson wrote, "I never before knew the full value of trees. Under them I breakfast, dine, write, read and receive company." (Courtesy of Al Martner.)

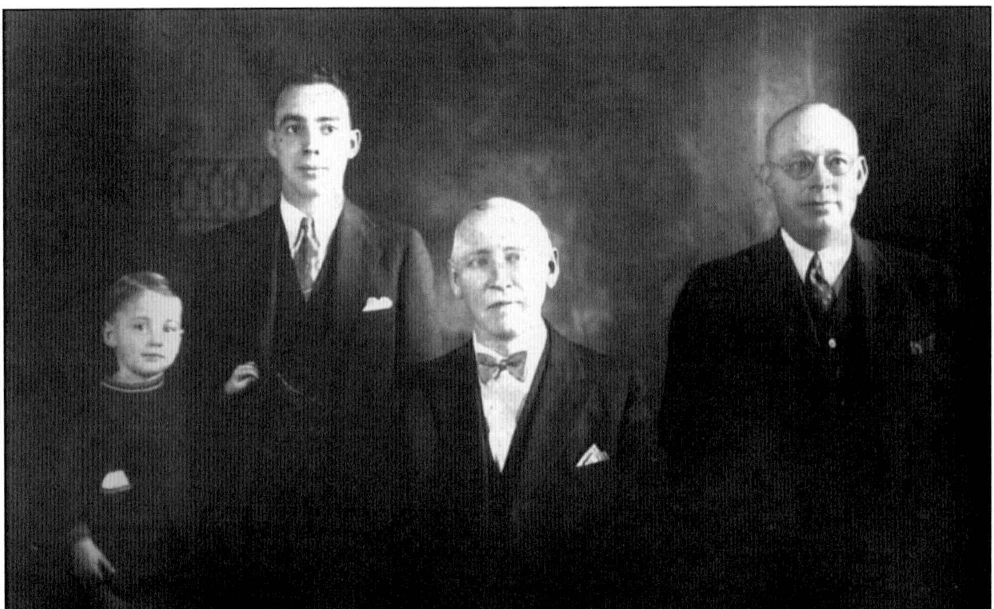

Four generations of the Martner family are shown in 1933. Pictured from left to right are Clyde Jr., Clyde Sr., Judge, and Charles J. Martner. They each were the spirit of manhood, leading them to deeds, to achievement, to happiness and to refined perfection. (Courtesy of Al Martner.)

What a jaunty pose! This 1920 photograph shows a young Mabel Johnson Martner. She lived and grew up in Montgomery, enjoying the marsh scenes. Was she going swimming in the Fox River? There were a few wetlands or marsh areas because most had been tiled or drained. At one time, however, approximately a third of Kendall County consisted of such areas. (Courtesy of Al Martner.)

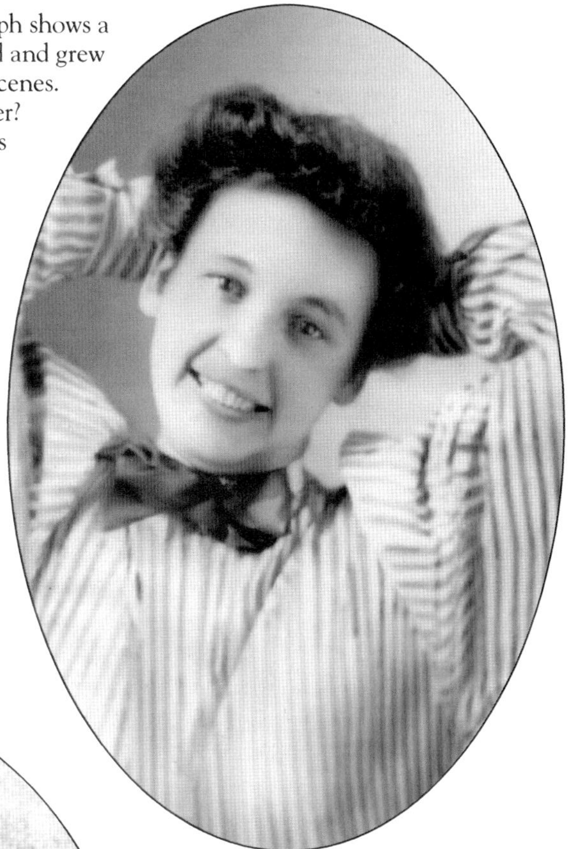

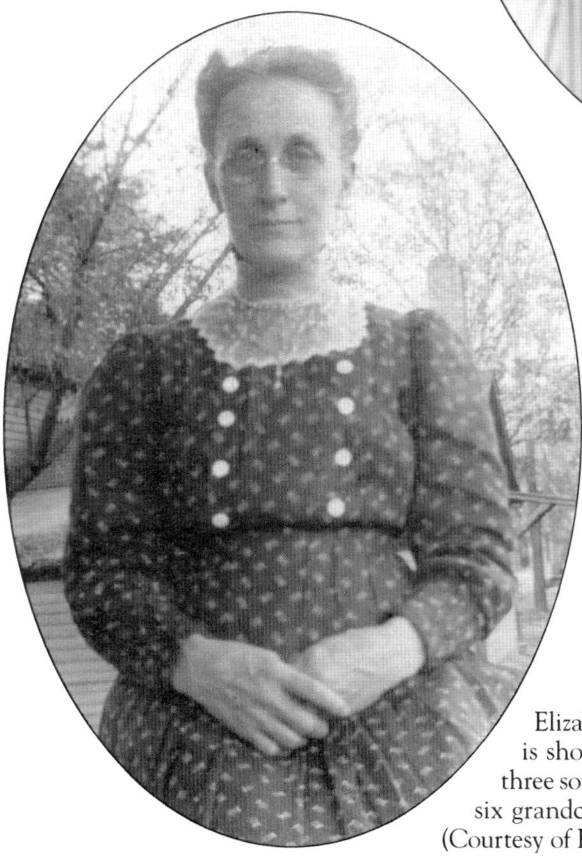

Elizabeth Cordelia Smith LaDew (1855–1936) is shown in this 1910 photograph. She bore three sons, George, Robert, and Charles. She had six grandchildren and eight great-grandchildren. (Courtesy of Ron LaDew.)

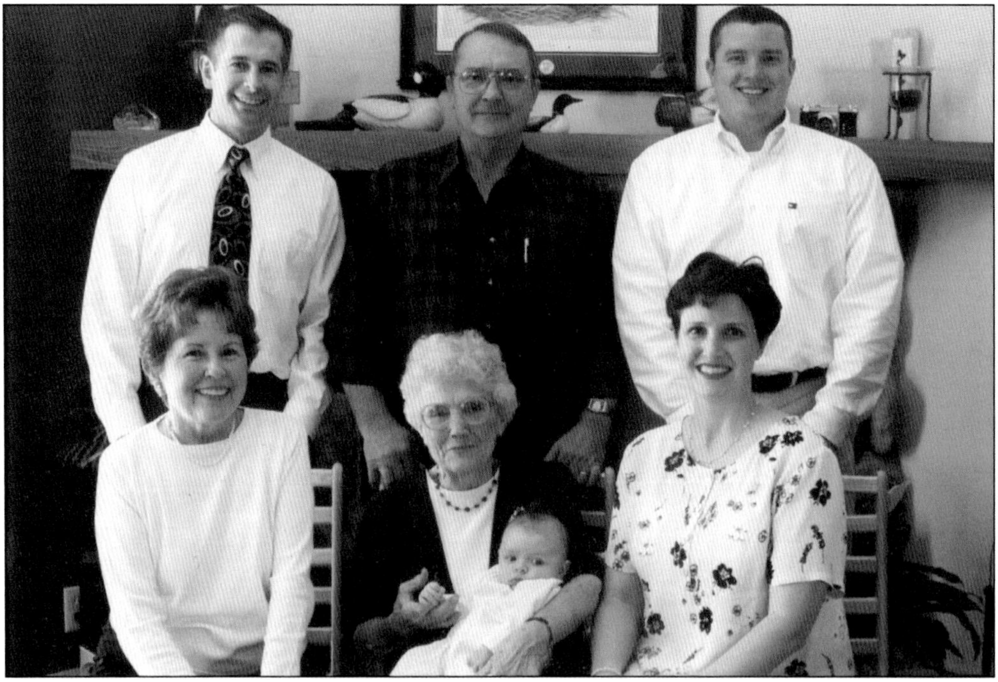

The Al Martner family gathered in 2001 at home to celebrate the baptism of baby John. The house was located at 308 Fairwind Court in Montgomery. Pictured from left to right are (first row) Barbara, Eleanor (holding baby John), and Jill; (second row) Randy, Al, and Michael. Baby John was baptized at St. Patrick's Church in Yorkville. (Courtesy of Al Martner.)

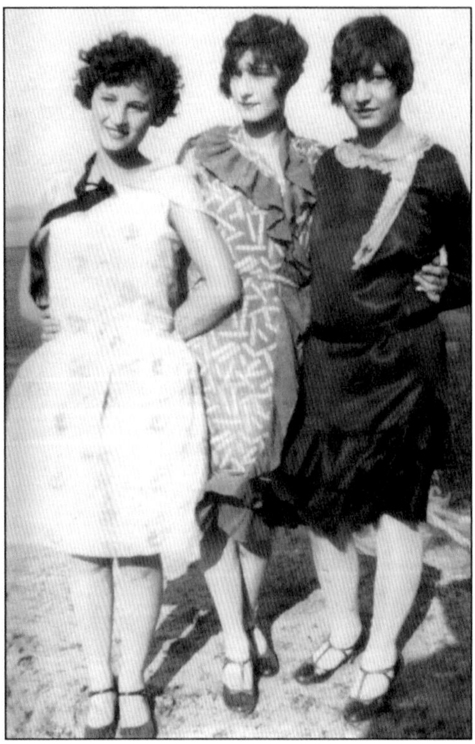

This 1930 photograph shows cousins Frances Scubic, Jenne Korelc, and Jenny Scubic striking a whimsical pose at Carbon Hill, Illinois. Jenne was born on February 16, 1913, and was the daughter of Ann Smrekar Korelc and Martin Korelc. (Courtesy of Jenne Korelc Olden.)

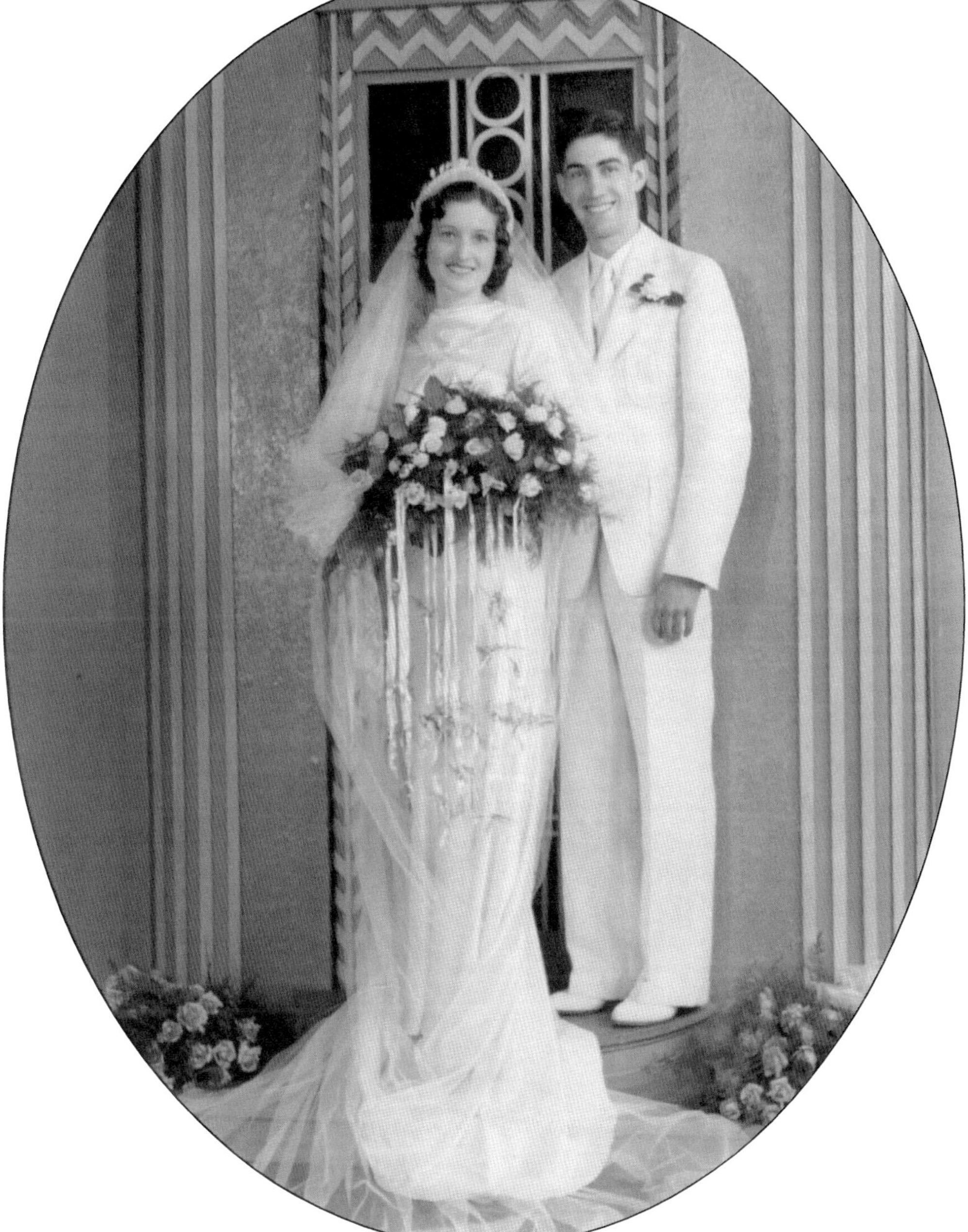

Jenne Korelc and Joseph Olden were married at Assumption Catholic Church in Coal City, Illinois, on June 5, 1937. They took a honeymoon trip to Chicago. Their three children are Dennis, Dianne, and Debbie. They have four grandchildren and four great-grandchildren. Joseph went to his rest in September 1991. (Courtesy of Jenne Korelc Olden.)

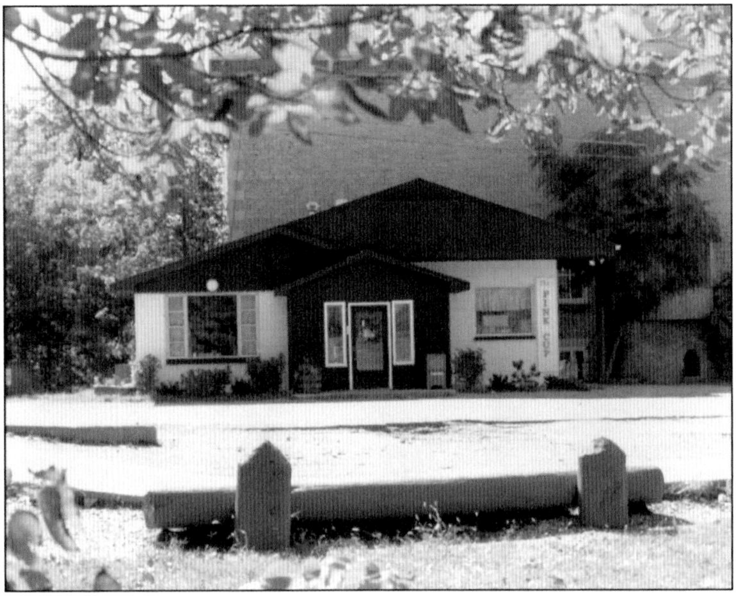

Jenne and Joseph Olden moved to Montgomery from Sard Avenue in Aurora in 1970. They opened the Pink Cup Restaurant in 1960, working at the restaurant for 28 years. The restaurant was open from 5:00 a.m. to 3:00 p.m. Mondays through Saturdays, and was closed on Sundays. This photograph shows the restaurant in 1975. (Courtesy of Debbie Olden Gibson.)

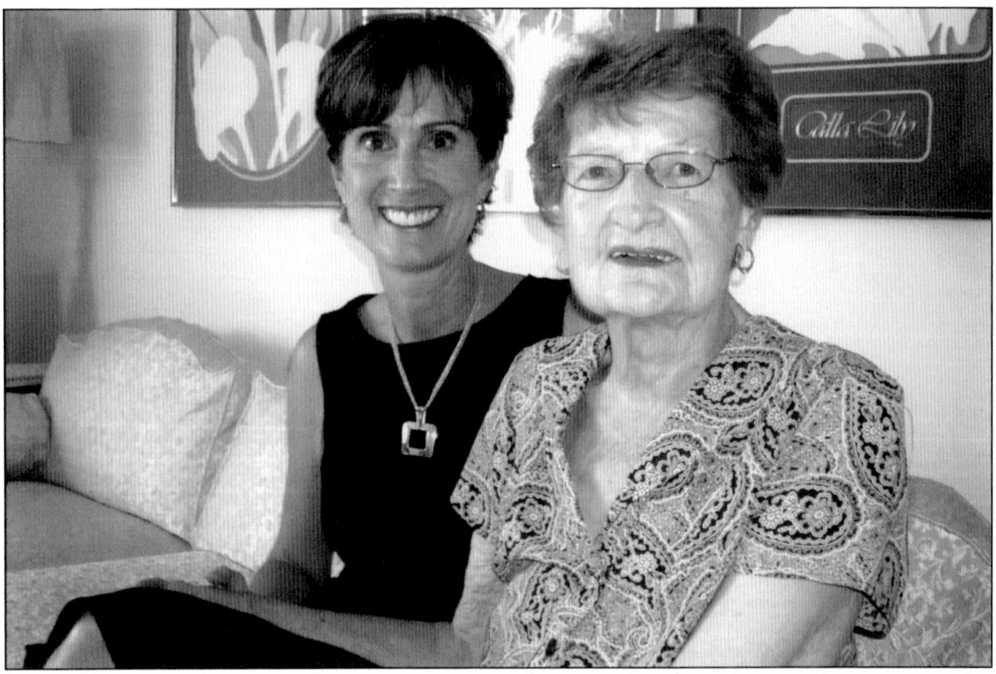

Jenne Olden (right) and her daughter Debbie strike a delightful mother-daughter pose in the summer of 2010. Jenne, who was 97 years old at the time of this book's publication, gave birth to Debbie when she was 41 years old. Jenne still loves to bowl with her eight-pound bowling ball and usually scores over 100 at the Parkside Lanes in Aurora. (Author's collection.)

Shown is the Pink Cup Restaurant's menu. Many years earlier, in 1888, when personal incomes increased, residents preferred dairy and meat products to oil and cereals. A local restaurant like The Pink Cup provided a meal of pork chop, ham, liver, or bacon that cost 5¢. Sides were also priced at 5¢ each, like oatmeal and milk, a third of a pie, or ham and beans. (Courtesy of Debbie Olden Gibson.)

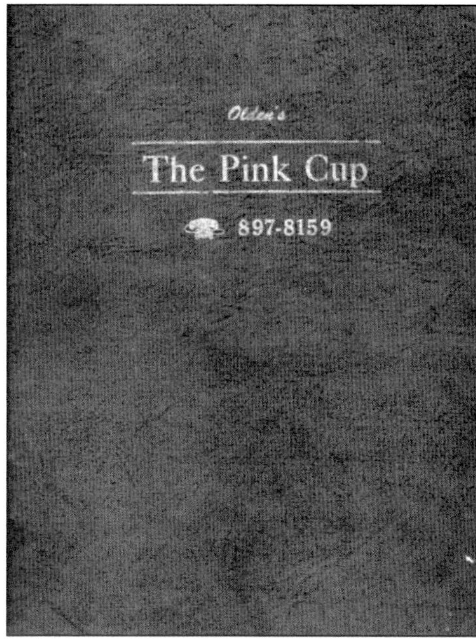

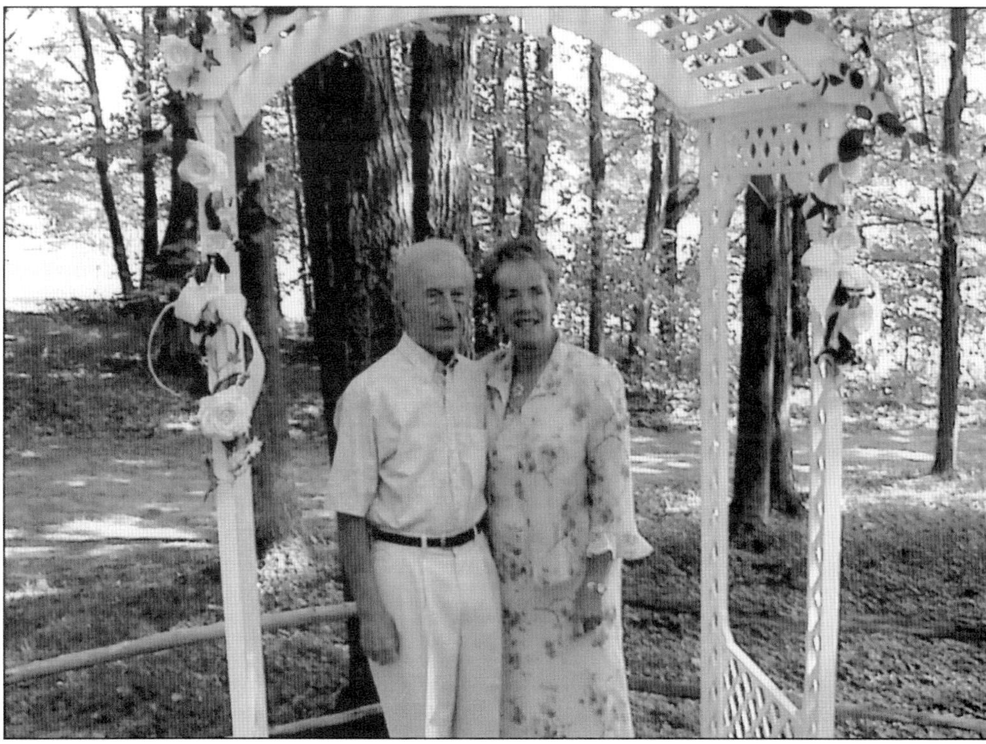

Marjorie Brooks Colley and John Wilson were married on July 3, 2004 in Boyne City, Michigan where Marjorie was raised. John has been a Montgomery resident for over 50 years. Marj was director of the Aurora YWCA from 1985 to 2000. She was born on January 3, 1939. John was born on June 6, 1925. Marj holds a master's degree in business management from Aurora University. John worked at his father's business Metropolitan Printing at 55 S. Lake Street in Aurora until retirement in the early 1980s. (Courtesy of Marjorie Colley.)

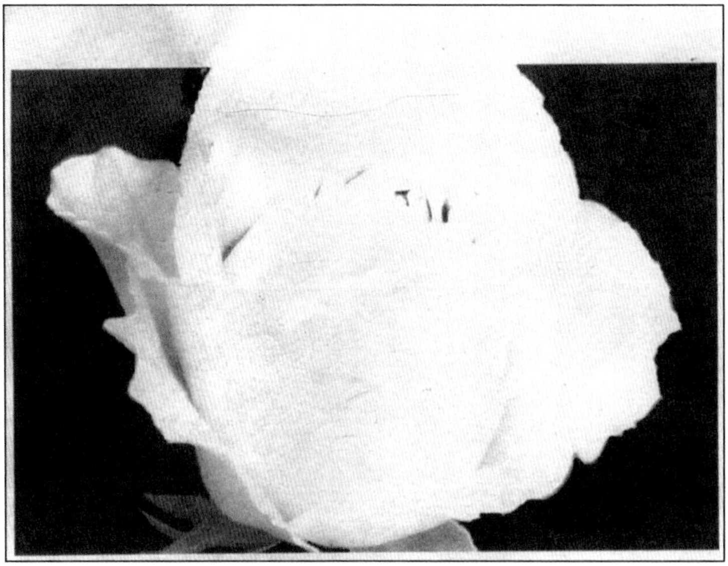

Marjorie Brooks Colley began taking photography classes at the Fox Valley Park District and discovered her talent with that medium. She won first place at the Aurora Art League in 2003 and 2005, and won first place at the Town and Country Show in 2009. She is a former member of the Kendall Arts Guild and the Fox Valley Arts Council. (Courtesy of Marjorie Colley.)

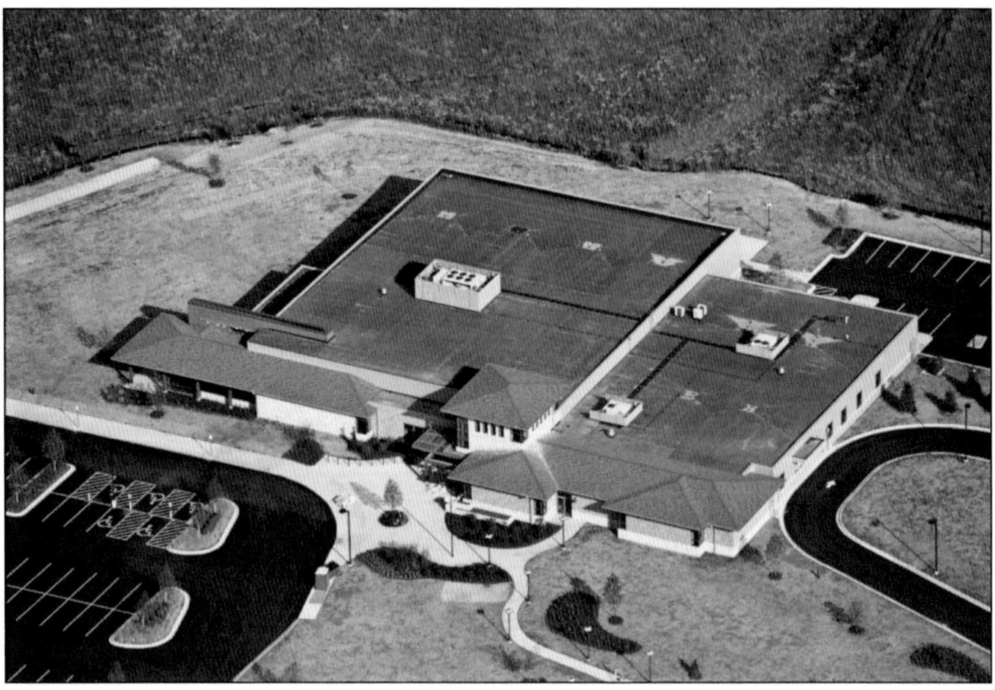

Construction of the new Montgomery Branch Library of the Oswego Library District is shown in an overhead photograph taken by McShane-Fleming Studios, Chicago. Ground-breaking was June 2008. Since the library's opening, the campus has been visited by 529,969 people. The library owns 32 public computers. (Courtesy of Frederick Quinn Corporation and McShane-Fleming Studios.)

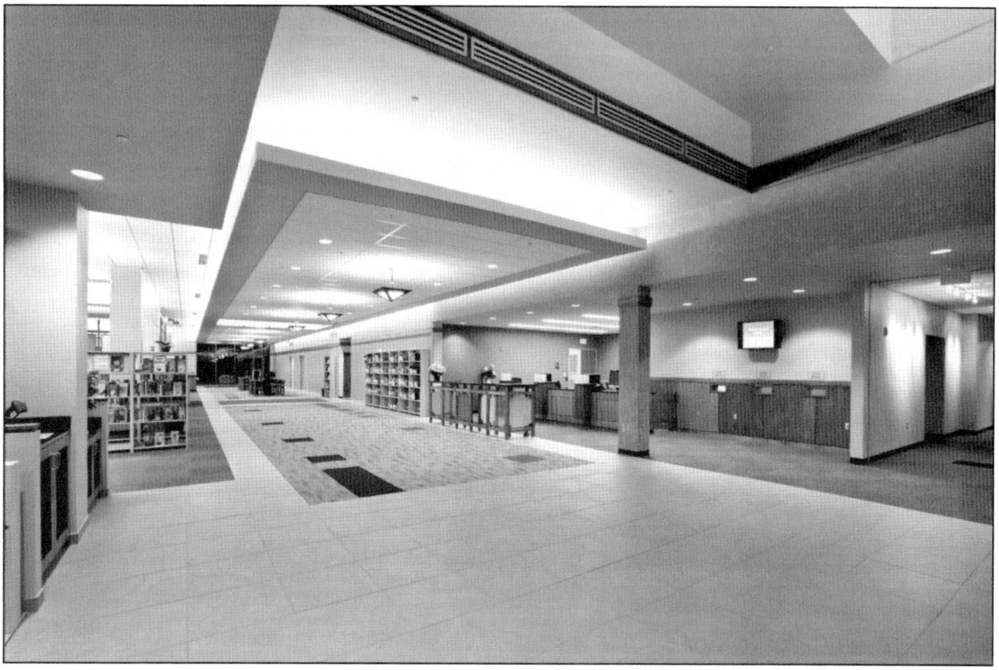

An interior view shows the spacious and modern entrance of the new Montgomery Branch Library. The contractor was the Fredrick Quinn Corporation. The building cost $6.8 million. Seven acres of land was donated by the Village of Montgomery and a local developer. The official ribbon cutting was held on August 23, 2009. (Photograph by McShane-Fleming Studios.)

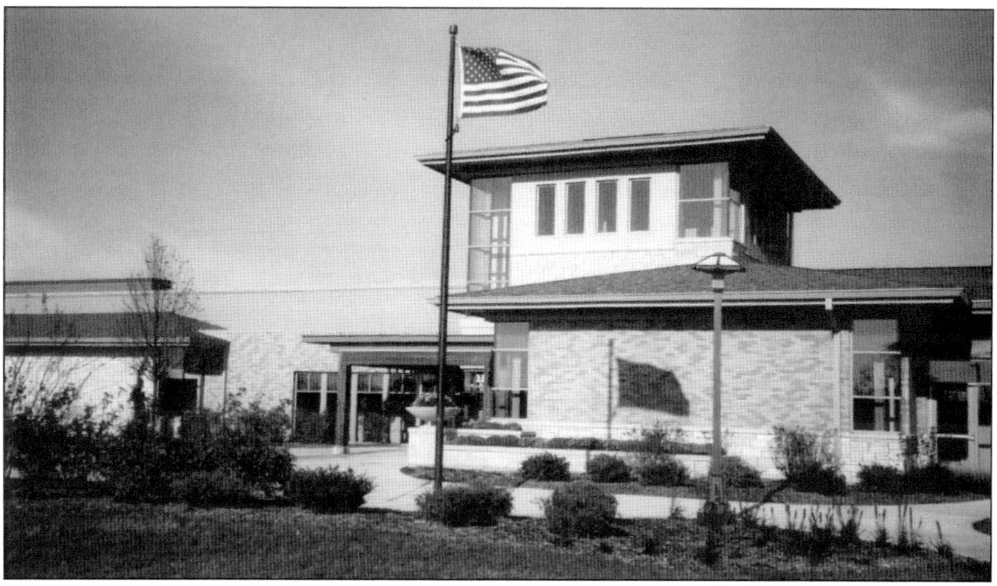

This is an exterior view of the Montgomery Campus Library. The history of the Oswego Library began in 1899, when the woman's club started bringing a basket full of books in each morning. In 1928, the Rank Building was donated to the village and used as the library. In 1964, the Oswego Township Library was formed, and $35,000 was raised to build the first library. In 2006, a library bond was passed for a new library in Montgomery on Route 30. Sarah Skilton is the library director. (Author's collection.)

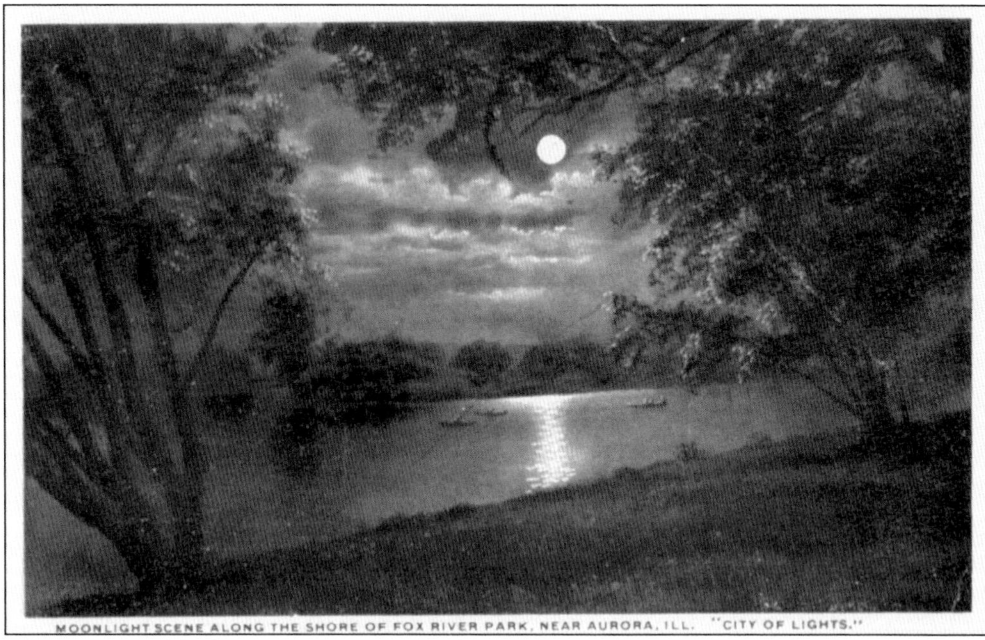

Oh, the glory of the long summer's moon! This postcard shows an evening at the Fox River Park in August 1923. (Courtesy of the Oswegoland Heritage Society and Little White Museum.)

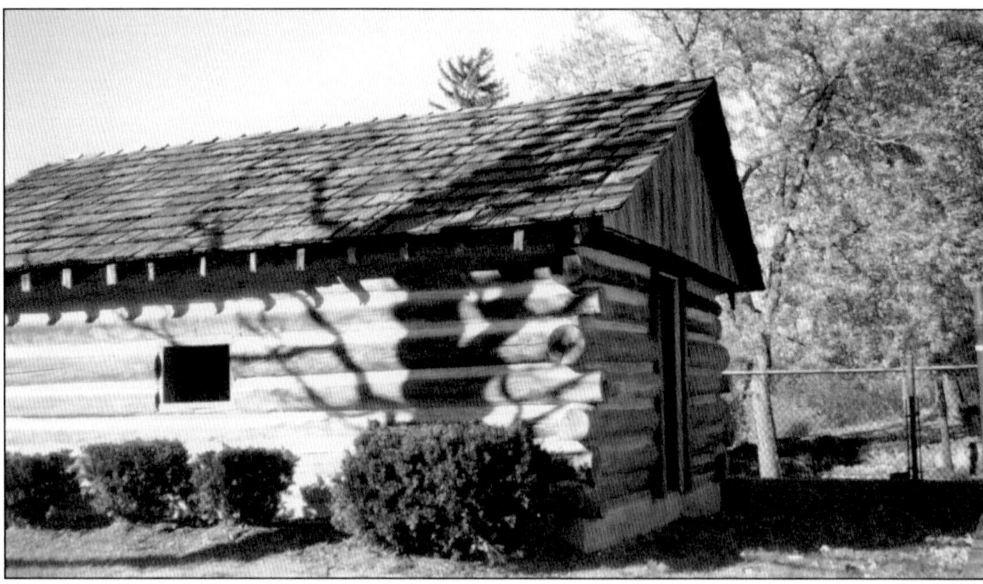

The first log cabin on this site was built by William T. Elliott, who arrived from Connecticut in June 1834. He was single and did not have anything in his pockets but $15 and a few blacksmith tools. He married Rebecca Pierce after meeting her at a hotel owned by Elijah Pierce, who was also one of the village's first settlers. Elliott and Rebecca's daughter Emeline was born on August 5, 1836. After moving on his claim, Elliott paid $10 for clearing the land. This photograph depicts a replica of that original cabin, and it is located by the Dieterle Memorial Home. (Author's collection.)

Eight

Such a Pleasant Little Town

The days may come, the days may go / But still the hands of memory weave the blissful dreams of long ago.

—"Sweet Genevieve" by George Cooper

Commerce in Illinois made small progress from 1818 to 1830. Steamboats commenced running in 1816 on the river, and by 1830, there were one or two small boats running up the Illinois River and as far as Peoria. Merchants sold dry goods and groceries, skins, hides, furs, some tallow, and beeswax. By 1840, the entire state had been settled except for a few prairies far from timber. The wilderness ceased. Before 1842, towns of intelligence, polish, and eloquence had around 1,500 inhabitants, and these towns included Chicago, Galena, and Springfield. There were many opportunities for education, and common schools flourished in many places. Churches were rapidly established and the church-going bell was often rung. One writer commented, "It seems to me that the people of Illinois may now justly be proud of their State. Their legislatures have improved in knowledge, public spirit, and patriotism ever since 1840."

In Montgomery, family life was valued, and it was a close-knit society where neighbors helped other neighbors. In the 1840s, a schoolteacher earned $200-$300 a year. In lieu of money, teachers also accepted wood, cornmeal, flannel, or cloth as payment. In the late 1800s, hobbies included quilting, making rag carpets, apple and pumpkin cutting, corn husking, wood chopping, and barn raisings.

Rail fences and osage orange hedges became symbols of settlement. There is such value to local history. To those who read it, it gives a larger and more intelligent view of the conditions now realized. "Today is ever the child of yesterday," wrote the sage. In 1858, Montgomery was incorporated as a village. On August 21, 1858, the first Lincoln-Douglas debate was held. The "Wedding March" by Felix Mendelssohn was first played at the January 25th wedding of Queen Victoria's daughter Victoria to Prince Friedrich of Prussia.

On the banks of the Fox River, settlers built homes and businesses, greeting their neighbors with helpful hands. "The Village of Montgomery is a pleasant little town in which to live," said former fire chief Charlie M. Gaylord.

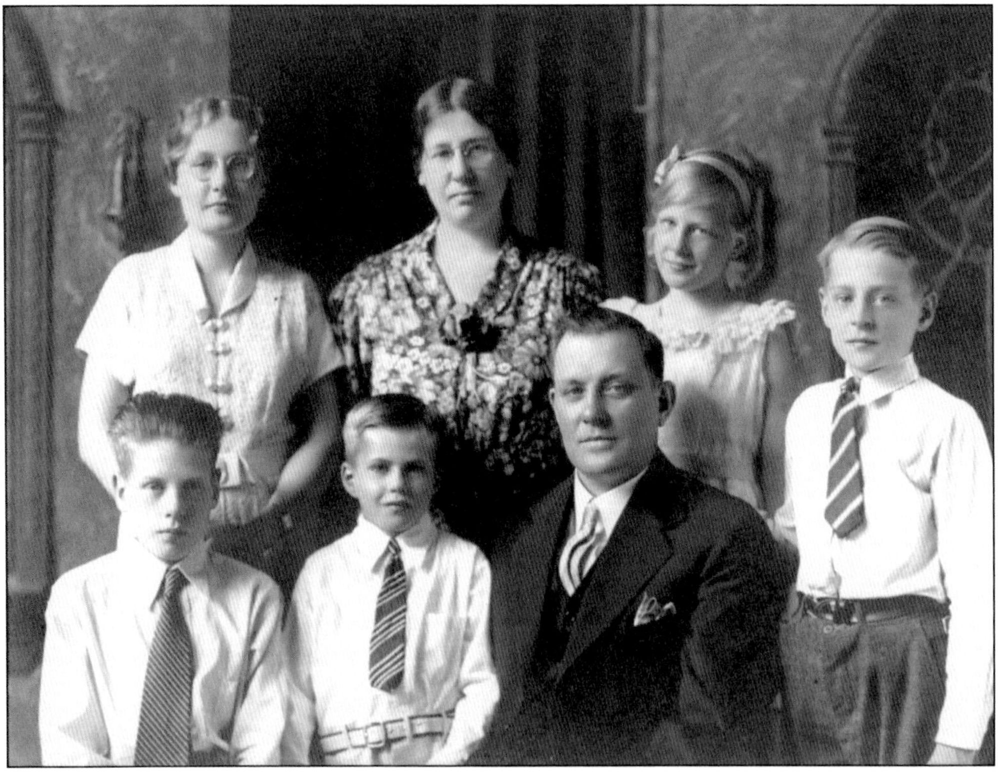

Shown is a delightful family portrait of the Albert Phillips family in 1938. Pictured from left to right are (first row) Herbert Phillips, James Phillips, and Albert Phillips; (second row) Dorothy Phillips Spring, Rose Phillips, Margaret Phillips Webb, and Albert Phillips Jr. (Photograph by E.E. Godfrey. Courtesy of Jim Spring and Nancy Spring Epley.)

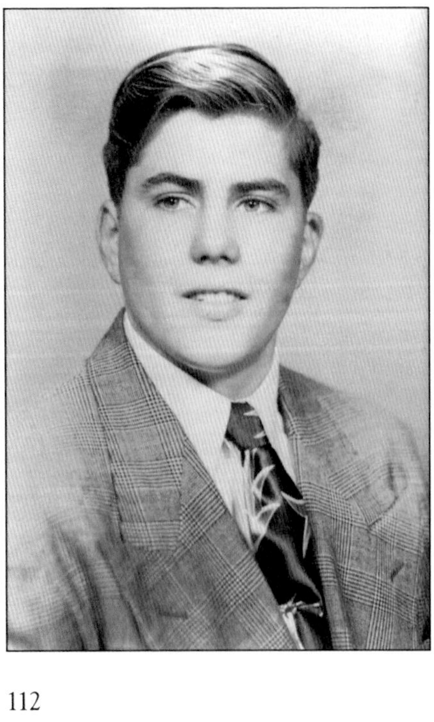

One sunny day in 1968, Jim Phillips took a walk and saw ducklings by the river. The following day, he saw that all the ducklings had died in the polluted water. Afterwards, he began his campaign against corporate businesses that polluted the Fox River. During his campaign, Jim called himself "the Fox" and left his signature on sewer outlets and smokestacks. In his book, *Raising Kane*, he wrote, "I am part of the river's spirit, and it is part of me." Jim's death date was October 3, 2001. (Courtesy of Jim Spring and Nancy Spring Epley.)

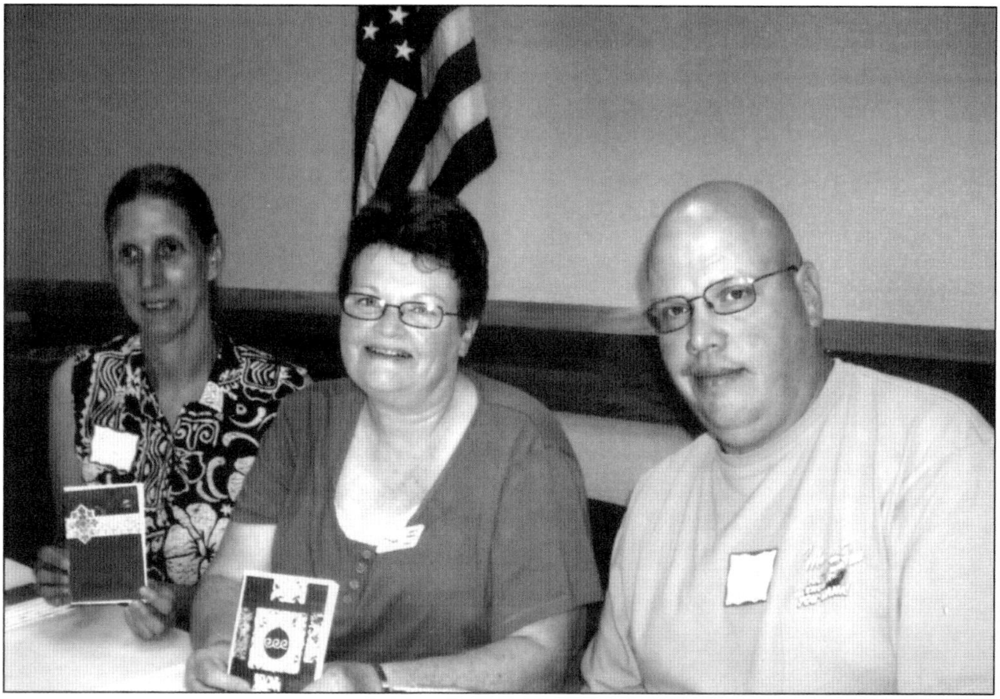

Stampin' From Our Hearts is a nonprofit organization that helps military personnel communicate with their families by providing them with handcrafted greeting cards. Each month, over 3,000 cards are sent to soldiers serving in Iraq and Afghanistan from all 50 states. Julie Wilson organizes each event, and some events are hosted at the Sugar Grove Library, which serves parts of Montgomery. Pictured from left to right are Jo Ann Davy, Julie Wilson, and Joe Bennett. (Author's collection.)

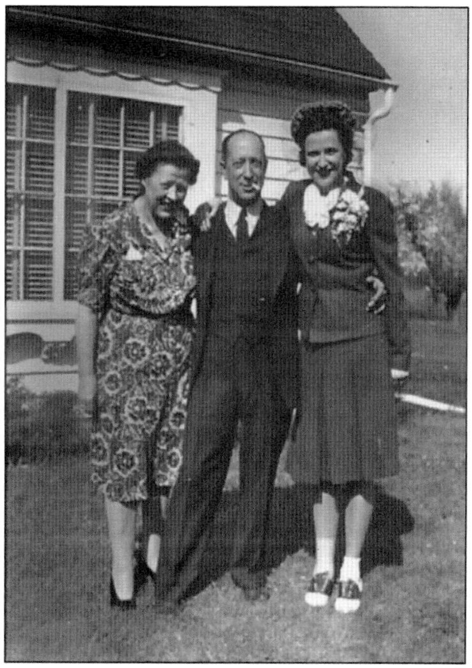

Shown are Agnes and Harry Baker with an unidentified friend on the right. They were standing in front of their home in Montgomery. They had one son named Shirley "Don" Baker. Don would later sponsor a semi-professional football team called the Aurora Clippers, and they played at Lyon Metal field for five years. During Saturday games, his son Brad recalls making 55 gallons of lemonade at home. The Bakers ran the laundry and dry cleaners located at 1400 Southeast River Road. They had 10 trucks and 60 employees. (Courtesy of Helen Baker.)

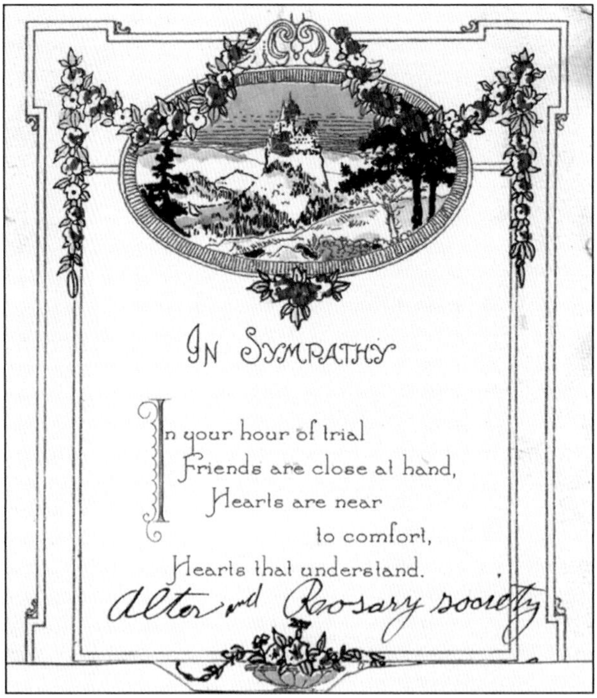

The Chicago, Burlington & Quincy Railroad donated land for the Riverside Cemetery in 1852. The Montgomery Cemetery Association was organized in 1869. The earliest recorded burial at the premises was for Dewitt Gray, who was born in 1820 and died in 1841. His father, Daniel Samuel Gray, set aside an acre of land that served as a cemetery. Dewitt's fiancée, Angeline Van Alstine, married his cousin Rufus Gray in January 1844. This is a Mass card from 1931. (Author's collection.)

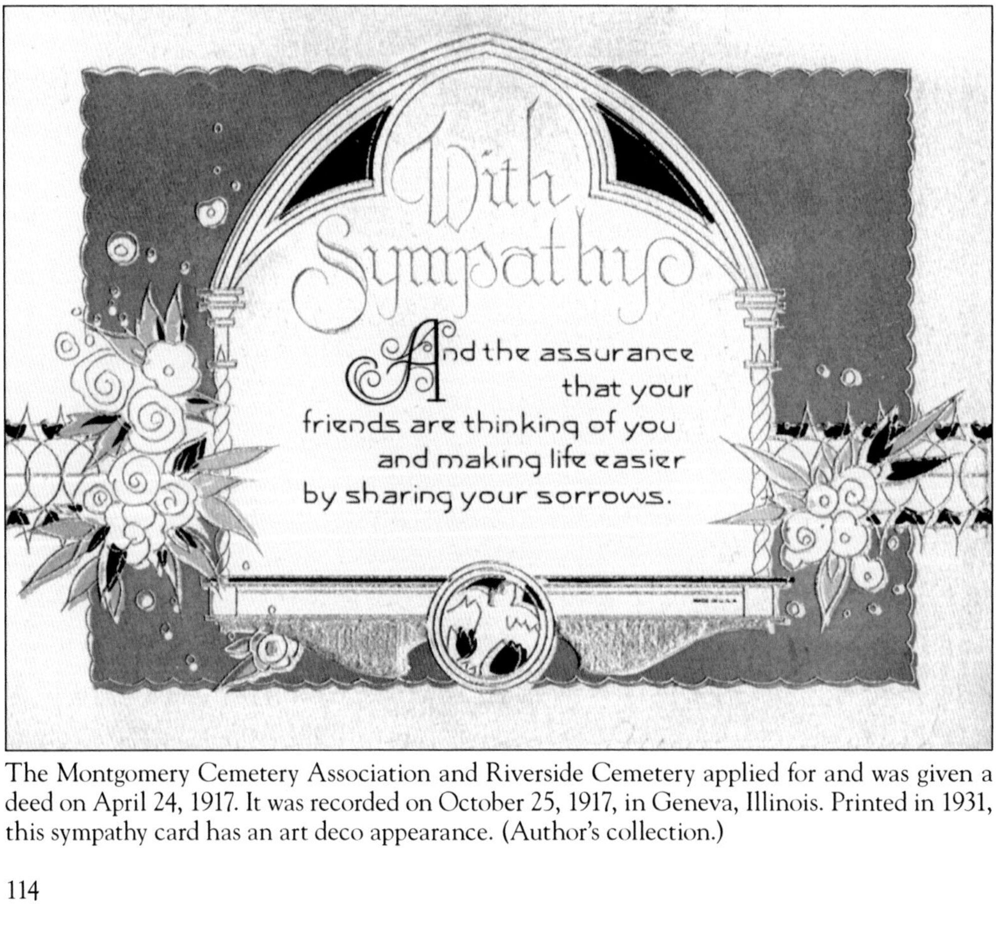

The Montgomery Cemetery Association and Riverside Cemetery applied for and was given a deed on April 24, 1917. It was recorded on October 25, 1917, in Geneva, Illinois. Printed in 1931, this sympathy card has an art deco appearance. (Author's collection.)

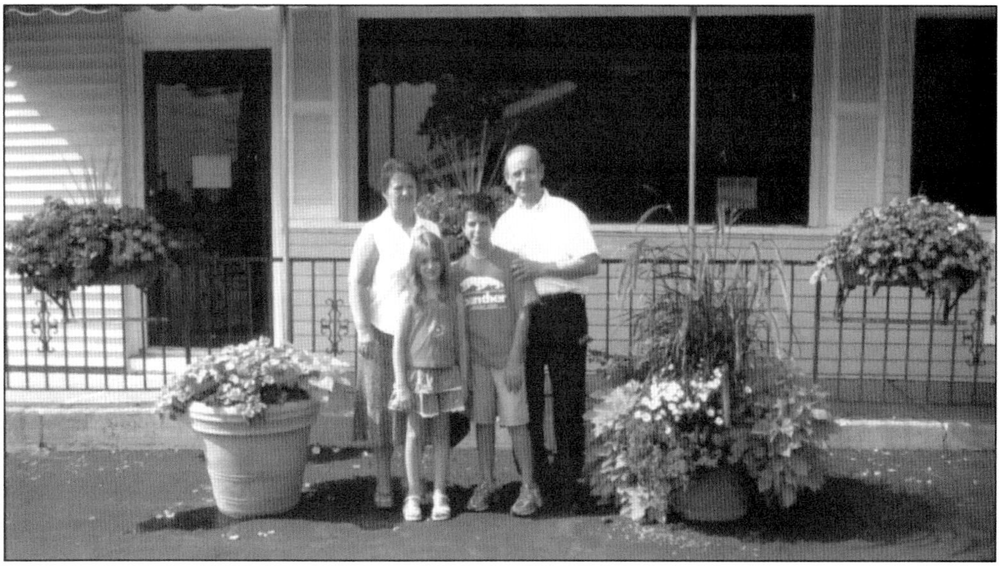

George Hiotis opened up his restaurant at 110 Webster Street in 1970. For over four decades, he has served thousands of residents and visitors from the area. The menu features home-style cooking with daily and senior specials. Customer favorites include the biscuits and gravy, potato pancakes, meatloaf, and the Friday's fish fry. George emigrated from Sparta, Greece, in 1957. He married Nancy on July 20, 1968, and they raised three children, Demetra, Louis, and Stacey. Shown are their two grandchildren Gus and Angela. (Courtesy of George Hiotis.)

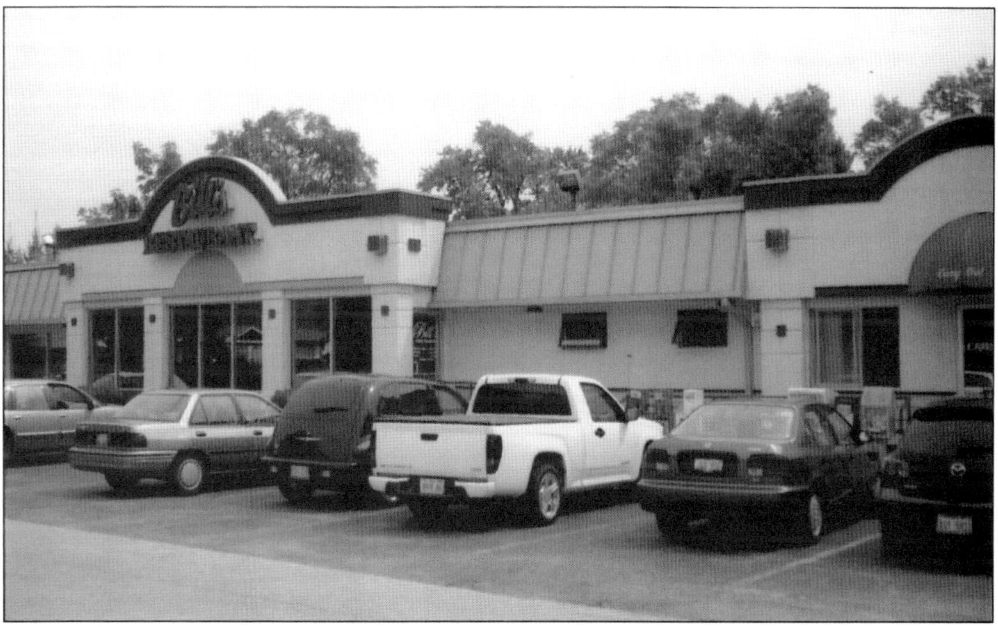

Bill's Restaurant opened in 1961 at 702 Montgomery Road. Its owner was Bill Castillo, and the restaurant started as a taco stand. After 28 years, he sold the restaurant to the Procopos family, and they owned it for 14 years. It is a casual and family-style restaurant with an eclectic menu. The restaurant had an external renovation after the 1996 flood, and then it had an interior restoration in 2003. Bill's reopened on August 3, 2010, by new owners Edgar and Yamin Reyes. (Author's collection.)

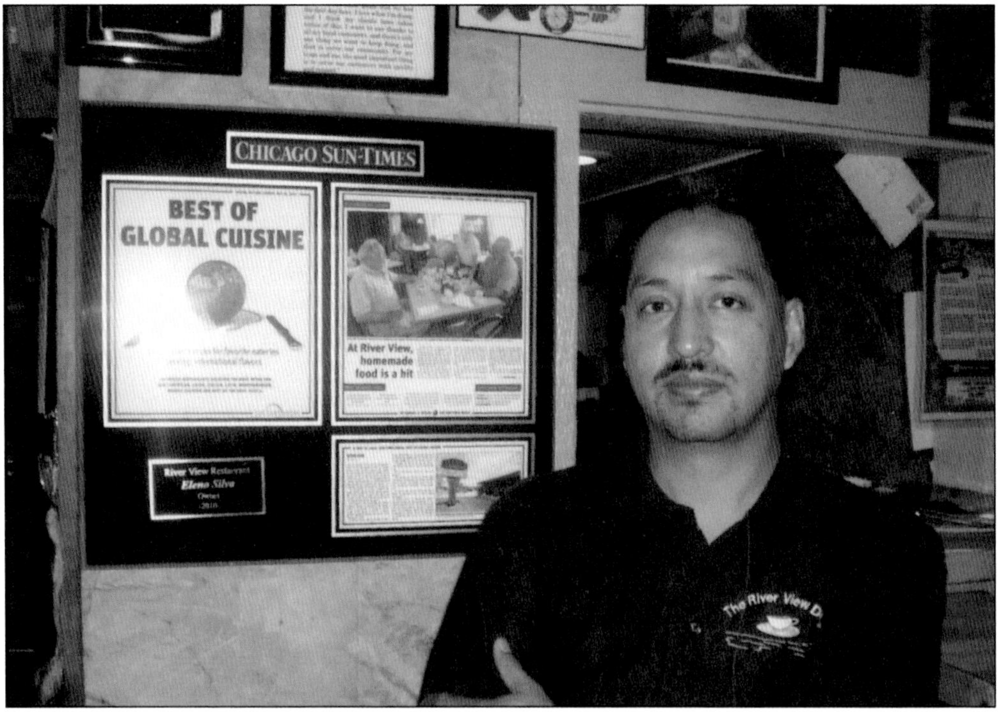

Owner Eleno Silva poses for a photograph in his River View Restaurant, which is located at 1420 Southeast River Road in Montgomery. He opened the restaurant in May 2004. Originally from Durango, Mexico, Silva immigrated to the United States and later began to learn the restaurant business as a dishwasher. He worked at the original Mitchell's Restaurant in Chicago. On May 16, 2010, the *Sun-Times Media* honored him as the reader's choice with the Best of American Cuisine Award. (Author's collection.)

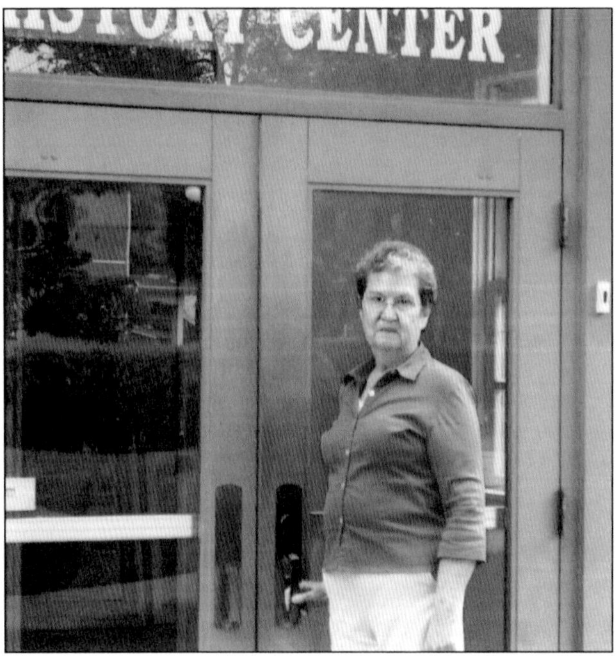

Shown is Barbara Mosley Peck at the Aurora Historical Society, where she worked and volunteered as a research assistant. Village residents have many attractions in the immediate vicinity, including the SciTech Museum, the Phillips Park Zoo, the Paramount Arts Center, the Hollywood Casino, the Blackberry-Farm Pioneer Village, and the Grand Army of the Republic Hall built in 1878. These locations are all located two miles north of Montgomery in Aurora, Illinois. (Author's collection.)

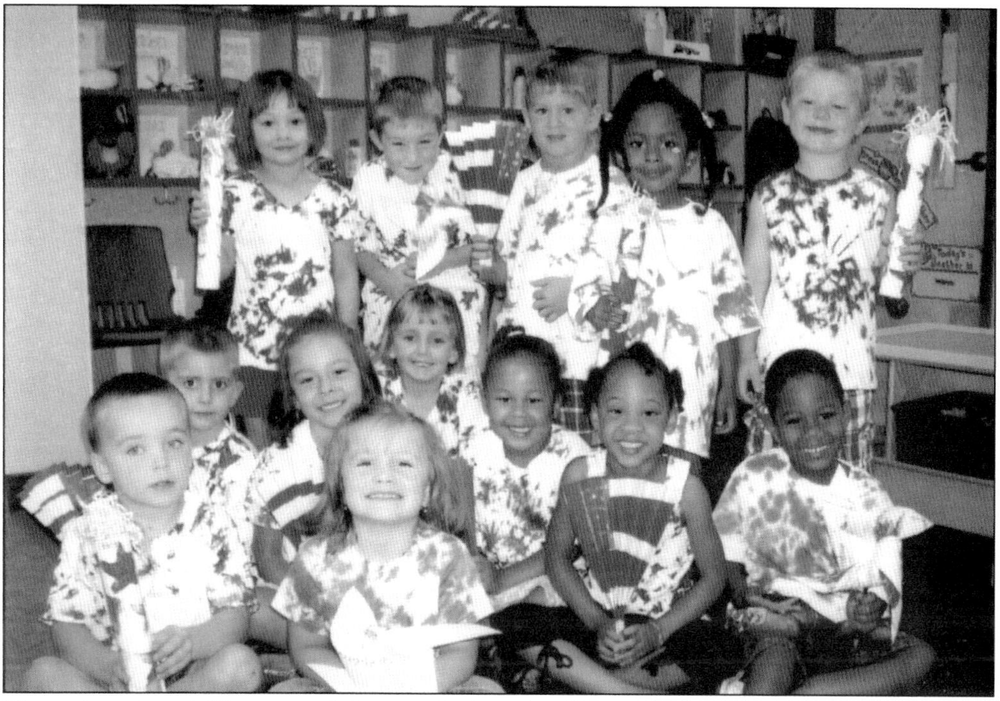

These charming children are celebrating the Fourth of July in 2010 with red, white, and blue tie-dyed shirts. Since August 3, 2009, the Rogy's Learning Place has been located at 2031 Mayfield Drive in Montgomery. Rogy's has been family owned and operated since 1972. They offer quality childcare that fosters a joy of learning. (Author's collection.)

Montgomery Fest celebrated its 25th year with a two-day event that culminated in a parade, concert, and fireworks. This photograph shows Illinois secretary of state Jesse White and Deon Allen. They were preparing for the Jesse White Tumbling Team's participation in the parade. (Author's collection.)

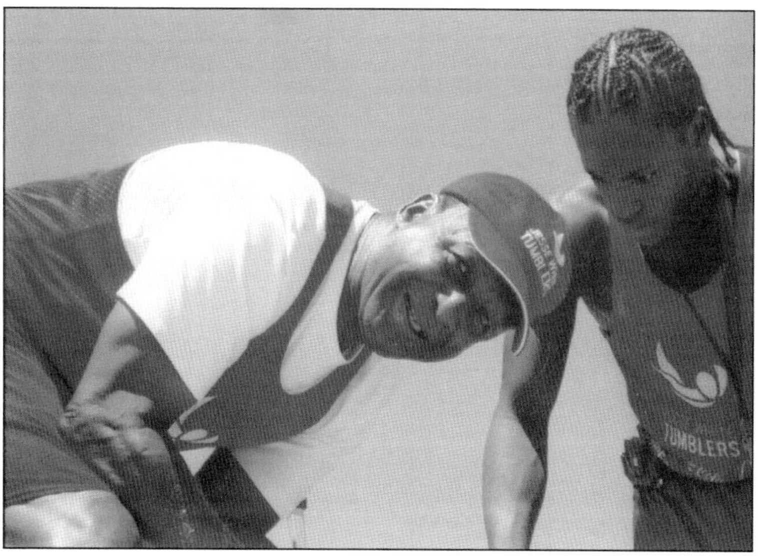

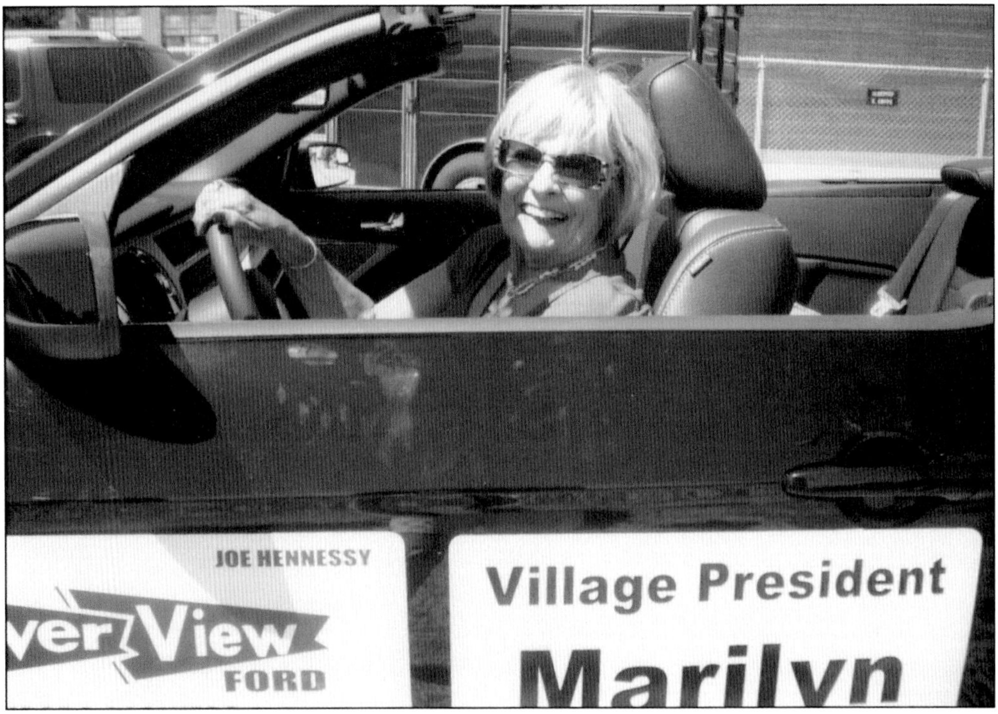

This photograph shows village president Marilyn Michelini participating in the Montgomery Fest parade on August 15, 2010. She began serving on the Kane County Board in 1982. Marilyn served on the Montgomery Board of Trustees until April 2001, when she was elected village president. Marilyn cooperates with five fire-protection districts, five school districts, three park districts, two library districts, two counties, four townships, one water-reclamation district, one drainage district, and one water authority. Marilyn serves on seven councils and committees, including the National Association of Regional Councils. (Author's collection.)

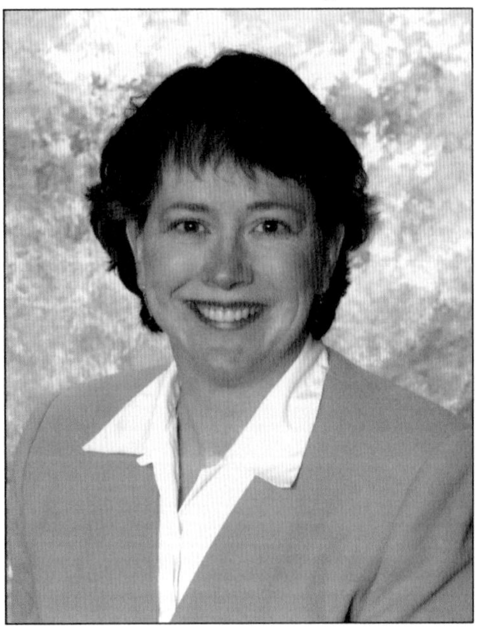

Anne Marie Gaura has been the village manager since May 1, 2000. She holds a master's degree in public administration from the Northern Illinois University. Her undergraduate degree is in organizational and corporate communications. Anne Marie worked in Lombard for nine years before taking her current position with the village. "I think one of the biggest changes in the last decade has been the speed at which we process information and the evolving policies," she said recently. (Photograph courtesy of Kausphoto.com)

Nine

CELEBRATING 175 YEARS

For those who are willing to make an effort, great miracles and wonderful treasures are in store. For them the gates of heaven are always open.

—Isaac Bashevis Singer

From the serene rolling prairies and virgin lands of northern Illinois in the 1830s to the present-day development of the Village of Montgomery, a great transformation has taken place. Most of that has been positive and life-affirming. However, with the current economic realities of budget deficits, of bank and real estate collapse, of drastic social and economic changes, it is important to recognize that this is a transition time, a time to reflect on the past accomplishments while noting that the current fabric of everyday life has changed dramatically. As the Village celebrates its 175th anniversary year, we know that our ancestors would not recognize life today in Kane and Kendall Counties.

Let us rejoice in our shared history.

There were many challenges in 2010. Lake Michigan now provides 77 percent of water needs for the area's population. There is limited ground water and surface water sources. In 2006, the unemployment rate was at 4.9 percent. Because of the recession, unemployment rose to 6.9 percent. In January 2010, the Kane County had an unemployment rate of 12.3 percent, and Kendall County had an 11.6 percent figure. Since December 1999, the state of Illinois has lost 305,000 jobs in manufacturing. In Kane County, there were over 5,000 foreclosures in 2009. During 2007 to 2010, there was a continual decline of sales-tax receipts.

While these economic realities show the need for fiscal restraint and accountability, public officials work daily to improve current conditions. Karen McConnaughay, chair of the Kane County Board, has brought community leaders together to identify the area's challenges and enact solutions. Under her leadership, Kane County has invested more than 80 percent of its budget to improve transportation and public safety. The county has constructed a long-overdue county jail and sheriff's office, built a new bridge over the Fox River at Stearns Road, and initiated the strengthening of emergency-response services. Also under her leadership, the county has maintained low debt and sufficient cash reserves. The Montgomery Economic Development Corporation, with the leadership of Charlene Coulombe-Fiore, has been instrumental in bringing new businesses to Montgomery. Pam Nagel is the executive administrator of the Chamber of Commerce. Montgomery's budget for 2011 is $19,766.830. The future is bright and filled with possibilities, and the Village will rebound from these current economic conditions.

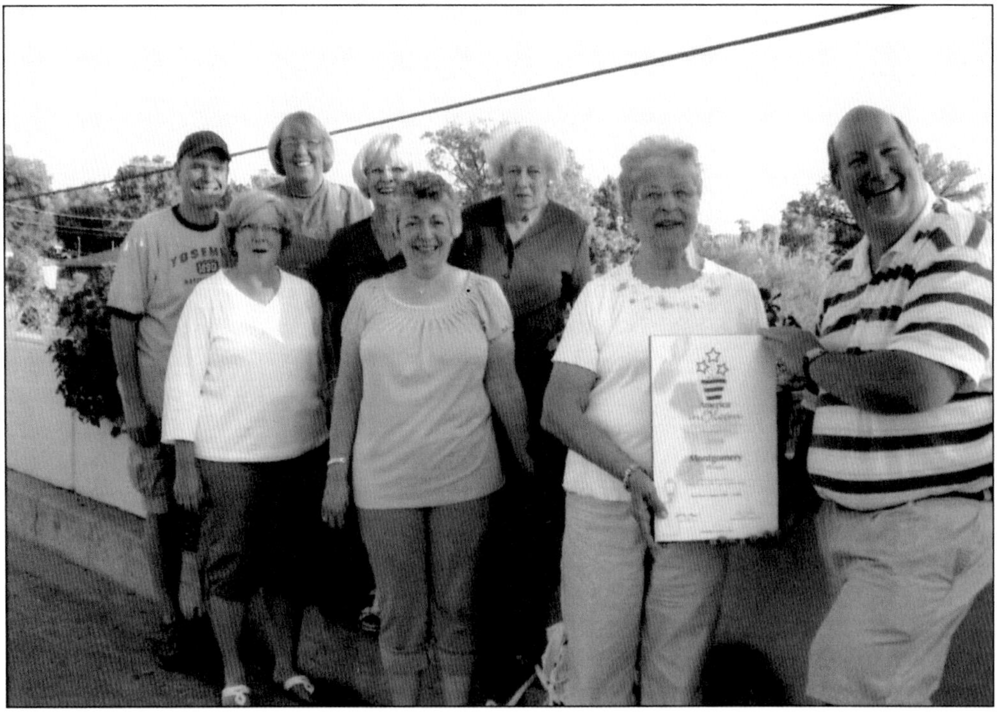

The Beautification Committee poses on a lovely August 18, 2010, evening beside the Mill Street Bridge. In 2004, the group won the America in Bloom Award by the Community Heritage Conservation. Pictured from left to right are Tom Yakaitis, village trustee Jeanne Felten, Patti Bulat, village president Marilyn Michelini, Donna Jones, Nancy Tranby, Alice Sutcliff (holding the award), and public works director Mike Pubentz. Missing from the photograph are members Brett Schaefer and Martha Larson. (Author's collection.)

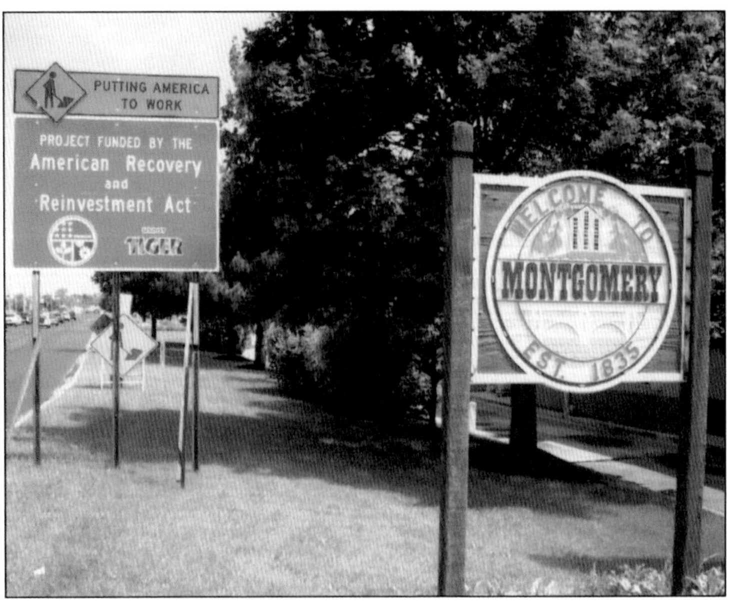

Shown is the welcome sign to Montgomery at the corner of Douglas Street and Route 30. The welcoming sign is next to a sign designated to the American Recovery and Reinvestment Act, which was a stimulus package enacted by the 111th Congress to create jobs, promote investment, and increase consumer spending. (Author's collection.)

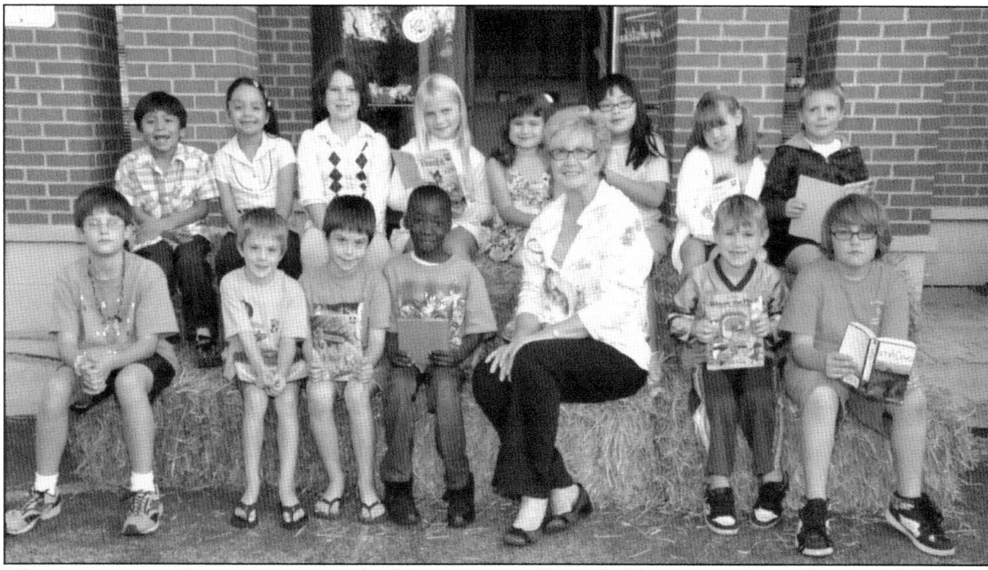

The summer-reading program at the Montgomery Branch library in 2010 offered children the chance to become an official Fox Valley Reader. Kay Hatcher, state representative for Kane, Kendall, and LaSalle Counties, sponsored this program at twelve libraries throughout her district. Pictured from left to right are (first row) Logan Metcalfe, Brighton Newman, Avarey Newman, Ayatunde Adekoya, Kay Hatcher, Sean Gannon, and Stephen Gannon; (second row) Juan Puga, Zenaida Puga, Abbi Vicich, Moira Gannon, Brooke Wegman, Amalia Marquhardt, Alyssa Voss, and Jake Voss. (Courtesy of Kay Hatcher.)

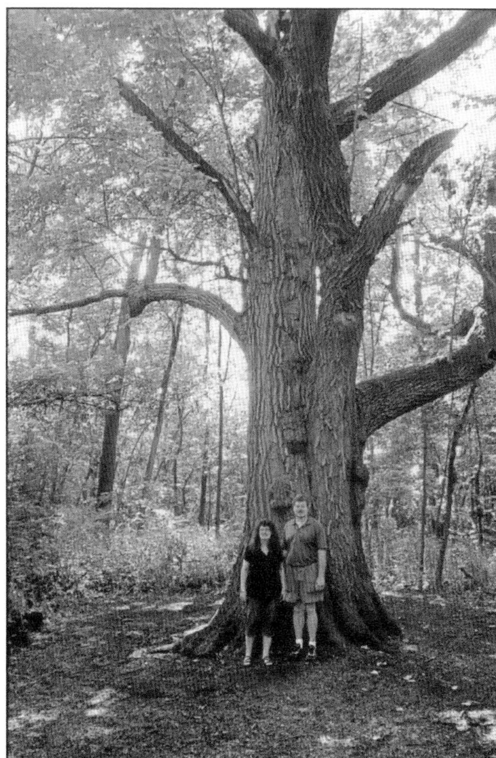

Imagine a red oak tree that has looked over the Fox River for the past 350 years. The homeowners of the tree are Virginia and Ron Potter. In 1660, several Indian tribes occupied this area, and it was called Illinois Country by early explorers. The Sioux, Assiniboin, Illinois, Maskouten, and Potawatomi tribes traded copper and fine bows with each other. Most notable among the Potowatomi was Waubonsie and Shabbona. And from a small acorn . . . (Author's collection.)

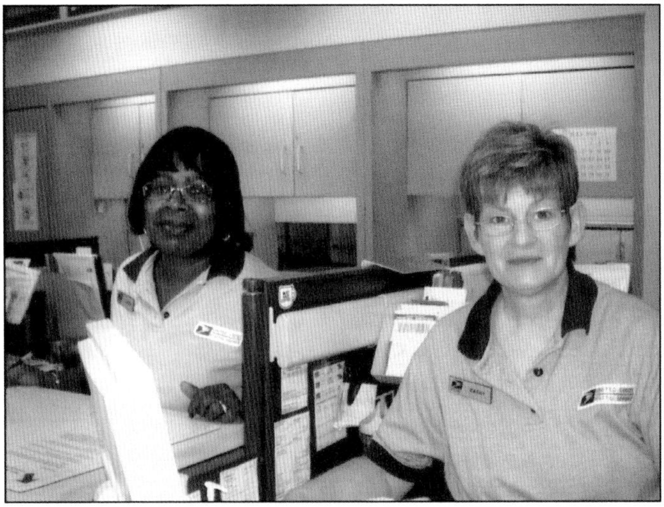

The letter carriers of NALC Branch No. 219 participated in a food drive on May 8, 2010, which collected 64,000 pounds of food and distributed them to several food pantries like the Interfaith Food Pantry and the Kendall County Food Pantry. Co-coordinators of the event were Sandhi Horton and Mary Kluber. Pictured at the Montgomery Post Office are, from left to right, Laura Phillips and Kathy Mason Dabney. (Author's collection.)

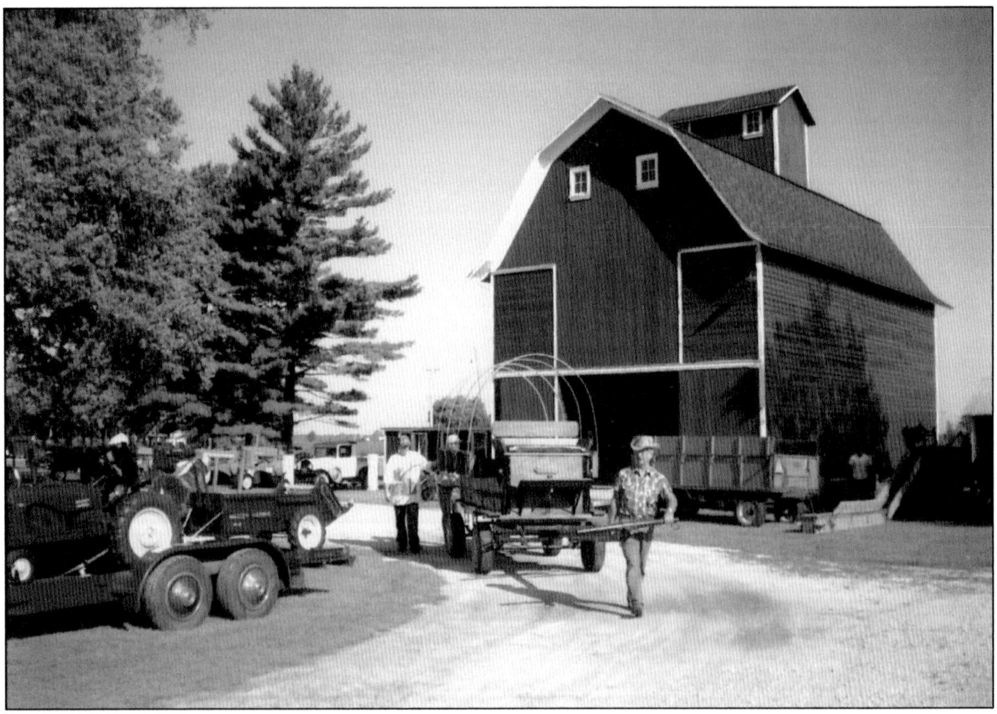

The Dickson-Murst Farm held its fourth-annual Spring at the Farm on May 16, 2010. Decorating the grounds are 45 rocking chairs that were donated and repainted cherry red. Bluegrass music, wagon rides, a plant sale, and a beekeeper with honey for sale created a day that many families enjoyed. In 2006, the Village of Montgomery received the Richard H. Driehaus Award from the Landmarks Preservation Council of Illinois for the preservation of this historic site. (Author's collection.)

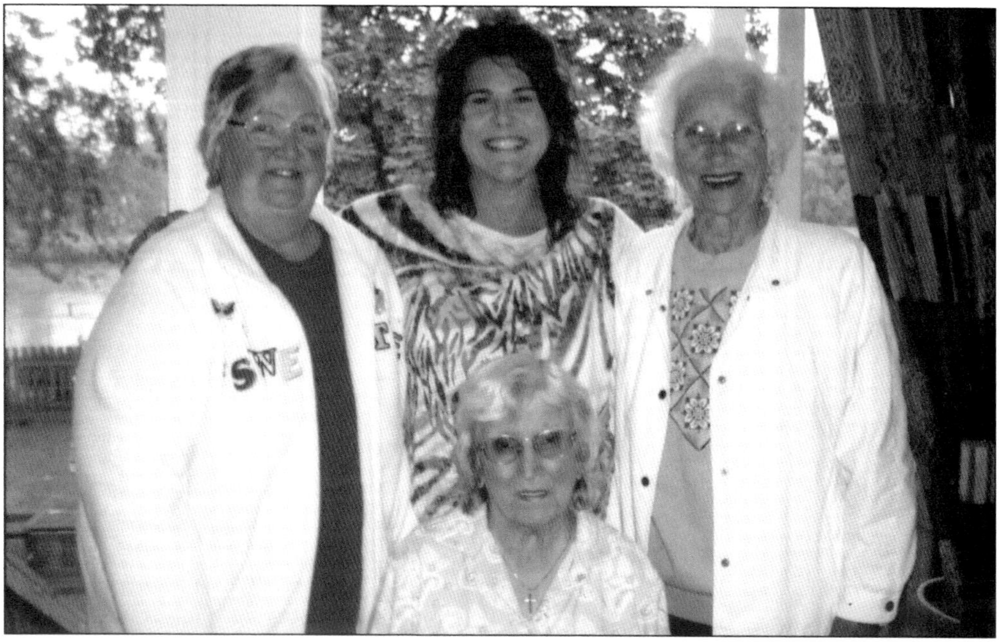

Dag Hammarskjold, secretary general of the United Nations from April 1953 until his death in a plane crash on September 18, 1961, said, "Friendship needs no words. It is solitude delivered from the anguish of loneliness." Pictured here are four dear women friends who live on North River Street, watching the Fox River flow gently by. From left to right are Jean Gibson, Cindy King Adams, Vivian Buchtler, and Jean Hart (seated). (Author's collection.)

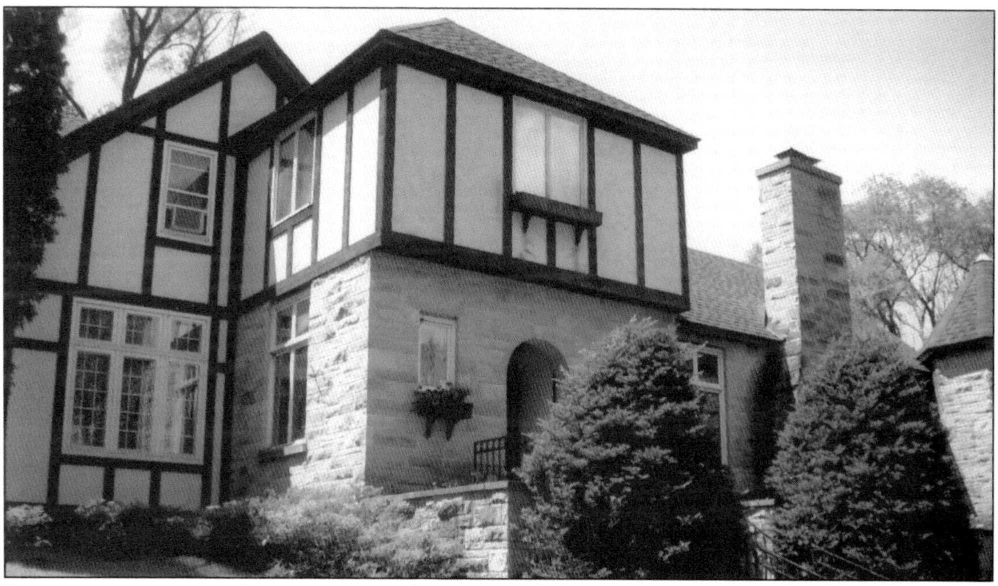

The current owners of Montgomery's Castle are Walter and Bonnie Sattler. They have lived there for the past 16 years. The original owner was Franklin Stark and he was a bachelor, a violinmaker, and a custom mill worker who made door and window frames. The home occupies 2.5 acres on the east side of the Fox River. It has five different roof levels and a turret with a circular staircase. There is a greenhouse and a dining room with French doors opening to the patio. (Author's collection.)

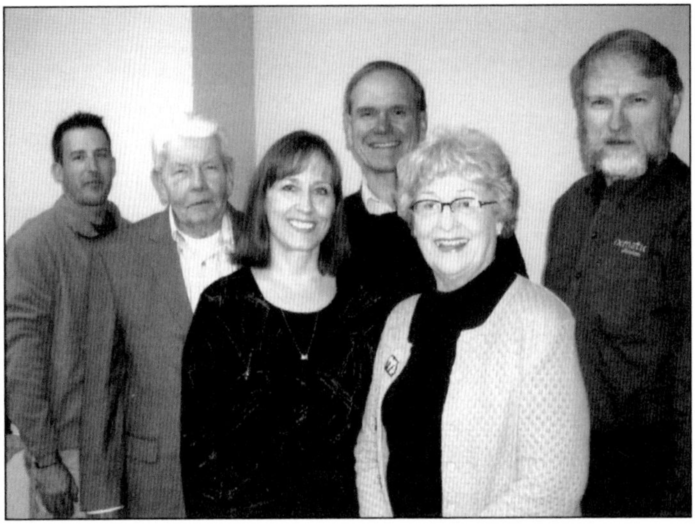

The Historic Preservation Commission gathered at Village Hall on November 15, 2010. Pictured from left to right are members Ken Eggert, Gene Michaels, Debbie Buchanan, Tom Yakaitis, Patricia Mosley Torrance, and John Aman. Missing from the photograph are Gretchen Countryman and chair Jeanette Lee. (Author's collection.)

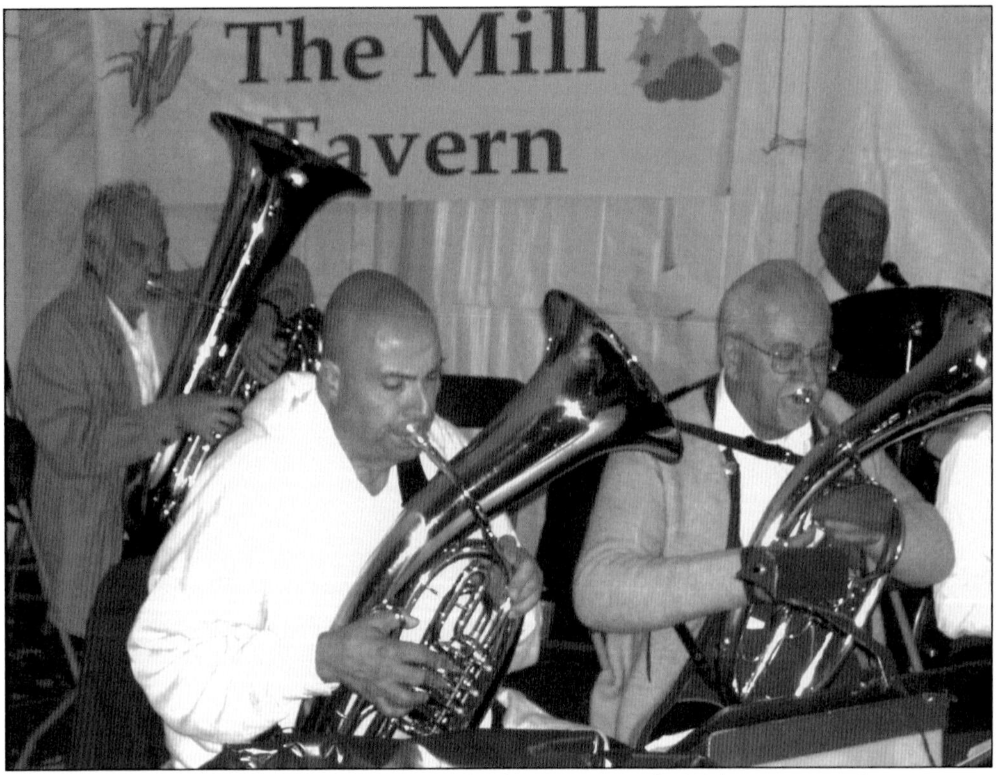

Montgomery celebrated its 11th-annual Oktoberfest in 2010 with 600 businesses and community members attending. It was hosted by the Greater Montgomery Area Chamber of Commerce. Pictured from left to right are Lenny Mack, Russ Nucio, Hans Schader, and Jim Drnek. The major sponsors of the event were Center Point Properties, Engineering Enterprises, Gusto Packaging, the LaKone Company, Suncast, Superior Beverage, The Mill Tavern, and the Bank of Montgomery. (Photograph by Kim Drnek.)

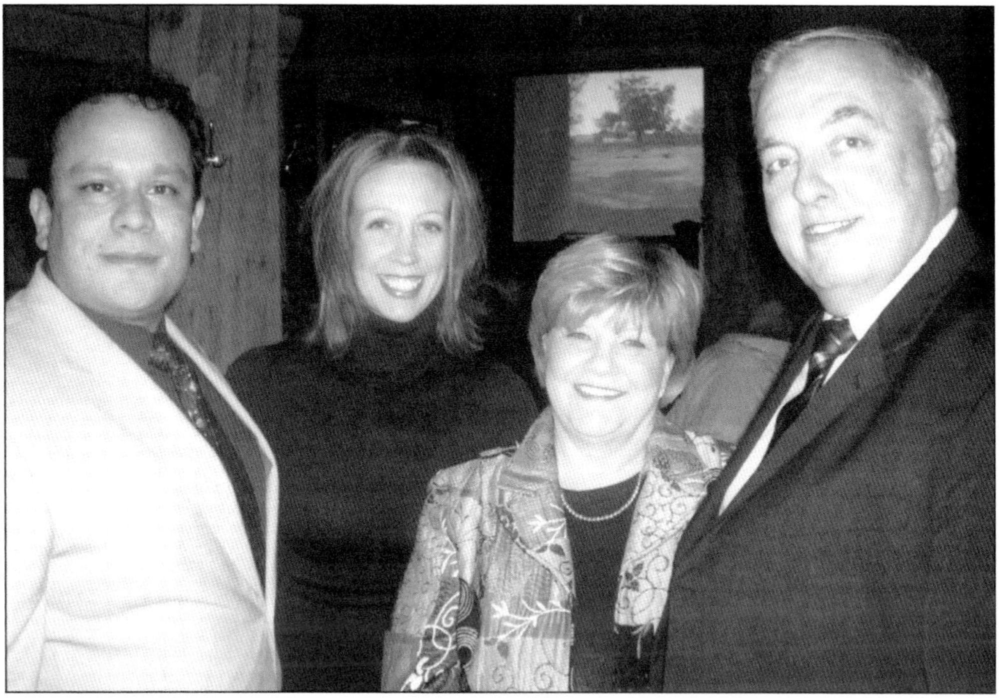

The Village hosted its 175th Anniversary Gala Reception at Gray's Mill on October 26, 2010. The hosts were Virginia and Ron Potter. Many certificates and plagues were awarded to the descendants of residents who lived in the area prior to 1910. Pictured from left to right are Rene Morales, Melissa Morales, Lyda Schmidt, and Dennis J. Schmidt. Dennis is the retired police chief and currently directs the driver's safety program at Waubonsee Community College. (Author's collection.)

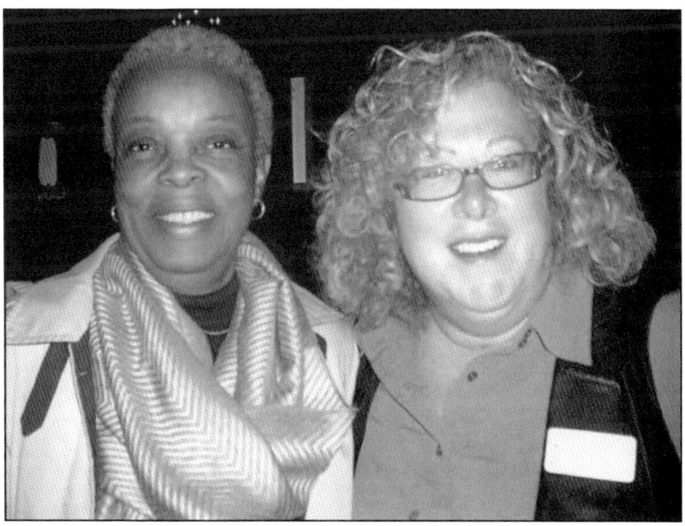

Pictured at the 175th Annual Gala Reception are, from left to right, Mildred-McNeal-James, who serves on the Plan Commission and Zoning Board of Appeals, and Charlene Coulombe-Fiore, executive director of the Montgomery Economic Development Corporation. (Author's collection.)

About the Author

Here is home. An old thread, long tangled, comes straight again.

—From "Cross Creek"

Jo Fredell Higgins is an internationally published writer and award-winning essayist, historian, and poet. Her photographs have won numerous awards. One was selected to be included in *One Day USA*, which was published by the US Conference of Mayors. Her photography exhibits have been shown at the Aurora Public Library, the Plano Public Library, the First Night Aurora, ArtWalk, and open house events at the Grand Army of the Republic Hall. Her poetry has been published in the women's poetry anthology *Her Echo, New Voices in American Poetry 1975*, in the Indiana Fine Arts Society's "The Poet," Morton Arboretum's *White Words of Winter* anthology, *A Different Drummer, Poems of the World* anthology, and in the *Downtown Auroran* magazine. Jo retired from Waubonsee Community College in 2007. She was the official photographer for Literacy Volunteers of America at the Illinois conference in 2002. Family Focus Aurora honored Jo for her community involvements in 2002. She was cited as an Amazing Youth Leader by the *Aurora Beacon-News*. Jo was a statewide judge for the Illinois Governor's Hometown Award. She served on the planning committee for the Midwest Literary Festivals in 2003 and 2004, and she led a panel discussion on adult literacy and signed copies of her Arcadia books. Jo presented a poetry workshop at the Aurora Public Library in conjunction with the national Make A Difference Day event in 2003. She was named Woman of Distinction by the YWCA in 2004. Jo's sixth book is the historical novel *A Song for Cecilia*. It will be released by Tate Publishing in 2011. She enjoys gardening, swimming, traveling, bicycling, and playing card games. Her daughter Suzanne and grandson Sean live in Madison, Wisconsin.

Bibliography

ABC Nightly News. "Illinois Spent $680 a Sign." July 14, 2010.

A Bicentennial History of Kendall County, Illinois. Yorkville: 1976.

Alexander, Dr. A.S. "Some Common Unsoundness. How to Buy and Care for Horses." 1917.

Anthony, Carl Sferrazza. *America's First Families*. New York: 2000.

Aurora Beacon News. 1931–2011.

Aurora City Directory: 1874–2011. Chicago, IL: 1874.

Bateman, Newton, LlD, and . *Historical Encyclopedia of Illinois*. Chicago, IL: Munsell Publishing Company, 1904.

Baumann, Paul, PhD. *The Fox River: A Bicentennial History*. Yorkville, IL: Kendall County Bicentennial Commission, 1976.

Beck, Bill. *The Kane County Bar Association: 1858–2008*. Virginia: 2008.

"Bishop Lane Will Dedicate St. Peter's Church Sunday." *Beacon-News*. October 27, 1966.

Boyd, Gregory A. *Family Maps of Kendall County, Illinois*. Norman, OK: Arphax Publishing, 2005.

Campion, Nardi Reeder. "Humble Legacy: Treasures in Lincoln's Pocket Don't Fit the Man of Myth." *Chicago Tribune*: April 12, 1988: Section D.

Chase, Wayne. *Records of Sacred Heart Cemetery*. Montgomery, IL: 1998.

Chicago Wilderness. *An Atlas of Biodiversity*. Illinois Conservation Foundation: 2000.

Coulombe-Fiore, Charlene, executive director. MEDC photo albums, 2003–2011.

Dieterich Wagner, Ruth. Unpublished documents. Montgomery, IL: 1930–1999.

"Extensive Sheep Yards." *Daily Express*. June 15, 1892.
"Farm Days to Remember." *Beacon News*. May 24, 2010: 12.
Farren, Kathy. *A Bicentennial History of Kendall County, Illinois*. Yorkville, IL: Kendall County Bicentennial Commission, 1976.
Fichtel, Michael. *Inscriptions of Sacred Heart Cemetery, Montgomery, Illinois*. 1980.
"Food Drive Bringing Community Together." *Beacon News*. July 13, 2010: 10.
Forever A Foundry. Aurora Metals, LLC, 1998.
Fox, Ray. *Raising Kane: The Fox Chronicles*. Montgomery: 1999.
Genealogical and Biographical Record of Kendall and Will Counties, Illinois. Chicago, IL: Biographical Publishing Company, 1901.
Greenaway, J.W. *Record of Aurora, Illinois in World War II*. Aurora: 1952.
Hanley, Matt. "Changes Coming for Catholic Mass." *Beacon News*. June 28, 2010: 7.
Higgins, Jo Fredell. "That Was a Good Year: 1917." *Naperville/Lisle Business Journal* 1.
Kane County Urban Development. *Architecture and Historic Urban Neighborhoods on the Fox River*. 1976–1977.
Kaus, Dean, and Lyle R. Rolfe. *Valley with a Vision*. Maryland: 1998.
Jensen, Richard J. *Illinois: A History*. Chicago, IL: 2001.
Living with Wetlands. The Wetlands Initiative. 1998.
Oswegoland Heritage Association, Roger Matile, ed. *Oswego Township*. Charleston, SC: Arcadia Publishing, 2008.
Oswego Visitors Bureau. *Visitor and Community Guide: 2010–2011*.
Meyer, Sherry A. *The Historical Geography of Montgomery, Illinois in Words and Images*. The Montgomery Historical Committee. Missouri: Walsworth Publishing Company, 1990.
McCoy, W.H. *Aurora City Directory: 1904*. Keokuk, IA: 1904.
Michaels, Gene. *Hobos in Early Montgomery*. Spring 2010.
Montgomery Economic Development Corporation. *Montgomery*. Yorkville: 2008.
National Register of Historic Places Evaluation of the Simon and Janet Dixon Farmstead in Kendall County, Illinois. IHPA Log #0211210001HKE. January 2003.
Piggott, Cecil Jr. Personal letter to Grace Nicholson. 1949.
Portrait and Biographical Record of Kane and Kendall Counties, Illinois. Beers, Leggett & Co.: Chicago, IL: 1888.
Prairie Farmers Directory of Grundy and Kendall Counties, Illinois. 1917.
"Shearing By Steam." *Aurora Daily Express*. Chicago, IL: January 14, 1898.
"Sheep Capital? No bahhh-loney." *Beacon News*. June 18, 1985.
Shoger, Paul M. *Threshing Kings of Kendall County: 1875–1955*. Yorkville: 1976.
Singer, Isaac Bashevis. *Stories for Children*. New York: 1962.
Speculum. Senior class of 1931, East High School. Aurora, IL: 1931.
"St. Peter School of Aurora, A Lasting Tribute to Generosity." *Rockford Observer*. November 18, 1960.
Tepper, Michael. *American Passenger Arrival Records*. Baltimore: 1993.
The Heron. The Conservation Foundation. Fall 2009.
The Lyon News. April 1942. Vol. 13, No. 1.
The Railway Locomotive Historical Society Bulletin. Boston, MA: 1949 (76).
Tillson, Christiana Holmes. *A Woman's Story of Pioneer Illinois*. Chicago, IL: R.R. Donnelley & Sons Company, 1918.
USA Today. July 4, 2010.
Village of Montgomery. *175th Annual Cookbook*.
———. Ordinance No. 1325. July 23, 2007.
———. Application for Local Landmark Designation for Dickson-Murst Farm.
———. Annual Report to the Village Board and Community. May 1, 2008—April 30, 2009.
———. Board meeting minutes. August 24, 2009.
———. Board meeting minutes. 1858–1888. Courtesy of Helen Prester.
www.encyclopedia.chicagohistory.org
White, Lutz. *Now and Then*. October 18, 1931.
Zellie, Carole. *Architecture and Historic Urban Neighborhoods on the Fox River*. Geneva, IL: Kane County Urban Development, 1977.